Dr Jane McGregor is a freelance writer and researcher. She holds a PhD in history awarded by the University of London having studied with the aid of a Wellcome Trust scholarship at the Centre of History in Public Health, London School of Hygiene and Tropical Medicine. Her interest areas are public health and mental health.

Everyday Sociopaths

How Evil Spreads – And How
We Can Stop It

Jane McGregor

sheldon PRESS

First published in Great Britain by Sheldon Press in 2023
An imprint of John Murray Press
A division of Hodder & Stoughton Ltd,
An Hachette UK company

1

Copyright © Jane McGregor 2023

This book is for information or educational purposes only and is not
intended to act as a substitute for medical advice or treatment. Any
person with a condition requiring medical attention should consult
a qualified medical practitioner or suitable therapist.

A CIP catalogue record for this title is available from the British Library

Trade Paperback ISBN 978 1 399 80695 4
eBook ISBN 978 1 399 80694 7

Typeset by KnowledgeWorks Global Ltd.

Printed and bound in Great Britain by Clays Ltd, Elcograf S.p.A.

John Murray Press policy is to use papers that are natural, renewable and
recyclable products and made from wood grown in sustainable forests.
The logging and manufacturing processes are expected to conform
to the environmental regulations of the country of origin.

John Murray Press
Carmelite House
50 Victoria Embankment
London EC4Y 0DZ

www.sheldonpress.co.uk

This book is dedicated to Fin McGregor,
whose courage and fortitude inspired the book.

Contents

1 Introduction: what the book is about 1
2 Everyday sociopaths 15
3 A profile of the sociopath 32
4 Interactions of the sociopath 52
5 Just doing my job! The perils of blind obedience 76
6 Coping in the aftermath of a destructive relationship 121
7 Establishing boundaries and regaining control of your life 146
8 Dealing with complex family situations 176
9 Towards empathy 200

Useful addresses 229
Notes 230
Further reading 240
Index 242
Acknowledgements 248

1

Introduction: what the book is about

This book is designed to heighten awareness of the problems of sociopathic abuse – and equip you to spot, avoid or remove sociopaths from your life.

Sociopaths are individuals with little or no conscience or ability to empathize with others' feelings. One sociopath (some people prefer the term 'psychopath') in the course of their lifetime will affect many, many people in a myriad harmful ways: misdirecting whole groups of people, bullying work colleagues, abusing children, instigating domestic violence or traumatizing friends and family through a sustained campaign of emotional abuse. The purpose in writing the book is to reach out and offer supportive guidance to those who already have been targeted by a sociopath, and to forewarn and forearm others who want to reduce the likelihood of being a target of abuse themselves.

The book is also about harnessing your powers of empathy. On the one hand, empathic people prove eye-catching quarry to the sociopath; on the other, if the expression of empathy was more widely approved by society at large it could provide a powerful antidote to sociopathic abuse.

Sociopaths in society

For simplicity's sake, the term 'sociopath' is used in the book as a catch-all term. Because the medical profession continues to debate the exact features of this condition, I will not be exploring it in detail. The aim is to highlight not the condition itself, but the destructive effects of sharing your life with someone who has a sociopathic personality.

Sociopaths are chameleon-like and lurk freely among us. They pose a serious threat to humankind, harming individuals, families and communities the world over, affecting the health and well-being of millions daily. Yet, for reasons explored in this book, they exist largely unseen; and this lack of awareness and responsiveness means that the traumas they inflict upon their many targets go undetected.

Sociopaths exist in greater numbers than you might suppose, although it is hard to know for sure just how many there are. Since most estimates are derived from data based on specific sub-groups like prison populations rather than the general population, and the condition has been subject to regular redefinition, estimates for sociopathy in society vary considerably and are likely to be set too low.

Martha Stout, a psychologist who treats the survivors of psychological trauma, informs us in her valuable book *The Sociopath Next Door* that 4 per cent of the general population are sociopathic. This estimate is derived from a large clinical trial involving primary care patients in the US, which found that 8 per cent of men and 3.1 per cent of women met the criteria for a diagnosis of anti-social personality disorder (AsPD), one of the terms used to describe those displaying sociopathic traits. The frequency of the condition was higher (13.4 per cent for men and 4 per cent for women) for those people with a history of childhood conduct disorder (a precursor of adult sociopathy).[1] Meanwhile researchers Paul Babiak and Robert Hare estimate that 1 per cent of the population have the condition, with another 10 per cent or more falling into what they call the 'grey zone'. In their book *Snakes in Suits*, Babiak and Hare suggest that the prevalence is likely to be higher in some groups including the business world, the philosophy and practices of which encourage sociopathic traits such as callousness and grasping behaviour.[2]

Australian psychologist John Clarke has been working along the same lines as Babiak and Hare. In his book *Working with Monsters* he reports that up to 0.5 per cent of women and 2 per cent of men could be classified as sociopathic (like Babiak and Hare he prefers the term 'psychopath').[3] A British study has estimated the prevalence of sociopathy in the general population at just under 1 per cent, although like other studies, this study found that prevalence is higher among certain groups including prisoners, the homeless, and people who have been admitted to psychiatric institutions.[4]

As you can see, estimates of sociopathy in the general population vary from less than 1 person in 100 to 1 in 25. Even at the most conservative end of the estimates, this translates into a possible 3.34 million sociopaths in the US and 671,000 in the UK. Worldwide it equates to a figure of 80 million. So the fact that sociopathic abuse remains such an overlooked problem is surprising, if not shocking. The cruelty of sociopaths finds no bounds, for there is no recourse, treatment or punishment to permanently stop them.

Sociopaths in power threaten the very existence of humanity. Adolf Hitler, the Austrian-born German politician who became the dictator of Germany from 1933 until his death in 1945 is one such example. During his dictatorship, he initiated the Second World War in Europe by invading Poland in 1939, was closely involved in military operations throughout the war and central to the perpetration of the Holocaust, the genocide of about six million Jews and millions of other victims.

You might suppose that we learn important lessons from history, but sadly this is often far from the case. In 1982, the prospect of a future ruled by the seriously morally inept was the subject of a British government exercise. This exercise was revealed in 2014 with the release of previously secret documents into the public domain. The exercise, which was named

3

'Operation Regenerate', imagined many cities flattened, millions killed by the blast and millions more suffering from radiation sickness. Released documents from the exercise revealed a proposal to install sociopaths in positions of authority, in the event of a shattering nuclear war. During the exercise officials played war games to envision what the impact of an attack would be upon law and order in society. Maintaining law and order, it was predicted, would become increasingly difficult as police would be busy helping victims of the radiation fallout. These predictions led a scientific officer in the Home Office to suggest the police could recruit another group of people to help restore order – sociopaths, or psychopaths as the report called them.[5] The documents reporting on the exercise show the scientist reasoned that emotionally dead, calculating people with zero empathy for other people or any moral code, would be exactly what was needed by a society trying to rebuild itself after an atomic bomb catastrophe. Advocating sociopaths because they are 'very good in crises', the Home Office scientist wrote in the report: 'These are the people who could be expected to show no psychological effects in the communities which have suffered the severest losses ... They have no feelings for others, nor moral code and tend to be very intelligent and logical.'

What this scientist failed to recognize is that sociopaths don't pursue goals for the sake of the common good; instead, they pursue self-interest whatever the human cost. Apparently the suggestion by the scientist failed to find support in the corridors of power. One critic of the idea stated that sociopaths were 'too dangerous, whether or not recruited into post-attack organization'.[6] This inability of many to see past the sociopath's superficial charms is one of the reasons sociopaths rise to power. In whatever way they manage to dress things up, in reality they are anti-social, not pro-social. We ignore them and this truth at our peril.

Sociopath-induced distress and trauma

Individuals who have been targeted by a sociopath often respond with self-deprecating statements like 'I was stupid', 'What was I thinking?' or 'I should've listened to my gut instinct'. But being involved with a sociopath is like being brainwashed. The sociopath's superficial charm is usually the means by which they condition people. On initial contact a sociopath will often test other people's empathy, so questions geared towards discovering whether you are highly empathetic or not should ring alarm bells. Those with a highly empathetic disposition are often targeted because they pose a threat. Those who have lower levels of empathy are often passed over, though they may be drawn in and used by sociopaths as part of their cruel entertainment, as discussed later in the book.

Those living with a sociopath usually exist in a state of constant emotional chaos. They may feel anxious and afraid, not knowing when the sociopath will fly into a rage. The sociopath meanwhile carries on untouched, using aggression, violence or emotional bullying to abuse.

Sociopathic abuse is always targeted abuse. The sociopath is a chameleon and will present different personas to different people. Sociopaths are often aggressive, though not all of them exhibit violent or criminal behaviour. Aggression is not limited to men either; sociopathic women can be aggressive and violent too. Sociopaths make up between 20 and 25 per cent of the prison population, committing more than twice as many violent and aggressive acts as other criminals do. According to Robert Hare, the author of *Without Conscience*, in the US male and female prisoners who are sociopaths commit more than twice as many violent and aggressive acts as do other criminals and are responsible for more than 50 per cent of all serious crimes. When they get out of prison, they often return to crime. The reoffending rate of sociopaths is about double that of other offenders and for violent crimes it is triple.[7] Sociopaths are often sexual abusers. They will act on the slightest of their urges and typically aren't put off by things that normal people would find repulsive or repugnant. This leads them to try out deviant sexual behaviours. They may be involved in abuse of children, seduce friends' spouses, and, of course, sexually abuse others. Rape is an example of the callous, selfish use of violence by sociopaths. In his book *Without Conscience*, Robert Hare estimates that about half of serial rapists are sociopaths and that this behaviour results from a potent combination of uninhibited expression of their sexual desires, a craving for power and control, and perception of the victims as objects of pleasure and satisfaction.

As well as inflicting physical trauma on others, there is the added and less visible burden of sociopath-induced emotional trauma, which if left unchecked can lead to anxiety disorders, depression and post-traumatic stress disorder (PTSD). Indeed, research in the field of neuroscience shows that verbal abuse during childhood can be just as harmful as other forms of mistreatment. It can have a lasting effect on the structure of the brain and lead to anxiety, depression, hostility, learning deficits, behavioural issues and drug abuse.[8] Chronically traumatized people often exhibit hyper-vigilant, anxious and agitated behaviour. They may also experience insomnia and assorted somatic (bodily) symptoms such as tension headaches, gastrointestinal disturbances, abdominal pain, back pain, tremors and nausea. Exposure to and interaction with a sociopath in childhood can leave lifelong scars, including a deep mistrust of other people and anxiety in social situations. Yet for all these problems, no one knows the true extent or depth of mental anguish suffered by those on the receiving end of chronic sociopathic abuse, because in the majority of cases the physical and mental health problems either go undetected or the root cause is overlooked.

Sociopathic abuse thus has a substantial public health dimension and as such warrants far more attention than it attracts at present. The public need to be more alert and equipped to counter the problem and to stop sociopaths from interfering in adverse ways in other people's lives. Furthermore, effective responses and interventions are required to reduce the range and extent of sociopathic abuse suffered by people the world over.

Defining the problem

As stated at the outset, this book is not about sociopaths or the condition per se; it is about surviving the harm they cause. I only set out to define the condition loosely, because I am not convinced that current terminology and labels are especially useful. The distinctions between labels like sociopathy, anti-social personality disorder, borderline personality disorder (BPD), narcissistic personality disorder (NPD)[9] and psychopathy are blurred and confusing. In fact it is my hope at some point that psychiatry will get away entirely from the existing labels and redefine them all as personality types along the empathy spectrum – something that is discussed further over the next few pages. Nevertheless some discussion of the changing conceptualization of sociopathy is justified, so next some key turning points in defining the problem are discussed.

The idea that there are people who look human but are not, and who exist without empathy or concern for the rest of humanity, was first mooted in 1801 by the physician Philippe Pinel (1745–1826).[10] In his work *A Treatise on Insanity*, Pinel named the condition *manie sans délire*, which roughly translated means 'madness without delusion'. Some time later, an English doctor, J. C. Pritchard (1786–1848), ascribed the term 'moral insanity' to the condition. Pritchard described it as 'a form of mental derangement in which the intellectual faculties [are uninjured] while the disorder is manifested principally or alone in the state of feelings, temper or habits ... The moral principles of the mind ... are depraved or perverted, the power of self-government is lost or greatly impaired, and the individual is ... incapable of conducting himself with decency and propriety in the business of life'.[11]

Nearly 100 years on, in 1941, American psychiatrist Hervey Cleckley published *The Mask of Sanity*, a book which first described the diagnostic criteria for the 'psychopathic personality'.[12] This was based primarily on experience with adult male psychopaths hospitalized in a closed institution. From his observations, Cleckley drew up a set of diagnostic criteria, including superficial charm, a lack of anxiety or guilt, undependability or dishonesty, egocentricity, an inability to form lasting intimate relationships, a failure to learn from punishment, poverty of emotions, a lack of insight into the impact of one's behaviour and a failure to plan ahead. Interestingly his definition of a psychopath made no reference to physical aggression or breaking the law.

Cleckley's best definition of psychopathy comes in a later edition of the book, in which he described a psychopath as 'a biologic organism outwardly intact, showing excellent peripheral function, but centrally deficient or disabled'. This rather elegant description pinpoints how hard it is to spot sociopaths given their ordinary outward appearance.

Subsequent to Cleckley's book, revisions of the classification were made by the American Psychiatric Association (APA). The classification of psychopathic personality was changed to that of sociopathic personality in 1958. In 1968 it was changed again to anti-social personality. After this Robert Hare elaborated on Cleckley's work to create the Psychopathy Checklist (PCL) and later a revised version, the PCL-R, which became the 'gold standard' assessment measure used to diagnose psychopathy. The PCL-R, which remains the standard measure today, identifies as typical of the psychopath interpersonal deficits such as grandiosity, arrogance and deceitfulness, affective deficits (lack of guilt and empathy), and impulsive and criminal behaviours.

The terms 'sociopath' and 'psychopath' often are used to reflect the user's views on the origins and determinates of the clinical syndrome or disorder. Some experts are convinced that the condition is forged entirely by social forces and call the condition **sociopathy**, whereas others are convinced that it is derived from a combination of psychological, biological and genetic factors and hence prefer the term **psychopathy**. I use the term **sociopathy** as a social label to describe a malady that has the potential to afflict the whole social body.[13]

Debate surrounding sociopathy and psychopathy and whether they are the same or different continues unabated today. The current edition of the *Diagnostic and Statistical Manual of Mental Disorders (DSM-5)*, released by the American Psychiatric Association in 2013, lists both sociopathy and psychopathy under the heading of Anti-social Personality Disorders (AsPD). In *DSM-5* and the *International Classification of Disease, Eleventh Revision (ICD-11)* there is no individual diagnosis for psychopathy or sociopathy. Instead, both are recognized as elements of Anti-social Personality Disorder. These disorders share many common behavioural traits, which leads to some of the confusion. Key traits that sociopaths and psychopaths share include: a disregard for laws and social mores, a disregard for the rights of others, a failure to feel remorse or guilt, and a tendency to display violent or aggressive behaviour. Some experts regard the current definition as describing criminality rather than sociopathy. Plenty more people can be diagnosed with AsPD than sociopathy or psychopathy, leaving the condition closer to the parameters of 'normal' human behaviour. In contrast the terms 'sociopathy' and 'psychopathy' help maintain the idea that the condition is distinct and extreme, hence serving to reassure the rest of us that the problem exists only in small numbers and only at the margins of society. In reality though, sociopathy probably exists on a continuum.

Adding to the debate, some theorists speculate that people behave cruelly not because they are intrinsically evil (a concept many consider outmoded), but because they lack empathy. According to Simon Baron-Cohen, an expert in developmental psychopathology at the University of Cambridge, limited or zero empathy may result from physical and psychological characteristics but empathy deficits can be turned around if people are taught to be more empathic.[14] He points to the need to identify treatments (as yet none are available but trials have been conducted with families of children with conduct disorder, a child version of sociopathy) that will teach empathy to those who lack it.

Putting empathy under the microscope – or rather the modern-day gadgetry of functional magnetic resonance imaging (fMRI) – Baron-Cohen explores new ideas about empathy in his book *Zero Degrees of Empathy*. He suggests that the level of empathy most of us experience varies according to the conditions we face at any given moment, although all of us have a predetermined level of empathy which we generally return to (our pre-set position, if you like) on what he calls the **empathy spectrum**. This spectrum ranges from six degrees at one end, down to zero degrees at the other:

- **Position 0** No empathy and hurting others means nothing to them.
- **Position 1** Capable of hurting other people but have some regret if they do.
- **Position 2** Has enough empathy to inhibit acts of aggression.
- **Position 3** Compensates for a lack of empathy by covering it up.
- **Position 4** Low to average empathy.
- **Position 5** Slightly higher than average empathy.
- **Position 6** An almost unstoppable drive to empathize. Very focused on the feelings of others.

At six degrees we have highly empathic people, while at zero degrees we have the sociopath. For his research Baron-Cohen constructed an Empathy Quotient or EQ test that is intended as a measure to determine how easily you pick up on and how strongly you are affected by others' feelings.

Baron-Cohen also suggests that deep in the brain lies the **empathy circuit**. This is thought to involve at least ten inter-connected brain regions, all regions of what is termed the 'social brain'. The first is the medial prefrontal cortex (MPFC), which is thought of as the 'hub' for social information processing and considered important for comparing your own perspective to someone else's. The functioning of this circuit determines where we each lie on the empathy spectrum, Baron-Cohen suggests. This idea relates to the earlier work of Giacomo Rizzolatti, a renowned Italian neurophysiologist. Rizzolatti demonstrated the existence of a system of nerve cells which he called **mirror neurons**. His work with primates showed that these nerve cells were fired not only when the animal performed an action, but also when it saw another animal performing the same action. This suggests that empathy involves some form of mirroring of other people's actions and emotions. Using fMRI, scientists have identified which regions of the brain appear to be involved in the mirror neuron system.[15]

Scientists have been quick to equate mirror neurons with empathy, but this may be pushing the idea too far. We are still some way from understanding exactly how social and biological determinants interact. Besides, mirror neurons may just be the building blocks for empathy. Other mechanisms may be involved and be just as, if not more, significant. For instance, one region of the brain, the amygdala, is considered to be important in the empathy circuit (in fact we have two amygdala in our brains, one in each hemisphere). The amyg-dalae appear to play a key role in emotional learning and regulation processing, and are vital in cueing us to look at other people's eyes when we want clues about their thoughts and emotions.

Empathy is a multidimensional construct and requires the ability to perceive, understand, and feel the emotional states of others. According to most models, empathy consists of at least three core components:

1 The ability to recognize emotions in oneself and others via different communicative cues such as facial expressions, speech or behaviour
2 A cognitive component, also referred to as perspective taking or theory of mind, describing the competency to take on the perspective of another person, whilst maintaining the essential distinction between self and other
3 An affective component, that is, sharing of emotional states with others or the ability to experience similar emotions as others.

Sociopaths are very good at reading the minds of their victims. That is, they have the ability to *see* things through the eyes of another person (cognitive empathy or what some have called 'cold' empathy). This is what affords them social intelligence (situational awareness, understanding of social dynamics). What they lack is the ability to share emotional states with others (emotional or affective empathy). In other words they lack the *feelings* that otherwise would permit them to experience and empathize with the emotional states of other people. This is clearly seen in deception. You have to be good at mind reading before it would even occur to you want to deceive someone. This suggests that in sociopaths the cognitive part of empathy is functioning very well, but the fact that they don't have the appropriate emotional response to someone else's state of mind – the feeling of wanting to alleviate distress if someone's in pain – suggests that the emotional or affective part of empathy is not functioning normally. For example, sociopaths are known not to empathize with other people's fear. It is thought that there are differences in brain structure that mark out those at the opposite ends of the empathy spectrum. Research by Professor Abigail Marsh of Georgetown University's Department of Psychology in Washington DC found that sociopaths have dysfunction of the amygdala (reduced volume) that impairs their ability to generate a fear response and identify other people's fear. Interestingly, this is in contrast to altruists (those who show selfless concern for the well-being of others), who have larger amygdala volume than that of non-altruists. These findings suggest individual differences may have an underlying neural basis.[16]

Outline of the book

This book alerts you to the ruses and manipulations socio-paths use and shows you how to invest in your empathic powers to keep them at bay. In Chapter 2, the tell-tale signs of sociopathy and sociopathic abuse are introduced by pro-viding accounts drawn from real-life situations. In Chapter 3, 'A profile of the sociopath', the character of the sociopath is scrutinized in order to help you 'see' the problem behaviour for what it is. By reading the narratives and information about sociopaths' common traits it's hoped that you will begin to understand the characteristics of the sociopath and socio-pathic behaviour.

In Chapter 4, 'Interactions of the sociopath', sociopaths' rela-tions with other people are analysed. In particular, I draw the reader's attention to the existence of the Sociopath–Empath–Apath Triad (SEAT). This is important to appreciate because sociopaths' interactions frequently involve not only the chosen target (often a person with a high level of empathy), but an apathetic third party referred to in shorthand as an 'apath'. How these three players interact is discussed in detail, as is the unfortunate reality that sociopaths frequently enlist the help of apaths in their cruel sport.

In Chapter 5, the dangers of blindly following orders and following the crowd are discussed together with psychological and social influences on human behaviour. Chapter 6, 'Coping in the aftermath of a destructive relationship', is about the early days following sociopathic trauma. In this chapter I include things to watch out for and ways to cope in the immediate aftermath of an association, friendship or intimate relationship with a sociopath.

Chapter 7, 'Establishing boundaries and regaining control of your life', focuses on the process of recovery and looks at measures to help you get life back on track, while in Chapter 8 complex family situations are discussed. Chapter 9 explores the potential of empathy as a powerful corrective and remedy for sociopathic abuse. Useful addresses and further reading are also included at the back of the book.

2

Everyday sociopaths

How do sociopaths work, and how can you spot them in everyday life? The purpose of this chapter is to heighten your awareness of the nature of sociopaths. Many sociopaths wreak havoc in a covert way, so that their underlying condition remains hidden for years. They may possess a superficial charm, and this appeal diverts attention from the more disturbing aspects of their nature.

Another reason that their real natures remain hidden is that many of the behaviours exhibited by sociopaths are seen in ordinary people too. Quite a lot of people cheat on their partners, have addiction problems, steal and lie, but not everybody who does so is sociopathic. Sociopaths are more numerous than is generally supposed. We encounter them on a daily basis, even if we don't register the fact. They may be politicians or celebrities, your neighbour, your partner, your boss, someone you met online or the person next to you in the checkout queue. So, it is quite probable that if you don't know one intimately, you have fleeting contact with a few.

The following accounts of sociopathic behaviour are drawn from real-life situations. Though they do not constitute an exhaustive account of everyday sociopaths or encounters, they reflect the kind of sociopathic behaviour and abuse that goes on in the course of everyday life.

Sociopaths come in all shapes and forms – young and old, men, women and even children – and can be hard to spot. I hope the following case histories illustrate just how individuals may be systematically targeted until they feel they can barely trust their own sense of reality – what is called 'gaslighting' (see Chapter 4). Sociopathic abuse is targeted abuse of individuals or groups. Sadly, it can wreck lives, though I hope to show that victims can become survivors, even if at huge cost.

Romance fraudster

A gambling-obsessed con artist told a nurse, Sarah, that he was a secret agent before fleecing her out of her entire savings of £50,000. The fraudster's victim thought she had met the 'perfect man' when she was swept off her feet by her 'confident, friendly and hugely likeable' suitor. But after gaining access to her bank accounts, he plundered her savings and then fled to Spain. Luckily, he was caught eventually, and made to pay for his crimes though many fraud cases go un-investigated.

Those with a kind and caring disposition can easily fall foul of a con artist and their ruses. In this case, Sarah fell under the charmer's spell then let him move in with her. He told her he was due a £320,000 divorce settlement and would start paying his way when it came through. He then asked her for several short-term loans and promptly repaid them – building up her trust before gaining access to her finances; positively reinforcing the view he could be trusted,

To play on the impression that he was a generous soul (perception managing is what they do best), he took her out for meals and was careful to show the 'wads of cash' in his wallet. Confident he had her in his clutches, he told her he was an 'old fashioned man' and wanted to manage her accounts so she would be spared the trouble. At this point she was persuaded not to look at her bank account as it would spoil the surprise, he was planning for her 40th birthday. In a bid to further conceal his antics he intercepted and hid all her post to prevent her seeing her account balances. Wickedly, he even asked her parents to help him raise the money for a deposit on a house, but cheques he wrote to repay the money were not honoured. And that wasn't all. When Sarah confronted him, he pretended to have taken an overdose and was taken to hospital (another tactic, 'playing for pity'), but blood tests showed that he did not require treatment.

Behaviourally, positive reinforcement tactics such as paying for meals and prompt payment of the loans helped reinforce the idea that he is a man to be trusted and safe to be with. Negative reinforcement is used to maintain compliance, such as the staged overdose. He plays on her compassion and her pity when it is Sarah who is the real victim in this. These tactics serve to strengthen the false narrative that Sarah has come to believe and sees her surrender repeatedly to the con artist's perspective and clutches.

This behaviour is like that of the con artist Anna Sorokin, who took the name Anna Delvey and tricked the New York elite out of hundreds of thousands of dollars. Delvey faked being a German heiress and socialite. She was convicted in 2019 of defrauding companies out of $275,000 during a ten-month spending spree and spent time behind bars.[1] The so-called Tinder Swindler is another example of this sort of abuse. Shimon Hayut, a convicted fraudster used dating apps to meet multiple women, then established lines of credit and loans in their names, leaving them holding the bills. How did he manage to get away with it? Hayut appeared happy to jump from one identity to another to keep his scheme running. He was convicted of fraud under his birth name but conducted his Tinder con under the name Simon Leviev, claiming to be the son of wealthy diamond magnate Lev Leviev.

Sociopaths online

Sociopaths can and do exploit people online. It is the easiest way to target the vulnerable and the young. Claire enjoyed making new friends online:

> 'When I was fourteen, I was feeling really low and lonely. I found it difficult to mix with people and I wasn't sure why. I'd been bullied at school because people thought I was different, and I spent a lot of time on my own. I used to go online a lot. I enjoyed making new friends online as I found it easier than talking to people face to face. It made me feel less lonely. I used to add people that I didn't know, and I had never had any problems before. I got a friend request from a girl I didn't know and added her. I don't know how she got my number, but I had previously put my number on Facebook asking people to add me. We talked quite a lot for a few days about general things and built up a friendship.
>
> After a few days the conversation turned. She kept asking for me to send her a naked picture. I wasn't very confident and was more likely to do something like that without questioning the reason why,

so I just sent her one without thinking about it. She kept asking for more. When I said 'no' she threatened to put the one she had on Facebook. I was very worried as I didn't want my friends and family to see it. I didn't hear anything for a couple of days, so I didn't think she was going to do anything with it but then I heard that she'd set up a group under my name with the naked picture of me on. Anyone who searched for me could find it.'

Some apps in the virtual reality metaverse are 'dangerous by design', according to the NSPCC.[2] The metaverse is the name given to games and experiences accessed by people wearing virtual reality headsets. The technology, previously confined to gaming, could be adapted for use in many other areas from work to play.

Sociopathic parent

Motherhood did not come naturally to Rebecca's mother. She didn't feel any real affection for her baby daughter and hated most aspects of caring. Worst of all she hated the attention her baby daughter received from her father. And as Rebecca got older, her mother's resentment towards her took a dark and sinister turn.

Whenever Rebecca didn't do as she was told, her mother would give her the coldest, hardest stare and say in the most vindictive voice, 'I'll remember that when you want something.' She would lock Rebecca in a cupboard under the stairs, and once in a fit of rage she hacked off chunks of her daughter's curly hair. To divert attention from the abuse, Rebecca's mother ensured that Rebecca was always well dressed and that her manners were impeccable. In another attempt to deflect attention away from Rebecca, her mother developed an extreme case of agoraphobia and other phoney disorders, so no-one saw them out and about together. Instead, she took anti-depressants by the bucketful and took to her bed.

As Rebecca grew up, her mother did all she could to keep her away from her father, who loved his daughter dearly. But Rebecca's father was oblivious to his wife's resentment of their father–daughter closeness. This blindness extended to not seeing the injuries that she inflicted on Rebecca, though most were concealed beneath her clothes. Rebecca, by contrast, was all too aware of her mother's resentment, and tried hard not to rock the boat. She said nothing about the bruises or traumas she endured. The abuse continued all through Rebecca's childhood and had a corrosive effect; over time she believed what her mother said about her, that she was a worthless human being.

By the time Rebecca was in her late teens she was emotionally spent but she left school with excellent grades and secured a place at a university, many miles from the family home. She flourished away from her mother's abuse. After university everything was working out. But for Rebecca there was still one unresolved problem and that was the increasing distance between her and her father. Her mother employed all manner of tactics to block contact between them. She intersected mail, arranged long weekends away when Rebecca might visit, and made it a policy to always answer the phone. In consequence father and daughter seldom spoke and eventually a wedge formed between them.

Years later, after a lengthy period of estrangement, Rebecca's father's health took a sudden turn for the worse. He was rushed to hospital where he died. In a final act of cruelty her mother didn't tell Rebecca until after the event when she informed Rebecca that because of her selfishness her father had been persuaded to write her out of his will.

Sociopathic partner

Amanda painfully discovered that the man she married was a sociopath. The warning signs were there early but at first, she was dazzled by his charming irresistible facade. He had all the qualities that she had been searching for. He was confident, intelligent, successful, good looking, socially skilled. When he asked her to marry him, she couldn't say no. She had no idea of the real nature of the bargain that she was striking, or that she was easy prey.

Over the next few years, her husband inflicted emotional abuse and showed a controlling nature, but this was hidden from public view. It was only a few months into their marriage when he stopped being charming and revealed another side to his character. He became very callous and controlling. He managed her bank account and told her who she could see. She noticed how he stepped on other people's feelings and exploited people. She didn't see for a long time that he had treated her badly too. If he got what he wanted, that was all that mattered. At work he was successful and had the right connections and an impeccable image. Other people were mesmerized by him too.

This was all delusion – the greatest act in the world that most people believed, even Amanda's relatives. No one would guess that in the darkness of her bedroom late at night, she was brutalized psychologically; derided, criticized and treated like dirt. Amanda was always in fight or flight mode – there was no let up. Her blood pressure went sky high; she got frequent infections and flu. She couldn't sleep at night and would wake up with a start. 'What is he going to do next?' she kept asking herself.

Sadly, it took a decade of abuse before Amanda recognized that she was married to a psychological abuser. She ignored numerous affairs and indiscretions before she finally accepted that he didn't give a damn about her. In fact, when she finally found the courage to leave him it was barely any time before he replaced her with a new girlfriend whom he swiftly moved into the home!

It took Amanda a surprising amount of time to come to her senses, for he had eroded her confidence and made her question her senses. Once she was awake to the reality of her situation however, she found courage to make plans in secret to get out of the marriage. She sought legal and financial advice and was able to protect the assets she had. Thankfully, her life is much more secure now and she's glad she got out of the marriage before he did more harm.

Sociopathic child

Jilly woke up from a nap during the afternoon with a kitchen knife poking her neck. Her ten-year-old son, Thomas, whom she adopted as a baby, was at the other end of the knife.

'Were you trying to hurt me?' she asked. Thomas only smiled. This wasn't the first such incident involving Thomas. And she knew it would not be the last.

Thomas, with multiple medical issues and emotional problems as a child, always had a dark side. Maybe it's because the first several months of his life were in a hospital with little physical contact, let alone intimate bonding. He was severely disturbed and had inappropriate ways of relating socially. Thomas never bonded with Jilly, and never really liked her. Despite years of her love, affection and attention, he often called her the B-word. Or wished she would die. And a couple of weeks ago he punched her in the face.

Jilly feared her own son. She had thought that love could fix everything. She and her husband, Richard, had been foster parents for 20 years, allowing all kinds of kids with all kinds of problems into their home.

Though Thomas had threatened her in the past, he had never threatened Richard. With Richard he was well behaved and always denied his abuses of Jilly. On this occasion she called the police who pretty much told her that Thomas is her responsibility, and they couldn't take him. Jilly and Richard agree that Thomas will hurt somebody. They worry about what to do for the best.

Sociopathic traits in children are not as uncommon as you would think. This sort of behaviour – cruelty in children – is one of the last taboos. Despite the occasional sickening story appearing in the news, it doesn't receive much public attention. Sociopathic traits in children are thought to have a hereditary, physiological and environmental basis and are discussed in Chapter 8.

Sociopaths at work

Andy was recruited as a finance officer at a large UK charity. From his first day, he charmed the pants off his seniors and ingratiated himself to anyone with influence.

Andy was responsible for paying charity bills but was not an authorized signatory on the charity's bank account. One day a few months into the job, he accessed one of the senior management team's bank account login details and set up fake payees in the name of genuine third parties. In this way he fraudulently obtained over £30,000 in a few months. Apparently, there was no review or oversight in place to catch his embezzlement.

Nothing came to light until one day about 18 months into the job a junior member of staff became suspicious. Aware that his colleague was suspicious, he set about creating distractions. His first act was to report that his phone and laptop had gone missing from his office. He claimed that they had been stolen from his desk after a meeting in which the junior colleague with suspicions was present. Andy banked on the rest of the team finding it inconceivable that he would make up such things. Then he spread malicious gossip about the staff member, in a bid to discredit her in the event she came forward and reported her suspicions to his seniors.

The charity CEO felt the alleged theft warranted investigation and he called in the police though there was insufficient evidence to see anyone charged. In this way, Andy was successful in isolating the woman whose instincts told her that he was up to no good. His actions caused the woman significant stress and not long after the police investigation, she went off-sick from work.

After embezzling the charity out of further funds to the tune of £80,000 over the course of the following year, Andrew finally resigned from the job. Everyone congratulated him and wished him well in his new job: a more senior role in another large national charity.

So how did Andrew get away scot-free with fraud and damaging his colleague's reputation? We allow authoritative and convincing people to strongly influence our behaviour, something a sociopath is eager to exploit.

Today, the dangers in most work settings aren't so often physical, but rather the dangers come from people who threaten one's job, emotional safety or esteem. There are minor threats, like hidden agendas; and then there are sociopathic ones, like ostracism, blame, public embarrassment, bullying, humiliation and betrayal. These are especially menacing when initiated by a superior who has direct control over your survival at work. The anti-social behaviour used by corporate sociopaths is particularly destructive for projects that are the collective product of many minds. To be successful, co-workers form a collaborative social system powered by emotional energy, knowledge, meaningful relationships, creativity and trust-based collaboration. Anti-social environments crowd out the helping behaviours that normally fuse workers into a tight collaborative team.

Sociopathic leaders

Are politicians natural-born sociopaths? Some think so. In 2016, Oxford psychologist Dr Kevin Dutton ranked a number of leaders for sociopathic/psychopathic traits using a standard psychometric tool, the 'Psychopathic Personality

Inventory-Revised' (PPI-Revised). The psychometric tool was developed to assess these traits in non-criminal (e.g. university students) populations, though it is still used in clinical (e.g. incarcerated) populations as well. He found Donald Trump ranked above Adolf Hitler, but lagged a little way behind Idi Amin, Saddam Hussein and Henry VIII. He also found Hillary Clinton ranked between Napoleon and Nero.[3]

As well in 2016 another academic, David Wilson, a professor of criminology from Birmingham University analysed the behaviour of former prime minister Tony Blair.[4] Wilson remarked that after his landslide victory in 1997, Blair had shown a growing appetite for military adventurism, as shown in his interventions in Sierra Leone, Kosovo and Afghanistan. But the Iraq invasion took this approach to a whole new level. Wilson suggested that Blair was willing to do anything to gain the approval of the US President whose power and prestige dazzled him. He pointed to Blair's behaviour after the *Chilcot Report* (the public inquiry into the nation's role in the Iraq War) was published in 2016. In the wake of the devastating findings of the report, and the evidence of hundreds of thousands of deaths in Iraq and the wider region, Blair still professed that he would take the same decisions again. Wilson describes Blair as a man who is deeply in denial. In psychological terms, Wilson reported, 'He is using denial as a defence mechanism to block out reality, and thereby assuage the inevitable guilt that would surely consume him if he faced the truth.' Wilson described Blair's behaviour as driven by a personality that was deluded, narcissistic, manipulative, needy and messianic.

The way we look at the personalities of leaders past and present has altered since the turn of the twenty-first century when the general view of sociopathy/psychopathy began to shift. Where once sociopathy was understood in terms of remorseless criminality, sociopaths came to be viewed as, not a discrete group of malevolent people separate from the rest of us, but as personalities existing on a continuum of lack of empathy. From this newer perspective sociopaths in certain spheres (e.g. politics, corporations) are increasingly accepted. Indeed, apologists for sociopaths in leadership claim that sociopathic traits in politics and the corporate world are desirable and advantageous. Presumably this is because they are risk-takers. This view normalizes sociopathy in society and in leadership roles gives it preference.

Experts such as Nick Haslam, professor of psychology at the University of Melbourne, argue that everybody has social intelligence (the ability to understand social cues and the motivations of others and oneself in social situations), thus all have the ability to manipulate and exploit others in the way some politicians appear to do.[5] However, this latter point – that everyone has the ability to manipulate and exploit others – is doubtful. Not all people have the same degree of social intelligence and for many, their natural empathy puts pay to exploitation of others, as their conscience just won't allow it. Furthermore, some individuals have great difficulty understanding social cues and the motivations of others; for example, those on the autistic spectrum. On account of this difficulty, they are more likely to be exploited than be manipulators themselves.

Haslam suggests much of the sociopathic leaders' poor, even morally defective behaviour, 'reflects the nature of the job, which calls for and rewards calculation, manipulation and the exercise of naked power'. This view and acceptance of sociopathic behaviour in certain spheres like politics and the corporate world fails to deal with the inevitable consequence of following malign leaders; social intelligence in the absence of emotional intelligence leads humanity into a moral void, a situation that is inescapably destructive. Sociopaths are insincere however much they dress things up and profess to have a social conscience. Their limited repertoire of emotions doesn't include moral emotions like guilt, shame or compassion. Sociopaths in leadership roles don't adhere to the social contract; in reality, they exploit it. So, if we propel sociopaths to the top of the social hierarchy we risk being led by social monsters, as history has repeatedly shown.

Sociopathic leaders seek to dominate the narrative so find ways to withhold information. They act covertly; conceal their corrupt activity by restricting information and hiding evidence, all the while keeping secret their true personality by wearing a mask of sincerity. The Founding Fathers of the United States were often worried about the tendency of republics to degenerate into demagoguery and tyranny. James Madison (1751–1836), one of the architects of the US Constitution, believed that an educated public is essential to maintaining the health of a nation. 'A popular Government, without popular information, or the means of acquiring it,' he said, 'is but a prologue to a farce or a tragedy; or, perhaps both.' A people 'who mean to be their own Governors,' said Madison, 'must arm themselves with the power which knowledge gives.'[6]

The normalization of sociopathy in leadership is a worrying trend. In recent years psychologists and psychiatrists, who up until now have been responsible for defining the problem of sociopathy, have had little to say about sociopaths in politics, especially leaders close to home. In fact, curiously there's been a reluctance to discuss them at all, perhaps for fear of psychological comment being merely partisanship in professional disguise. During the American election of 2016, for example, an election that saw Donald Trump come to power, questions were asked about whether psychiatrists should assess the mental state of political candidates. However, since 1974, the American Psychiatric Association has held it to be a violation of medical ethics for psychiatrists to make public statements about public figures whom they have not formally evaluated. This rule against making psychiatric diagnoses of public figures is called the Goldwater rule.[7] It derives from an event of 1964, when the editors of *Fact* magazine asked more than 12,000 psychiatrists to render an opinion about whether the Republican candidate, Barry Goldwater, was psychologically fit to serve as president of the US. More than 2,000 psychiatrists responded. Many of them concluded that Goldwater was mentally unfit for the presidency. Some even argued that Goldwater had a psychosis such as paranoid schizophrenia, though it should have been clear even to a lay audience that Goldwater was not schizophrenic. For this reason, American voters cannot turn to psychiatrists to help judge the character or the mental health status of American political candidates.

There is similar reluctance by psychiatrists in the UK to diagnose or label the personalities of politicians and prominent public figures. This failure to alert the public to potential danger may be due, in part, to professional defensiveness. Nevertheless, because the designated experts are reluctant to call out sociopaths, it has a silencing effect on society. Silence from experts has a way of making it appear as if no threat exists at all. This said, it is often counterproductive to call someone a sociopath, as anyone who has done so knows. Preferable to name calling is to call out the sociopath's anti-social behaviour. This can be done by anyone who sees it and is prepared to call it out – there's no need to wait for an expert to tell you what you detect about anyone. Calling it out allows others to initiate ways to protect themselves from harm.

Historically, psychiatry has been the leading profession involved in defining and treating mental health disorders including those of the anti-social kind. Yet, one of the reasons for psychiatry's reluctance to engage in public debate is that there is confusion within the profession about the best way to engage and treat people with anti-social personalities. Psychiatry lumps together personalities under an umbrella term, 'personality disorder'. It groups together individuals that 'think, feel, behave or relate to others very differently from the average person', according to the NHS website.[8] This means that the group of people identified as having personality disorder covers a range of personalities across the empathy spectrum and divide. Recently an advertisement for an upcoming conference on personality disorders, run by the Royal College of Psychiatrists, was promoted on social media. The conference was primarily aimed at general psychiatrists. Its advertising poster described personality disorder as '... the thorn in the flesh of many clinicians'.[9] It went on to say, '... the majority avoid contact with health professionals but nonetheless cause considerable distress both to themselves and those around them'. The rest of the advertisement outlined the programme of the event, which included discussion of the limitations of definitions and treatment of personality disorders. A person claiming to have a personality disorder complained on the social media platform that the wording of the conference poster was unacceptable. What then followed was an outpouring of apologies from psychiatrists and the poster was swiftly removed. When one commentator said he could see nothing wrong with the wording, having a family member with a personality disorder who had wreaked havoc on the lives of those around them, his words and view were passed over. This online exchange typifies the inability of psychiatry to properly grapple with sociopathy in culture. Waiting for experts to tell us what to think and do – for example, waiting for psychiatrists to diagnose the challenging person in your life and give their expert advice – often means we bypass our instinctive responses and delay getting out of harm's way.

As said in the introductory chapter of this book, psychiatry has redefined sociopathy repeatedly in an attempt to maintain control of determining what it is and treating it. Except for the rare few mental health professionals (psychologists in the main) who speak up about sociopaths in everyday life, there seems to be at play a form of self-censorship. In wishing to keep a stranglehold on the treatment of disordered personalities as a specialty of psychiatry, the profession makes repeated attempt to redefine them, to the point where the distinctions between the various diagnostic labels are not useful and are blurred. Psychiatry has found no useful way of treating sociopaths. It fails in the task of modelling effective interaction with personalities who lack sensitivity for others and have poor social boundaries, and it fails in its expert role in promoting public mental health because it neglects to alert the public and equip them with ways to contend with sociopaths in daily life.

Psychiatry has not yet come to terms with the consequences of sociopathy being of greater prevalence than previously supposed. Sociopathy is no longer regarded as a fixed trait of the few but considered to evolve on a continuum (absence of empathy by degree), thus it likely affects more people. Furthermore, there may be a subconscious bias at play; psychiatry like all professions, is not immune to the problem of sociopathy in its ranks and among its leaders. A grim example emerged in the social environment in which the psychiatric profession evolved in Germany with the onset of Nazism. Psychiatry and its theories became an instrument used to legitimize the authoritarian state's drive to isolate those who threatened to disrupt society or were considered 'economically unproductive'. This development ultimately strengthened the racial hygiene ideology of the Third Reich and facilitated the extermination of an estimated 100,000 mental patients.[10] Ideas do not exist in a vacuum, they spread and merge over time and place. We need to be on the constant lookout as ideologies, even in medicine, can be taken up and exploited for malign purposes. Neither antisocial traits nor empathic ability are assessed at recruitment into psychiatry, or in any specialty of medicine at any stage in a doctor's career. Medical doctors, psychiatrists, psychologists, scientists, experts of all varieties, don't have the moral high ground or possess greater empathy on account of their qualifications or intellect.

The pervasiveness of sociopathy among leaders is a serious unresolved problem that impacts us all. The expert leader not only mesmerizes, but also confounds others with their authoritative pronouncements. We are afraid to appear stupid or be the odd one out who doesn't go along with it when a new phenomenon or view gains ground, so we don't speak out. Worse still, some use the opportunity to join in with the abuse, the leader's pronouncements giving them license.

Having high intelligence or IQ doesn't provide immunity from sociopathic ruses. Individuals working in academia are as likely to be taken in by sociopathic fraudsters as anyone else. Perhaps more so, because education is structured in such a way as to encourage conformity. Deciding what knowledge someone needs is an exercise in having power over someone. Assessment, specifically, is grounded in power structures. Learning, as it's been traditionally perceived by our culture, is a sorting process. It separates the expert from the novice. It is an exercise in 'them' (passive recipients of knowledge) and 'us' (experts who tell people what to think and do). Arguably, it has little to do with the promotion of intelligence or thinking for oneself.

Established professional groups in stable societies may enjoy **stability privilege**, where members view themselves as superior and become complacent. Having one's guard down, owing to a belief that 'no threat exists in our community' is perhaps why colleagues of the prominent public figure, child sex-abusing, BBC presenter and charity fundraiser Jimmy Savile, didn't raise concern about the abuser in their midst. In 2022, a documentary, *Jimmy Savile: A British Horror Story* highlighted the mesmeric appeal of Savile, a man who sexually abused up to 1,000 young girls and who police consider one of the country's most prolific sex offenders. The documentary shows archive footage of the presenter making, what are in hindsight, extremely disturbing comments. At one point, Savile is heard saying, 'I am a voluntary helper ... Sometimes, when nobody's looking, I help the lassies.' In truth, he gloated about his sexual abuses and exploits, yet those in his thrall were either blind to the true meaning of his words or for reasons one can only guess at, chose to look the other way. The BBC was later blamed for having a 'culture of secrecy'. In its subsequent report, released in 2013, 90 pages were blacked out though the BBC Director General at that time, Tim Davie, went on record as saying: 'Redactions are not about protecting the BBC's reputation.' Former prime minister Margaret Thatcher and the Royal Family were blamed for lending Savile credibility.[11]

Financial gain in the form of charitable donations by Savile may have silenced dissenters in the NHS and prevented them from reporting him. Overlooking financial inducement as a factor that influenced the silence on Savile's abuses, coupled with complacency within the institution that the NHS doesn't harbour abusers in the ranks (Savile worked as a hospital porter and volunteer) probably led to the gross ethical failures that later became apparent. Complacency within the caring professions also may be why the serial killers GP Dr Harold Shipman, and nurse Beverley Allitt went undetected by their colleagues and got away with murder. It is also perhaps why, in a recent case that sparked national outrage, the Metropolitan Police did not see Wayne Couzens, the murderer of Sarah Everard, in its ranks, although evidence later emerged from messages exchanged between Couzens and colleagues that some officers knew of his deviant views and colluded with him. Collusion amongst police officers is a recognized phenomenon. There is thought to exist a 'blue wall of silence', a term used to denote the informal code of silence among police officers not to report on a colleague's errors, misconducts or crimes, including brutality. All three aforementioned killers successfully hid within the safe confines of their respective professions and held power over their victims on account of the status afforded them by their benign roles.

Our society relies upon all manner of experts to think for us and tell us how to behave. We are governed in visible and not so visible ways. Sometimes the leader's route to power bypasses democratic processes and they are not recruited or promoted up the ladder in a fair and ethical way. Invariably there are no checks carried out with regard to the suitability of their personality to the role. This is often the way in modern politics where charisma and a sense that 'this person will get the job done at all costs' are given priority. Nevertheless, it happens in other spheres too like academia, medicine and the police – areas that in various ways exercise social control. Who leads us impacts on the behaviour of the rest, sometimes in deeply concerning ways, and has serious consequences for society as I discuss later in this book. Next up in the following chapter, the characteristic behaviours of everyday sociopaths like the ones described here are laid out for closer inspection.

3

A profile of the sociopath

To deal with sociopaths effectively you first need to open your eyes – which is why, in this chapter, the sociopath is put under the microscope. In the tale 'The Emperor's New Clothes' by Hans Christian Andersen, two weavers promise the Emperor a new suit of clothes that is invisible to those who are stupid and unfit for their positions. When the Emperor parades before his subjects all the adults, not wishing to be seen in a negative light, pretend they see the Emperor's elegant new clothes. The only truthful person in the crowd is a child, who cries out, 'But he isn't wearing any clothes!'

In this chapter it is hoped that you will see sociopaths in the same way the boy in the tale sees the Emperor – naked, and as they really are. Very young children often have this ability – they'll say things like 'That's unkind, stop it', or 'I'm telling on you, you bully', when they see behaviour that defies the social boundaries that they have been taught.

But as children get older, most find it gets harder to take such a bold stance. From infancy we are trained to 'toe the line', to conform to society's standards and rules. We are conditioned to keep quiet, which often means turning a blind eye or putting up with abuse. The boy in the tale represents those who see the problem behaviour for what it is and find the courage of their convictions to make a stand. 'Sight' becomes insight, which turns into action. Awareness is the first step in limiting the negative effects of contact with a sociopath.

Traits of the sociopath

Superficial charm

Have you ever come across someone with magnetic charm? Perhaps alongside this they affect an air of importance and have a grandiose view of themselves? Sociopathic charm is not like any other. It is not in the least self-conscious.

The power to mesmerize or hypnotize often is a marked feature of sociopaths. At the very outset sociopaths utilize this hypnotic ability to tread over the issue of consent, whether it be the granting or the withholding or refusing of it. The targeted person or group who fall into an hypnotic trance are incapable of free self-willed action. This mesmeric paralysis explains the apparent inscrutability of a situation such as sexual abuse or domestic abuse – a complexity that often escapes our social understanding, leaving us incapable of grasping the full extent of the victim's horrifying predicament. Victims can remain hypnotized by their abusers for a lengthy period before they eventually wake, as is apparent in the case study of Amanda and her sociopathic partner presented in Chapter 2. It took Amanda over ten years of marriage to come to her senses and leave.

This hypnotic incapacitation also affects individuals with allegiance to religious cults and extreme political groups (e.g. Hitler's mesmeric influence on the Nazis and German population). Though it is frequently observed and often talked about, there's been little research on the mesmerizing influence of sociopaths. What is understood however, is that the initial charm offensive with its mesmeric impact enables **brainwashing** to take place. It usually starts with one person or persons (the targeted individual or group) being guided by another (the mesmeric sociopath) to respond to suggestions for changes in subjective experience, alterations in perception, thought or behaviour.

The term brainwashing was first used in the 1950s to describe how the Chinese government appeared to make people cooperate with them. Research into the concept also looked at Nazi Germany, at some criminal cases in the US, and at the actions of human traffickers. In her book *Brainwashing: The Science of Thought Control*, Dr Kathleen Taylor asserts that the techniques used to influence others include isolating the individual and controlling their access to information, challenging their belief structure and creating doubt, and repeating messages in a pressurized environment.

Sociopaths use this hypnotizing skill to great effect. They rarely exhibit social inhibitions, so they hardly ever get anxious or tongue-tied. Nor are they afraid of offending you. They aren't held back by the social convention that ensures most of us take turns in talking. They talk at you, confident that you will agree with everything they say.

Often they have a lot to say. A 'conversation' with a sociopath can feel like a bombardment. To the untrained ear sociopaths' pronouncements sound authoritative because they tend to use words and phrases intended to make them sound knowledgeable, but which on dissection sometimes prove nothing more than gobbledygook. This is how child abusing BBC presenter Jimmy Savile got away with abusing young girls, because he distracted the public with a bedazzling, whacky persona. Sociopaths with political ambition learn how to seduce whole populations in this way, and can be temporarily highly effective, long enough to get elected, but are usually very harmful in the long run.

When you first meet a sociopath, you may be impressed by their good manners. They tend to be charming at first, may go out of their way to please you and often fall back on flattery. These tactics are designed to draw you in. But beware, for they are not what they appear, which is why sociopaths are often called 'social chameleons'. It seems counterintuitive that someone so charming can be so dangerous, but many people are duped this way. Being charming is a sociopath's most potent trait. Targets often later remark that they were overwhelmed by the sociopath's charm offensive. They may seem larger than life, a go-getter, an adventurer. Their grandiose air and smooth conversation add to the illusion of being in the presence of someone special. They make you feel boring and insipid by comparison.

Everything a sociopath does is calculated to have an effect on you. Just as their charm is superficial, so too is everything else about them. The smile *looks* phoney because it *is* phoney. The sociopath has blunt emotional reactions and fakes emotions to appear sincere. The only natural smile you will see exhibited by a sociopath is a sneer as they derive pleasure from seeing others suffer.

It is hard to recognize when people have no shame for they usually conceal their lack of conscience well. The sociopath will make it their business to know how a person can be manipulated, hence their use of flattery and charm. It is quite common for sociopaths to create a sense of similarity and intimacy. They use it to blindside those in authority and those they use to do their bidding. As a consequence, no one guesses the sociopath is manipulating everyone behind the scenes, or if they do they are active and sadistic participants conniving in the ruse.

Predatory behaviour

Sociopaths are predators and hostile competitors. They have an insatiable hunger for power, money, sex and exploitation. This hunger is accompanied by base emotions such as fury, rage, envy, which stimulate them to attack their target with ferocity in order to gain their prize. Humans evolved as predators although through time they diversified their diets and behaviours. It is thought that cooperative behaviours emerged when humans lived by hunting game and gathering wild plant foods, so it paid dividends to cooperate and share among the group. Human cooperation is adaptive and solves problems of survival. Aiding parental care and social bonding, empathy is best seen as evolving in the context of cooperation and as a driver of pro-social behaviour. Numerous lines of evidence suggest that these variations in human traits and behaviour, as seen in the personalities along the empathy spectrum, are best explained by the heritable characteristics over successive generations over millennia and by cultural and local norms.

A sociopathic predator doesn't feel concern (empathy) for its prey for that would only get in the way of the satisfaction and enjoyment of the kill. What skills the predator require to successfully down their prey are perceptiveness (ability to spot prey) and cool calculation (the ability to manipulate a situation based on social intelligence). Predatory sociopathic behaviour therefore can be viewed simply as stimulated by hunger (an internal drive) and driven by opportunity.

There are infinite opportunities to use and abuse people in this calculated way when you are an apex predator at the top of the hierarchy. Apex predators exert a top-down control on individuals in the group. With few individuals awake to the dangerousness of the predator amongst them, sociopaths are free to target prey at will. As with other archetypal predators, they devour pretty much anything they can prey on. Without the limitations of a conscience they don't hesitate to hunt the young and vulnerable. Nonetheless, predators select their prey wisely to maximize success and minimize their chances of getting caught.

Motivated by the thrill of using, dominating and emotionally hurting others, the sociopath's actions are extraordinarily devastating to their victims. Some neglect their families and children and allow them to suffer cruel consequences (as in the case study of Rebecca's mother in Chapter 2). Their sexual behaviour is often predatory, deviant and involves power and domination. Sociopaths often have a precocious sexuality and this is one of the early behaviour problems. As they get older, sociopaths continue to engage in frequent, casual sex for they crave excitement. But just because there is sex doesn't mean there is love. There will never be any true intimacy or emotional sharing involved. Nor do sociopaths recognize the concept of consent. They may use sexual violence then make victims feel as though they are somehow to blame. Sociopaths also make their victims feel that what happened to them wasn't 'real' sexual violence.

Whilst psychiatrists have been reluctant to call paedophiles (those who sexually abuse children) sociopaths, the undeniable truth is individuals who target the young and molest children do as sociopaths do – they abuse power, manipulate and harm their victims. The child sex abuser's chosen strategy of manipulation, such as grooming (preparing a child for a meeting and abuse), along with the abuse itself, is justified by making excuses. They often redefine their actions as mutuality, arguing that the sexual contact is consensual, and exploit the power imbalance inherent in all adult–child relationships. Sociopaths always treat others, whether they happen to be adult or child, as objects of manipulation and view the harms they cause in pursuit of their selfish goals as irrelevant and inconsequential.

The need for stimulation

Another characteristic of sociopaths is their need for constant stimulation. They seek thrills through sex, drug-taking, ferocious competition with others, and engaging in all manner of risk-taking activities, including crime. They become bored easily, perhaps because their emotional repertoire is so limited. Their heads are not full of the kind of emotions that distract the rest of us (fear, guilt, love, joy, etc.).

Sociopaths have a very limited emotional range and are noted for their shallowness and fleeting attachments. Consequently they don't get other people's 'neediness' and see no point in showing emotions or sharing feelings except as an act of manipulation. Instead, and to fill the void, they tend to seek stimulation from external sources. They engage in 'mind games' (a struggle for psychological one-upmanship), and employ behaviour to specifically demoralize or empower their target. In this way they undermine their targets' confidence in their own perceptions. We saw this in the case studies presented in Chapter 2, in particular where the con artist played psychological games on his victim, Sarah. We saw it also in the case of Amanda who was married to a sociopath. It took years before she realized she had been psychologically abused and found the courage to leave. The sociopath may invalidate other people's experience: not only its significance and content, but also the person's capacity to trust their recollection of events, hence making the person feel guilty for holding their original view. Such abusive mind games may include discounting (denial of the person's reality), diverting, trivializing, undermining, threatening and anger. The sociopath's tactics and modus operandi are discussed in more detail in Chapter 4.

Not all competitive people are sociopathic, clearly. What we are talking about here is covert aggression and hostile competitive behaviour where the sociopath misuses others in order to beat off rivals and pushes ahead regardless of whether others get hurt or not. Because they are indifferent to others, sociopaths do not display a proper sense of social responsibility. They develop strategies which allow them to ignore social convention, reason and evidence in the pursuit of some personal goal. Sociopaths may well believe they exhibit extraordinary social responsibility. Indeed some have a Messiah complex, believing themselves to be some sort of saviour and unfortunately society often colludes in this, as was evident in the case of child sex abuser, Jimmy Savile.

A parasitic lifestyle

Another commonly observed characteristic of the sociopath is a parasitic nature. To someone targeted by a sociopath with strong parasitic tendencies it can feel quite literally as if life is being sucked out of them. Parasitic behaviour is associated with passive aggression.[1] Passive aggressives do not deal with things directly. They talk behind your back and put others in the position of telling you what they would not say themselves. They find subtle ways of letting you know they are not happy. They are unlikely to show their angry or resentful nature. They conceal it behind a façade of affability, politeness and a show of well-meaning. However, underneath there is usually manipulation going on.

Types of passive aggression include **victimization** – a situation where the person concerned is unable to look at their own part in a situation and turns the tables to become the victim, or at least to behave like one; **self-pity** – the 'poor me' scenario; **blaming** others for situations rather than being able to take responsibility for one's own actions; **withholding** usual behaviours or roles in order to reinforce to the other party that you are angry; and **learned helplessness**, where a person acts as if they cannot help themselves. It is common for someone acting in this way to deliberately do a poor job of something to make a point. The important thing to note is that passive aggression is a destructive pattern of behaviour and a form of emotional abuse. Such behaviours cause great distress to the target, who often feels overburdened with guilt and responsibility.[2] The con artist in the case study of romance fraud from Chapter 2 drew heavily on passive aggressive tactics. He pretended to have taken an overdose and in consequence was taken to hospital.

Manipulative behaviour

Sociopaths are often **socially intelligent** (i.e. they have the capacity to understand others and social situations), which is how they usually get on well and go undetected in the social realm. They know just how to influence others, but lack feeling for other people. This means they have no qualms in exploiting and manipulating others for their own gain.

Sociopaths often abuse their targets in a covert fashion. Psychological manipulation is a mainstay of the sociopath, who uses behaviour to influence or control others in a deceptive and dishonest way. Advancing the interests of the manipulator, often at another's expense, such methods are exploitative, abusive, devious and deceptive.

Manipulators may control their victims through **positive reinforcement**, which involves employing praise, superficial charm, superficial sympathy (crocodile tears) and excessive apologies, money, approval and gifts, attention and the use of facial expressions such as a forced laughter or smiles, all for public recognition; again, this relates to the behaviour of the romance fraudster in Chapter 2. Another approach is **negative reinforcement** – removing the person from a negative situation as a reward; for example, 'You won't have to pay all those bills if you allow me to move in with you.' Yet other means are **intermittent or partial reinforcement**, used to create a climate of fear and doubt, and **punishment**, including nagging, intimidation, threats, swearing, emotional blackmail and crying as ways of playing the victim.

A sociopathic manipulator can cause you to believe you are going crazy. If you find yourself in a relationship where you think you need to keep a record of what's been said and begin to question your own sanity, likely as not you are experiencing emotional manipulation. A sociopath is an expert in turning things around, rationalizing, justifying and explaining things away.

They lie so smoothly and argue so persuasively that you begin to doubt your own senses. Over a period of time this is so eroding it can distort your sense of reality. The sociopath can make you feel guilty for speaking up or not speaking out, for being emotional or not being emotional enough, for caring or for not caring enough. Manipulation is a powerful strategy. Most of us are conditioned to check ourselves, and we are usually our own worst critics. If accused of being in the wrong or acting imperfectly we do whatever is necessary to reduce our feelings of guilt.

Another powerful strategy is to demand sympathy from us. The sociopath plays the victim remarkably well. However, they seldom fight their own fights or do their own dirty work. In the earlier case example of the sociopathic partner (Chapter 2), Amanda's husband manipulates her family so they don't see that there is abuse going on at home. Manipulators also use verbal abuse, explosive anger or other intimidating behaviour to establish dominance or superiority; even one incident of such behaviour can condition or train the target to avoid upsetting, confronting or contradicting the manipulator.[3]

Sociopaths are always on the lookout for individuals to scam or swindle. The authors Babiak and Hare outline the sociopathic approach as having three phases.[4]

The assessment phase

Some sociopaths will take advantage of almost anyone they meet, while others are more patient, waiting for the perfect, innocent target to cross their path. In each case, the sociopath is sizing up the potential usefulness of an individual as a source of money, power or influence. Some sociopaths enjoy a challenge while others prey on people who are vulnerable. During the assessment phase, the sociopath determines a potential target's weak points and uses these to lead the target off course.

The manipulation phase

In this phase the sociopath has identified a target and the manipulation begins. At this time a sociopath may create a persona or mask, specifically designed to 'work' for their target.

A sociopath will lie to gain the trust of their target. Sociopaths' lack of empathy and guilt allows them to lie with impunity; they do not see the value of telling the truth unless it will help them get what they want. As the interaction with the target proceeds, the sociopath carefully assesses the target's persona. This move gives them a picture of the target's traits and characteristics so they can exploit them. The target's persona may also reveal insecurities or weaknesses they wish to hide from view.

The sociopath will eventually build a personal relationship with the target based on this knowledge. The persona of the sociopath, the 'personality' the target is bonding with, does not really exist. It is built on lies, carefully woven together to entrap the targeted person. It is a mask, one of many, customized to fit the target's particular expectations. This act of manipulation is predatory in nature and often leads to severe physical or emotional harm for the person targeted. Healthy relationships are built on mutual respect and trust; the targeted person believes mistakenly that the 'bond' between them and the sociopath is of that kind, and that this is the reason their relationship is so successful. So when the sociopath behaves disrespectfully or there are breaches of trust, such incidences are overlooked.

The abandonment phase

This is when the sociopath decides that their target is no longer useful. They then abandon their target and move on to a new one. Sometimes, perhaps not surprisingly, targets overlap. The sociopath can have several individuals 'on the go' as it were: one who has just been abandoned, but who is kept in the picture just in case the others do not work out; another who is currently being played; and a third, who is being groomed in readiness.

Lying

Truth and whether it is universal (meaning widely accepted facts that do not change over time, circumstance, location and so on) has been debated throughout time. And nowadays some even argue that we have entered a post-truth era; post-truth being defined since 2016 in the *Oxford English Dictionary* as 'relating to or denoting circumstances in which objective facts are less influential in shaping public opinion than appeals to emotion and personal belief'.

One truth that is universal, however, is that truthfulness eludes some. To ethically reason and arrive at truth requires a person to possess a conscience; that entity identified as existing within ourselves that helps us decide how to act towards others and is essential for promoting pro-social behaviour. To call our times a post-truth era suggests that we live in an unconscionable and sociopathic age where deceit is commonplace and truth telling is exceptional.

A problem with denying the existence of truth is that it fails to live up to what we know to be 'true' in our own consciences, our own experiences and what we see in the world. If there is no such thing as truth, then there is nothing ultimately right or wrong about anything. Inevitably, one person's sense of right would soon clash with another's. What happens if I put many lives at risk, or people are free to do whatever they want – murder, rape, steal, lie, cheat, etc., and no one could say those things are wrong? There could be no government, no laws and no justice. It would be catastrophic.

The difference between a truth and an untruth is understood only by those who wrestle with a conscience and as often stated in this book, sociopaths lack conscience. Without this entity a lie is no different from a truth – hence different narratives, perspectives and opinions are used in any which way that serves the sociopath's self-interests.

Sociopathic liars lie to gain something. Their lying is often calculated and cunning. Sociopaths don't care who their lies will affect, as long as the lie fits their purpose and achieves what they want. They may well know the difference between right and wrong, for they conceal their wrongs because they don't want to get caught, but without a conscience, the crux of the matter is they don't care – though they can be so good at lying that they believe their own lies.

Lying is an invaluable tool for a sociopath, who uses it to gain pity and sympathy. In fact, their lying shows no bounds. They use an assortment of tactics to deceive – they distort, evade, dissemble, prevaricate, confound, distract, minimize, confuse, wilfully misrepresent and purposefully misunderstand, often with a smirk of satisfaction. If you pay very close attention you may catch a sociopath in a lie because they have a tendency to tell different versions of the same lie to different people. However, the sociopath is apt to make sure that individuals who have been told different stories don't have the chance to meet or compare stories. They may even keep friends and acquaintances apart to minimize the risk of being exposed. And even if they are exposed, the sociopath doesn't baulk at telling a new lie to cover the old. We see this done frequently in the arena of politics and we see it in the case study of the con artist. Always remember when dealing with a sociopath that lying doesn't worry them one jot. Your feelings don't matter. The sociopath doesn't have the capability or desire to care about you or anyone else who is harmed by the lie. Nobody is 'special' to a sociopath unless they're serving them a purpose.

Sociopaths are likely to lie about previous relationships and situational circumstances. Don't be surprised if you find out that your sociopath boss never got a degree, let alone graduated from Cambridge, as stated in their CV!

Sociopaths are equally likely to lie about physical or mental abuse, especially if it will help them in a divorce or custody situation. Their lying is persistent lying. It doesn't matter if the lies are easily disproved, because for some illogical reason they are seldom challenged. The lies sociopaths create may be fantastic in nature, extensive, elaborate and complicated. Often there is a blurring between fiction and reality. The magnitude of the lie or its callous nature is irrelevant, and so are any consequences. Such characteristics have led researchers to conclude that the lying behaviour might be gratifying in itself, and the expected reward external.[5]

Con artists

Most sociopaths are con artists for they present a false persona and false picture in order to deceive. Sociopaths often acquire money through deception. They lie, cheat and fool people into thinking they've happened on a great deal or some easy money, when in reality the only person making anything out of the situation will be them. If that doesn't work, they'll take advantage of other people's weaknesses; loneliness, insecurity, poor health or simple ignorance. The sociopath's confidence tricks exploit other people's credulity, naïveté, compassion, vanity, confidence, irresponsibility and greed. Sociopaths often succeed in their cons because they induce errors of judgement in the victims. They frequently involve accomplices, who accept the perpetrator's plan because the accomplice is led to believe that they will gain money or receive some benefits by doing some task. How sociopaths rope in other people to engage in their ruses is discussed in Chapter 4 and Chapter 5.

Aggression and anti-social behaviour

The sense of entitlement that comes with sociopathy is astonishing to those who abide by the social laws and conventions of our culture. Where does the entitlement come from? It stems from self-absorption and selfish rage. When a sociopath is angry everyone knows it, for they can fly into terrible rages. Sociopaths exhibit anger or attempt to gain your pity when intent on deceiving you. They rely on the fact that your judgement will be affected by your conscience and feelings of guilt if you don't respond to the situation sensitively or fairly.

In the case studies presented in Chapter 2 there are many examples of anti-social behaviour and most are dressed up as something else by our expert manipulators. They exhibit concealed aggression, verbal aggression, passive aggression and when out of control, overt physical aggression.

Manipulation must occur for us not to 'see' the aggression and anti-social behaviour for what it is. The process obscures our view so that the sociopath can 'get away with murder'. Use of covert aggression is how Amanda's sociopathic husband, from the earlier case study, manages to get away with emotionally tormenting her while keeping his behaviour hidden from other family members and their friends. It is how Rebecca's mother got away with physically and emotionally abusing her daughter, for she hid it and manipulated everyone else, including Rebecca's father. It is how serial murders Beverley Allitt and GP Harold Shipman concealed their murderous intent. It is how Jimmy Savile got away with harming children for many years, and explains why his death was greeted with public outpourings of grief before his heinous crimes were revealed.

The sociopath's reliance on bullying and sabotage as an act of aggression frequently reveals itself in the workplace. Andy, from the case study of the workplace sociopath (Chapter 2), is very hostile in a covert way. He covers his tracks by faking a theft and convinces others to call in the police in order to intimidate his suspicious colleague. Although frequent in sociopaths, hostile competition and manipulation are in any case commonplace in society. The world of work in effect promotes it, and nowhere is this more apparent than in commerce and politics.

Cruelty to animals is also common among sociopaths. Nevertheless sociopaths are just as likely to use pets as a prop; as a way of convincing a new target of their kind-heartedness and trustworthiness.

Not all emotional displays are faked by the sociopath. As previously stated sociopaths can fall into terrifying rages, especially when their plans start to go awry or when backed into a corner. Their rages are often unrestrained tantrums – fury. This likely is as a result of arrested emotional development (stuck at an early stage of development) where moral emotions like guilt or shame don't hold them back. Violent outbursts can lead to physical abuse.

Recent research suggests that there are brain differences in individuals prone to aggression and bullying in adulthood. An international team of neuroscientists scanned the brains of life-long bullies and found that they appear to be physically smaller than other people's brains.[6] Using fMRI imaging lifelong bullies' brain cortexes were found to be substantially thinner and their entire brains had less surface area than the non-bully brains. The findings support the idea that, for the small proportion of individuals with persistent (lifelong) anti-social behaviour, there may be differences in their brain structure that make it difficult for them to develop social skills that prevent them from engaging in anti-social behaviour. A key exception was that the brains of people who exhibited anti-social behaviour as teenagers, but not as adults, showed no such abnormalities. The researchers suggest that those who are bullies only in adolescence, are generally capable of reform and can go on to become pro-social members of society.

Lack of empathy and remorse

Simon Baron-Cohen, author of *Zero Degrees of Empathy* defines empathy as an ability to identify what someone else is thinking or feeling, and to respond to their thoughts and feelings with an appropriate emotion.[7] What causes people to be capable of seriously hurting one another is not rightly understood, but when our empathy is 'switched off' and we operate solely on an 'I' basis (viewing the world as if only we existed), we are much more inclined to view other people as objects. This is the standpoint from which sociopaths are thought to see the rest of us.

As previously stated, Baron-Cohen suggests that we all stand somewhere on an empathy spectrum (from high to low) in a relatively stable position, though this is not immovable. In other words, you may experience quite a high level of empathy in general but your ability to empathize with others may display an occasional 'blip'. The good news is that for most of us our empathy is recoupable. For those with a long-standing lack of empathy, unfortunately it is not.

A side-effect of having no empathy is that sociopaths take no responsibility for their own behaviour. It is always about what has been done to them. One of the easiest ways to spot a sociopath is that they often attempt to establish intimacy through the early sharing of deeply personal information that is generally intended to make you feel sorry for them. Initially you may perceive this type of person as very sensitive, emotionally open, even a little vulnerable. However, that couldn't be further from the truth. Sociopaths are addicted to high drama. Life with a sociopath always entails having to deal with numerous problems and crises.

But don't expect the sociopath in your life to feel sorry for anyone but themselves. Sociopaths don't feel emotions like guilt, remorse or compassion. Their emotional experience appears to be restricted to base emotions like envy, self-pity, anger, resentment and rage. Sociopaths not only don't feel any concern for the effect their actions have on other people, but they are also unresponsive to other people's fear. Using neuro-imaging (fMRI) techniques that show which parts of the brain are active as someone is doing a particular task scientists have discovered that sociopaths exhibit less amygdala activity than control subjects when they view fearful faces. The amygdalae are two almond-shaped structures, one in each hemisphere of the brain that is important for emotion processing, especially how we experience fear and recognize it in others. Research by neuroscientist and psychologist Abigail Marsh and others reveals that sociopaths' brains are marked by a dysfunction in the amygdala; their amygdala is not only under-responsive to images of people experiencing fear, but is also up to 20 per cent smaller than average.[8]

Sociopaths who have been studied have been found to have a distinctive stare. Studies have documented that their pupils do not dilate when viewing scary or graphic images and that they tend to hold gazes for an uncomfortably long period – especially when engaging in deception or persuasion. A recent study published in the *Journal of Research in Personality* offers new insights into this stare, finding that those sociopaths who have been studied tend not to move their heads much. This is thought to be connected with dysfunction of the amygdala. Studies into general interpersonal communication have found that in normal circumstances head movement and direction can help convey agreement, dissent and confusion, while doing things like shaking your head or nodding can help emphasize a point. When combined with gaze, head movement can express even more complex functions, like the degree of emotion, social control and regulation of conversation (e.g. whose turn it is to talk). These new findings therefore suggest unique ways socio-paths communicate nonverbally and could offer clues into the neurological underpinnings of the condition. Researchers also found violations of personal space (e.g. standing too close) may reflect impairments in amygdala function as these are also characteristic of individuals with amygdala damage.[9]

Variation

Sociopathy and non-empathic acts are found in all populations on the planet. As stated, sociopathy exists on a spectrum. However, previous research on sociopathy has been over-reliant both on a male conceptualization of it as a medical disorder and on means of assessment developed, and primarily validated, with men.[10] There has been little systematic investigation of sociopathy in women. This means that since sociopathy is not routinely assessed in women the harmful potential of some sociopathic women can be overlooked.

This said, researchers have identified differences between sociopathic men and women. Researchers identify four key points in the way these differences manifest:

1 behaviour,
2 interpersonal characteristics,
3 underlying psychological mechanisms and
4 different social norms for men and women.

From the available literature it would seem that when women direct their aggression towards others, their victims are generally those within their domestic sphere of control – a partner, a family member, a child, a friend or a work colleague. In addition, much of the harm or aggression carried out by women involves manipulation of, or damage to, peer relationships through aggressive competitiveness, the withdrawal of friendship, ostracism, overt bullying, telling lies about the victim to promote their rejection by others and other acts of interpersonal aggression, in order to exclude the victim from the social group. In women, there is also a tendency to exhibit self-injurious behaviour.

Sociopath women are less likely than men to physically leave or move on from relationships (e.g. with a child or partner), and their damaging nature is less likely to be detected. Conversely, male aggression is more visible and more likely to result in arrest and punishment than is the case with women.[11] Manipulative men are more likely to run scams and commit fraud. When men direct their aggression toward others, its function most often is to damage the victim's sense of control or to dominate.

In the next chapter the sociopath's social interactions and how they use and abuse other people for their own sport are discussed.

4

Interactions of the sociopath

Instead of living for, in, and with yourself, as a reasonable being ought, you seek only to fasten your feebleness on some other person's strength.

Charlotte Brontë, Jane Eyre, *ch. 21*

In this chapter the sociopath's social interactions are analysed. In particular I'll be drawing your attention to the existence of what I've termed the Sociopath–Empath–Apath Triad (SEAT). Unremitting abuse of other people is an activity of the sociopath that stands out above the rest. To win their games, sociopaths enlist the help of hangers-on, which means that their interactions frequently involve not only the chosen target, but also a third party I call the **apath** – I explain why below.

The apath

In the context of any sociopathic interaction, those that collude in the sport of the sociopath are called 'apaths', short for 'apathetic'. Apathy is lack of feeling. An apath is the type of person most likely to do the sociopath's bidding. Being apathetic in this situation means showing a lack of concern or being indifferent to the targeted person. In Chapter 3, I highlighted the importance of 'seeing' the problem for what it is via the tale of 'The Emperor's New Clothes', which represents the collective denial and double standards that are often a feature of social life. The apath in this context is someone who is willing to be blind, i.e. not to see that the Emperor is naked.

Apaths are an integral part of the sociopath's arsenal and contribute to sociopathic abuse; sociopaths have an uncanny knack of knowing who will assist them in bringing down the person they are targeting. It's not necessarily easy to identify an apath from the outside. In other circumstances an apath may show ample empathy and concern for others, just not in this case. The one attribute an apath must have is some connection to, or some influence on the sociopath's target. Hence, close friends, colleagues, siblings, parents and other close relations can become accomplices to the sociopath and be instrumental in the downfall of the targeted individual.

How apaths, who may otherwise be fair-minded people, become involved in such destructive business isn't difficult to understand, though it can be hard to accept. The main qualifying attribute of the apath that renders them a willing accomplice is poor judgement resulting from lack of insight. This may be linked to reduced empathy for the targeted person. The apathetic person might bear a grudge, be jealous or angry, or have a sense of being let down by the individual concerned, and in consequence may be as keen as the sociopath to see the target defeated. Hence, the apath may be willing to join forces with the sociopath because they too has something to gain from the evolving situation.

At other times the apath doesn't want to see 'bad' in others, so chooses not to see it. On still other occasions, they might choose not to see because they have enough on their plate and don't possess the wherewithal or the moral courage to help the targeted person at that time. Or they might go along with abuse because they are 'just doing their job!' Usually, and whatever the reasons for their active or passive involvement, what happens during the course of interaction with a sociopath is that the apathetic person's conscience appears to fall asleep. Apaths walk in and out of situations in a trance-like state. It is this scenario that causes people blindly to follow leaders motivated only by self-interest. We excuse bullying, outrages, even murder, on the grounds that the leader knows best, regarding the injured and maimed targets not as fellow humans, but as objects, as 'its'.

This behaviour was demonstrated effectively in experiments carried out in the 1960s. In 1961–1962, Yale University professor Stanley Milgram set up an experiment to test the human propensity to obey orders. A person playing the role of 'teacher' was given a list of word pairs which he was to teach the 'learner'. The teacher was then given an electric shock from an electro-shock generator as a sample of the shock that the learner would supposedly receive during the experiment. The teacher began the experiment by reading the list to the learner. The teacher then read the first word of each pair and read four possible answers.

The learner was asked to press a button to indicate his response. If the answer was incorrect, the teacher would administer a shock to the learner, with the voltage increasing in increments for each wrong answer. If correct, the teacher would read the next word pair. The subjects believed that for each wrong answer, the learner was receiving actual shocks. In fact there were no shocks.

During the experiment, many people indicated their desire to stop and check on the learner, and some paused to question the purpose of the experiment. But most continued after being assured that they wouldn't be held responsible. A few subjects began to laugh nervously or exhibit other signs of extreme stress after hearing 'staged' screams of pain coming from the learner. If the subject indicated he wanted to halt the experiment, he was given verbal instructions by the experimenter, in this order:

> 'Please continue.'
> 'The experiment requires that you continue.'
> 'It is absolutely essential that you continue.'
> 'You have no other choice, you must go on.'

If the subject still wished to stop after hearing all four instructions, the experiment was halted. Otherwise, it was stopped after the subject had been given the maximum 450-volt shock three times in succession. In the experiments, 65 per cent of the 'teachers' administered the experiment's final massive 450-volt shock, though many were very uncomfortable doing so.

Afterwards, Milgram summarized the experiment in an article titled 'The perils of obedience', declaring:

> Ordinary people, simply doing their jobs, and without any particular hostility on their part, can become agents in a terrible destructive process. Moreover, even when the destructive effects of their work become patently clear and they are asked to carry out actions incompatible with fundamental standards of morality, relatively few people have the resources needed to resist authority.[1]

Milgram's experiments have been repeated many times over and yielded consistent results. What this evidence suggests is that a person of authority can strongly influence other people's behaviour. This is relatively useful in one way, as it makes it easy for an authority such as a government to establish order and control. But in the wrong hands such power and influence can have catastrophic consequences. The dubious nature of Milgram's experiments has attracted a great deal of ethical criticism, most importantly that he deceived the participants and didn't take adequate measures to protect them – indeed, within the context of this book, you might be forgiven for thinking such rather callous experiments have sociopathic tendencies. (Milgram's defence was that the results were unexpected and that their shocking nature, as much as the methods he used, may have evoked the criticisms.)

What the aforementioned experiment indicates is that some people are more malleable than others. Importantly, it tells us that a greater number of us lack a backbone than perhaps we would like to think. In fact the study, which has been repeated many times suggest that two thirds or more of us (a recent study discussed in Chapter 5 suggests the number has significantly increased) have a tendency to 'follow the leader', whether that leader is malign or benign. Within this majority group lurk the apaths, the foot-soldiers to the sociopath. Apaths are less able to see the situation for what it really is; their view of the bigger picture is obscured by their attitude to and opinion of the target, and by the sociopath's mesmeric influence.

Apaths are often fearful people; individuals who feel they do not possess the level of skill required to confront a challenge. They are the ones most likely to go with the flow, to conform and agree that the Emperor is wearing new clothes. But apaths may also fail to perceive any threat at all. A danger is of no importance if one denies its existence. An apath's response to a sociopath's call to arms can then result from a state of 'learned helplessness'. Apaths behave defencelessly because they want to avoid unpleasant or harmful circumstances. Apathy is an avoidance strategy.

Here's a case study to illustrate how apathy in others aids sociopathic abuse. A survivor of childhood abuse discusses her father's apathy:

> I always worshipped my father. To me, he was 'The Good One'. He didn't spend much time with me, but what time he did was treasured.
>
> When my mother was nasty to me, he would take me aside and explain that she hadn't been loved as a child, and that she didn't mean to hurt me, and really loved me, and that we must be very kind and understanding towards her. I only realized much later how harmful that was; it really set me up for my narcissist husband!
>
> Later my father developed a drinking problem. And then life became really complicated. My father let me down badly in the end.

Turning a blind eye is a common trait of the apath, as this next account makes evident:

George

George, an apath, was so used to his sociopathic wife, Marie, telling him what to do and what to say that he didn't see anything wrong in it. He learned to act defencelessly as a means of getting through life. Thus, it became more or less a habit to turn a blind eye if his wife challenged or threatened others, even if the person targeted happened to be one of his children. Marie bossed him about in order to keep control of her domain and possessions (these included family members, whom it has to be said she viewed as objects, not human beings). If she felt someone was getting too close to her foot-soldier husband, she would view them as a threat and start an offensive.

Her usual approach was to slyly make snide remarks and hurtful comments, or tell lies about a target's character. If the victim responded angrily, as naturally most would, she would turn to her husband and say 'See, George, I told you, she hates me', to which the husband would go along and lend support to her outrage. It is likely that the apath husband occasionally overheard the criticisms and accusations she directed at the targeted person but chose to ignore them. And she, accustomed to his passivity, had long ceased bothering to keep her remarks out of earshot. In the end he became so practised in self-trickery and so fearful of a showdown that he submissively went along with her every time.

In the case studies presented in Chapter 2, we see similar behaviour exhibited by Rebecca's father, who was persuaded by her cruel mother to write her out of his will. Children who have been abused can experience apathy in the form of helplessness, withdrawal, depression and by the silence that is enforced by the keeping of secrets. It can take a person many years before they come to the realization that their parent was abusive. In the case study of Amanda, whose husband was sociopathic, she very likely behaved in a helpless way before she finally woke up to the various forms of psychological abuse she had endured during their ten years of marriage. We also see apathy in her family. They are blindsided by her husband and didn't see the abuse that was going on. Apathy and indifference to abuse is a significant problem We see this in the failures of public institutions to address the lessons that need to be learned from the abuses of Jimmy Savile. In the chapter that follows this one, apathy and the role of apaths in aiding and perpetuating abuse, is discussed in more detail.

The empath

Not always, but quite often, the person targeted by the socio-path is an empath. To understand why this is, and what is going on when it happens, we first need to understand what an empath is. Most human beings have the ability to empathize, but some have more ability than others. Empathy is a vague and elusive concept. For US neuroscientist Jean Decety, empa-thy resembles 'a sort of minor constellation ... stars glowing in the cosmos of an otherwise dark brain'.[2] He is referring to the network of regions of the brain; the anterior cingulate cortex and anterior insula that light up orange on an fMRI scan when a person witnesses another in pain. Yet empathy is more than orange-lit bits of brain. It is something that makes us human, or rather, humane.

Empathy is a shared emotion. To show empathy is emo-tionally to put yourself in the place of another. It is a learned phenomenon that requires emotional control and the capac-ity to distinguish oneself from others. Most of us possess the automatic ability to perceive and share others' feelings. A baby listening to another baby cry will cry too. Unconsciously people mimic the facial expressions of those they see. The ability to empathize is directly dependent on your ability to feel your own feelings and identify what they are. If you have never felt a cer-tain feeling, it will be hard for you to understand how someone else is experiencing that feeling.

An empath, in the context that the term is applied in this theory and book, is a socially and emotionally intelligent indi-vidual. They are awake and alert to their surroundings. They are tuned in, perceptive and insightful. Empaths sense when something's not right, they respond to their 'gut instinct', and take action to alert or help other people. Going back to our folktale, 'The Emperor's New Clothes', the empath is the boy who mentions the unmentionable: that the Emperor is naked. He isn't wearing any clothes.

Back in the 1990s, researchers suggested that there was a positive relationship between empathy and **emotional intelligence**.[3] Since then that term has been used interchangeably with **emotional literacy**. What this means in practice is that empaths have the ability to understand their own emotions, to listen to other people and empathize with their emotions, to express emotions productively and to handle their emotions in such a way as to improve their personal power. In other words, they achieve balanced awareness, intelligently using both reason and emotions to arrive at socially appropriate responses.[4]

Empathy is a powerful communication tool that is often underused and undervalued in today's world. Yet the world needs as many empaths as it can find, for empaths are often mediators, and peacemakers. People are often attracted to empaths because of their compassionate nature. Even complete strangers find it easy to talk to empaths about personal matters because in general they make great listeners. A particular attribute of empaths is that they are sensitive to the emotional distress of others. Conversely they have trouble comprehending a closed mind and lack of compassion in others.

Empaths may find other people's indifference difficult to tolerate. Very highly empathetic people may find themselves helping others at the expense of their own needs. Empaths are pro-social and become disturbed by the cruelties and wrongs in the world around them, which can lead them to make a stand against bullies and wrongdoers.

Empathizing is a process. It isn't just about *feeling* concern for others, it is also about taking appropriate action to help others.

Put another way, empathy isn't empathy if there is no empathetic response. Empaths are prepared to stand apart from the crowd and put themselves in difficult situations, which sees some left to fight alone. Empaths who uphold strong interpersonal boundaries may become frustrated if other people don't respect these boundaries. Some, unwilling to deal with apathy around them eventually withdraw from the outside world and prefer solitude.

Those who have an unstoppable drive to empathize may exhibit extraordinary altruism. The *Oxford English Dictionary* describes altruism as 'disinterested or selfless concern for the well-being of others, especially as a principle of action'. A secondary definition from zoology identifies it as 'behaviour of an animal that benefits one or more others (typically of its own species), but which carries a cost for the individual concerned'. The possible beginnings of altruism can be seen in our closest living relatives, chimpanzees.[5] In an experiment in 2006 baby chimps were observed to quickly help a struggling adult, jumping to hand the adult an item that had fallen out of reach although they were given no reward or praise for doing so. This behaviour is observed in other animals too, including rats.[6]

Altruism is rooted in empathy. To help a friend in need is a necessary first step is recognition and connection with another person's state of distress. Empaths get cues as to the emotional state of other people by interpreting their facial gestures and movements. They may have a strong response to the sight of other people's fear and become motivated to help them. Empathy therefore can be seen as survival apparatus, enabling individuals to do their part to aid the survival of the group.

It is not fully understood what helps drive this behaviour but the evidence points toward a hormone called oxytocin in the amygdala. Oxytocin is responsible for generating maternal care and provides a consistent response to anything that looks infantile, including other people's babies, animal babies or even people who look like babies – like someone with a wide-eyed fearful expression. It could be that oxytocin in the amygdala is key to making the critical change of thinking in a empath from 'This person's afraid, I need to protect myself' to 'This person's afraid, I'm going to help them'.

The amygdala (the brain's centre of emotional processing), is especially important in how we experience fear and recognize it in others. As mentioned earlier in the book those who are extraordinarily altruistic have been found to have larger volume amygdala than normal, a finding that is reversed in sociopaths, who have markedly reduced volume (smaller) amygdala.

It's odd; most of us enjoy watching films and reading books about heroes who refuse to go along with the crowd, which suggests there is something admirable about people who make a bold stand, but in real life watching someone raise their head above the parapet often makes the rest of us feel queasy. Most people prefer the easy life and choose to maintain the status quo. What prevents many of us from acting on our consciences is fear; fear hems us in. By contrast, when empaths instinctively experience fear they respond to it by asking themselves what is the right way to deal with the presenting danger and summons courage. They pause, albeit momentarily, to consider whether fleeing the scene or helping out is the right thing to do. This is self-reflection and emotional intelligence in action – survival skills that are discussed later in Chapter 7.

It was interesting to discover, when doing the research for this book, how often people referred to empathetic types in problematical terms as 'too sensitive'. It is often said in criticism and as a put-down. In fact, there has been a considerable effort in popular psychology in recent times to problematize empathy, perhaps unsurprisingly given the prevailing selfishism and resultant lack of self-perceptivity that goes with self-absorption, which limits critique of self and with that, the present culture. I also found that there is some confusion over what the terms 'empath' and 'empathy' refer to. Some people are highly sensitive to their own feelings, but it doesn't necessarily follow that they show empathy towards others. Indeed, individuals with poor regulation of their emotions can find themselves unable to respond to others in an empathetic way because they are held back by emotional distress. Emotional instability can thus hinder an individual's ability to empathize. This is sometimes observed in people diagnosed with emotional instability disorder, more commonly called borderline personality disorder.

By contrast to others on the empathy spectrum, empaths whilst sensitive to the feelings of others, have characteristically strong emotion-management and perspective-taking skills. They utilize *all* component parts required for empathizing: emotional empathy, cognitive empathy and perspective-taking skills, to arrive at a pro-social response. Empathizing seen in this light is a process, the outcome of which is action to show concern in socially appropriate ways even if it means taking personal risk. Most empaths thrive very well because of their balanced thinking.

Empaths use their ability to empathize to boost theirs and others' well-being and safety. Problems arise for empaths, however, whenever there are indifferent sorts of people – apaths – in the vicinity. Empaths can be brought down, distressed and forced into the position of the lone fighter by the inaction of more apathetic types around them. Here is an everyday scenario involving an empath fighting unaided among apaths.

Cameron

Cameron spied a boy being bullied by a gang behind the cricket pavilion. Other boys must have witnessed the incident, as he saw several of them walk close by. Without hesitation Cameron shouted to the gang to stop kicking the boy. Cameron's friends, who had been laughing and poking fun at each other moments before, watched aghast and then one by one began to creep away from the scene. Suddenly the field was deserted and Cameron faced the gang alone. He couldn't walk away and leave the boy to get a kicking; his conscience would not allow it. So he braved their insults and name-calling and stood there, determined not to back down. The gang leader sensed his authority was weakened by Cameron's presence, so he told his bully-boys to let go of the victim: 'We'll get him later,' he said, 'when this ****'s not around to spoil things.' To Cameron's surprise and disappointment, when the boy was released from the gang's clutches, he was less than grateful that he had missed out on a beating. Cameron didn't know what infuriated him more: the boy's lack of gratitude or that his mates were nowhere to be seen.

The sociopathic transaction

Often empaths are targeted by sociopaths because they pose the greatest threat (they take risks that others won't). The empath is usually the first to detect that something is not right and express what they sense. As a consequence, the empath is both the sociopath's number one foe and a source of attraction; the empath's responses and actions provide excellent entertainment for a bored and listless sociopath going about their daily business. Cameron's story highlights what happens to empaths who become embroiled in the intimidations of a bully.

The world of the empath is not for the fainthearted, and it is easy to see why others walk away from these kinds of confrontational situations. In the context that is being discussed, empaths often find themselves up against not only the sociopath, but quite often a flock of apaths as well. Apaths hide among the two-thirds of people (maybe higher) who obediently follow the leader. On the basis of these traits apaths are afforded pole position in the sociopath's intrigues. But this prime spot comes at a price, for in what I call the **sociopathic transaction**, the apath makes an unspoken Faustian pact with the sociopath, and then passively (often through fear) or otherwise, participates in their cruel sport.

The Sociopath–Empath-Apath Triad

For a sociopathic transaction to be effective it requires the following threesome: a sociopath, an empath and an apath. I call this the **Sociopath–Empath–Apath Triad** (SEAT). The usual set-up goes something like this: the empath is forced to make a stand on seeing the sociopath say or do something underhand. The empath challenges the sociopath, who straight away throws others off the scent and shifts the blame on to the empath. The empath becomes an object of abuse when the apath corroborates the sociopath's perspective. Ultimately the situation usually ends badly for the empath, and sometimes also for the apath (if their conscience comes back to haunt them or subsequently they become an object of abuse themselves). Frustratingly, however, the sociopath often gets off scot-free.

Sociopaths rarely vary this tried-and-tested formula because it virtually guarantees them success. In fact, in almost every sociopathic interaction, this interpersonal exchange is enacted. The sociopathic transaction relies heavily on the apathy of those close to the event or situation and highlights the importance of the apath in the transaction, as indicated in Figure 4.1.

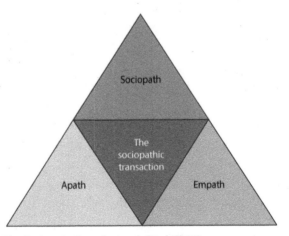

Figure 4.1 The Sociopath–Empath–Apath Triad (SEAT)

Sociopaths draw in apaths by numerous means: flattery, brib-ery, disorienting them with lies. A sociopath will go to any lengths to win their game. The best way to illustrate the interplay, and the ease with which apaths are pulled in, is by another short story.

Steve and Robin

Steve and Robin, both microbiologists at a prestigious university, were collaborators on an important vaccine trial. The head of department, Ben, was the principal investigator. An arrogant and surly man in his early forties, he was a taskmaster and bully, though lauded by the university bigwigs because his reputation for excellent research helped secure large grants. With this new project he hoped to gain substan-tially; an important new vaccine could see his status in his field rise still further and prove the catalyst for a glittering scientific career. His colleagues worked relentlessly on the trial collecting data.

With the early phase over, Ben set about drafting a paper on their preliminary findings for submission to a respected scientific journal. Unbeknown to his colleagues, Ben decided that the outcome didn't look nearly as tantalizing as he had hoped, so he falsified some key results in order to present their findings in the best possible light. On completing the first draft he sent out the paper for comment to his colleagues. Steve replied immediately by email and confirmed he was happy with the manuscript. In fact he used the opportunity to suck up to his boss, thanking him for writing the paper so swiftly. Robin, on the other hand, was aghast. He read it over and over, not-ing what he saw as colossal errors. With great urgency, he rattled off an email to Ben.

Receiving no immediate response, he phoned Ben. When Ben didn't pick up, Robin went to find him in person, discovering him in the cafeteria with Steve. He was already too late, however. Ben had just been poisoning Steve's mind, saying that Robin had challenged him over the accuracy of the results due to a long-standing grudge rooted in his own inefficiency. Ben had, he said, had to pull Robin up about his own work several months back.

Steve, however, was different, Ben implied – much more thorough. He intimated that Steve would be on course for promotion: 'Especially if we get this paper out and secure funding for the next stage trials off of it.' By the time Robin joined them, Steve, though initially shocked, had already been won over by Ben's swift flattery and insinuations.

Seeing Ben and Steve together at a table, Robin crossed the cafeteria to them. 'Hi, you two got a moment?' Briefly there was an awkward silence. Steve exchanged a look with Ben, who gave a slight conspiratorial smile, now that the transaction was done and the sport under way. 'Yes, we've got a few moments. We were just talking about the paper. By the way I did see your email, but if you look at the paper thoroughly I think you'll find that everything is correct.' Robin turned to Steve to see how he was reacting to this nonsensical account of the situation. Steve looked at him with a smug look on his face. 'I'm with Ben on this one, Robin. There are no flaws in the analysis or the write-up of the study that I can see. We should be grateful Ben got it turned round so quickly.'

Robin was totally floored. 'You can't be serious? You're happy for it to go off to be reviewed with all these serious errors in it? Our reputations will be left in ruins when this gets out.'

Robin decided to make a stand. He asked for his name to be removed as a co-author of the paper but was exasperated to learn that it was sent off to the journal anyway. More frustratingly still, it was published within a few months. Meanwhile the workplace became a source of stress for Robin as he struggled to cope with the backlash from colleagues who saw his intervention as an attempt to sabotage their work. People avoided him at break times, and when they did talk to him, the conversation was awkward and stilted.

Eventually Robin arranged a meeting with Ben to have it out once and for all. But when the time came for the meeting Ben took control of the agenda. 'Robin, I have to be honest with you, many of your colleagues are unhappy about the way you handled things and some have made complaints about the standard of your recent work. Furthermore your colleagues don't trust you to conduct yourself professionally after you attempted to sabotage their hard work. Mercifully the reviewers saw what a damn fine trial we'd conducted and didn't get wind of your attempted slur. We can't afford to have a saboteur on the team, someone so reckless they would put the whole research project at risk. So I've discussed this with the Dean and he agrees there's no future for you here, and no other way to deal with this. You've got to go.'

The 'gaslighting' effect and how it works

Let me now explain the sociopath's standard mode of operation. Sociopaths frequently use **gaslighting** tactics. In our story Ben (the sociopath) targets Robin (the empath) and uses Steve (the apath) as a corroborator in the abuse. The actions of both Ben and Steve have a 'gaslighting' effect on Robin.

Gaslighting is the systematic attempt by one person to erode another's reality. The syndrome gets its name from the 1938 stage play *Gas Light* (originally known as *Angel Street* in the US), and the 1940 and 1944 film adaptations. The 1944 film *Gaslight* features a murderer who attempts to make his wife doubt her sanity. He uses a variety of tricks to convince her that she is crazy, so she won't be believed when she reports the strange things that are genuinely occurring, including the dimming of the gas lamps in the house (which happens when her husband turns on the normally unused gas lamps in the attic to conduct clandestine activities there). The term has since found its way into clinical and research literature.

Gaslighting is a form of psychological abuse in which false information is presented in such a way as to make the target doubt their own memory and perception. Some psychologists call this, rather incongruously, 'the sociopath's dance'. It may simply involve the denial by an abuser that previous abusive incidents ever occurred, or it could be the staging of strange events intended to disorientate the target. In any event, the effect of gaslighting is to arouse such an extreme sense of anxiety and confusion in the target that they reach the point where they no longer trust their own judgement. The techniques are similar to those used in brainwashing, interrogation and torture, the instruments of psychological warfare. This is Machiavellian behaviour of the worst kind. A target exposed to it for long enough loses their sense of their own self. They find themselves second-guessing their own memory, become depressed and withdrawn and totally dependent on the abuser for their sense of reality.

Gaslighting is a deliberate manipulative ploy that occurs between one individual (the **gaslighter** – the sociopath in our case) and another (the **gaslightee**). The endgame for the sociopath is when the gaslightee thinks they are going crazy. If gaslighting goes on for months or even years before an individual realizes they're being gaslighted they may show obsessive-compulsive symptoms because they want to constantly check themselves and recheck themselves. The confidence-depleting nature of gaslighting can also contribute to increased anxiety in many or all aspects of the person's life, not only in the relationship. Many who are gaslighted berate themselves or feel the need to apologize all the time.

Anyone can become the victim of a sociopath's gaslighting moves. Gaslighting can take place in any kind of relationship – between parent and child, between siblings or friends, or between groups of people including politicians and the public or between colleagues at work. Going back to our analogy of the Emperor's New Clothes, it is the process of gaslighting that distorts our sense of reality and makes us disbelieve what we see. Even when the victim is bewildered there is a reluctance to see the gaslighter for what they are. Denial is essential for gaslighting to work.

Psychotherapist Christine Louis de Canonville describes different phases that the abuser leads the relationship through: the **idealization** stage, the **devaluation** stage and the **discarding** stage.[7] Gaslighting does not happen all at once, so if you suspect in the early stages of a relationship that you are being gaslighted, you can protect yourself by walking away. However, you need to be informed as to what those stages look like to make that choice. Let's now explore them briefly.

The idealization stage

During this early stage the sociopath shows themselves in the best possible light. But this phase is an illusion. The sociopath intends only to draw their target in. At the beginning of the relationship they are usually ultra-attentive, charming, energetic, exciting and great fun. If the context is a new romantic relationship, the targeted person may feel they love the sociopath intensely. It can feel like an addictive or hypnotic sort of love.

Caught up in the euphoria, they become hooked. If the context is a friendship, the person targeted may feel they have never in their life met anyone with whom they have more in common. In the workplace, the person may feel they have finally found a boss who sees their true potential. The target does all they can to gain the sociopath's special approval. The boss might tempt them along with words to the effect of 'I see a lot of me in you'.

The devaluation stage

Once the sociopath has assessed the target's strengths and weaknesses, the first phase is over and the devaluation stage begins. From here on in, the sociopath is cold and unfeeling. This phase begins gradually so the targeted person is not alert to the transformation. Nevertheless at some point it will begin to seem to the target that they can't do anything right. They feel devalued at every turn. Totally confused, the targeted person becomes increasingly stressed, unhappy, low in mood or depressed. The gaslighting effect is under way. Confused by the sociopath's behaviour, the targeted person tries harder to please their sociopathic abuser in order to get the relationship back on track. But no matter what they do, they only seem to cause the sociopath further injury. The target gets caught up in a spiral of sociopathic abuse where unpredictability and uncertainty are routine, until finally they become a shadow of their former self. The paradox of the situation is that the more distressed the target becomes, the more the sociopath enjoys the power of the situation, and the more powerful they feel, the more blatant and extreme their abuse becomes.

Devaluation can be delivered through many different forms and levels of attack. The targeted person has been conditioned, appearing in all intents and purposes to the outside world to be a willing partner in the sociopath's games. If they do manage to escape the sociopathic individual, they are at high risk of future entrapment by other sociopaths, because they are primed in a way that other sociopaths can spot.

The discarding stage

In the discarding stage, the game comes to its conclusion. By this time the sociopath has lost their ardour for the game, for they view the contest as already won. The target is reduced to an object, something to which the sociopath is totally indifferent; it is as if the targeted individual no longer exists. The targeted person on the other hand is left confused and raw with emotion. In the context of a romantic association the targeted person may scrabble around trying to find a way to rescue the dying relationship. But the sociopath resists all attempts to re-establish any connection, using bullying tactics such as silence or coldness in retaliation; they are probably already making moves to secure their next target.

The effects of gaslighting from the targeted person's point of view

During the process of gaslighting, the targeted person usually goes through some recognizable emotional and psychological states of mind. Psychologist Dr Robin Stern describes three stages those targeted go through: disbelief, defence and depression.[8]

Disbelief

The targeted person's initial reaction to gaslighting behaviour is one of complete disbelief; they cannot believe the sudden change towards them, or that they are being gaslighted. All they know is that something terribly distressing seems to be happening, but they can't figure out what. Blinded by the sociopath's promises or affections, the targeted person naturally trusts that their friendship or love is returned, but of course, this belief is based upon falsehood. In consequence the sociopath offers no sympathy or support when the target seeks to put the relationship right. Gaslighting doesn't need to be severe in order to have stark effects on the gaslighted person. It can be as subtle as being told 'You are so sensitive' or having it suggested that you are incapable: for example, 'You can't do that. You'll have to leave it to me.' Even though the targeted person knows on a rational level that these statements are untrue, their confidence is so eroded that they can't trust their own view. In extreme cases, those desperate for reassurance that they're not going mad become very dependent on their abuser for a sense of reality.

Defence

In the early stages of the devaluation phase the targeted person still has the emotional wherewithal to defend themselves against the manipulation. However, at some point they are thrown off balance by creeping self-doubt, anxiety and guilt. Becoming bewildered and unable to trust their own instincts or memory, they tend to isolate themselves because of the shame they feels. Eventually they are left unable to defend themselves from the unbearable gaslighting effect. One psychological condition that can result is called **Stockholm syndrome**. This got its name from a 1973 bank robbery in Stockholm, Sweden, when four bank employees were strapped in dynamite and locked in a vault. Much to their rescuers' surprises, the hostages developed more trust in their captors than in the police who were trying to rescue them. The term was subsequently coined by Swedish psychiatrist and criminologist Nils Bejerot, who was involved in the case. Stockholm syndrome can occur in situations where people find themselves held captive and in fear of their lives – not only thanks to sociopathic abuse, but also in kidnapping and hostage situations. It refers to the way in which someone in such a situation may bond with their captor as a defence mechanism – what is technically known as **traumatic bonding**. In order to cope with the discomfort of living in such madness and chaos, the targeted person – and apaths too if they are involved long enough – cope by rationalizing and excusing the sociopath's behaviour in order to reduce the conflict they are experiencing. It is a unconscious self-preservation strategy.

Depression

By the time someone has been systematically gaslighted, they hardly recognize themselves. In fact, many such people become a shadow of their former selves. They begin to feel that they can't do anything right any more, that they don't feel that they can trust their own mind or trust the opinion of others. So they withdraw into a distorted version of what is really taking place. Some escape into a state of constant low mood or depression. Depression is different from normal sadness – it is worse, as it affects the person's physical health and it goes on for longer. A lot of people who have been gaslit for a sustained period in this way go on to experience PTSD (see Chapter 6 for more on this). This is especially true of children of sociopathic parents and victims of child abuse.

In the aftermath of sociopathic abuse, people may experience an array of responses – shock, disbelief, deep sadness, guilt, shame, anger, fear, loneliness and an array of physical symptoms including panic attacks, flashbacks, anxious thoughts, fatigue and dissociation – although many also express relief at finally knowing what has been going on. Confidence erosion is another symptom that follows constant gaslighting. Gaslighted individuals live in fear of doing the wrong thing and making their situation even more dangerous. They become more cautious and doubt themselves. This often affects how they make decisions in their life. They commonly ask 'Am I too sensitive?', 'Why do I attract people like this?' or 'Am I to blame?'

Shame and blame are the hallmarks of gaslighting. The targeted person may become hyper-sensitive after the constant humiliation. They hear countless times from the sociopath and their foot-soldier apaths that they are 'too sensitive', mistaken or in the wrong so over time they begin to believe these lies about themselves.

Another negative side effect of having been gaslighted is that the targeted person finds themselves always apologizing, even for their very existence. This is, to all intents and purposes, a way of avoiding more conflict with the sociopath. Many children of sociopathic parents have a tendency to do this. It is not an act of politeness. Rather, it is a powerful strategy for staying safe, and a means of disarming the sociopath.

One more knock-on effect that must be faced as a result of having experienced gaslighting is the resulting joylessness, a melancholic view of life. Many people who have experienced the traumatic effects of gaslighting go through such physical and mental tortures that they suffer a personality change. They may end up feeling confused, lonely, frightened and unhappy. But rather than expose their vulnerability they hold on to it and keep their feelings in. Targeted individuals often experience great shame about their situation. When well-meaning friends and family members show concern or ask whether they are OK, they avoid the subject and withhold information in order to avoid further pain.

Shame in sociopathic abuse is a difficult issue. The shame that a targeted person feels is a normal response to the sense of failure they feel as a result of their inability to protect themselves (and dependents) from abuse. In addition, other people often have a 'blame the victim' mentality or take the attitude that the targeted person should 'just get over it', both of which demoralize the individual concerned. This shame can be interpreted by others as defensiveness, but in reality it is likely that the individual wishes to withdraw and socially isolate themselves out of fear and lack of trust of others.

Some people who have been gaslighted also experience difficulty in making simple decisions. Having to ask permission to do anything, not being allowed to express their own opinion, never being able to win an argument, constantly being chastised and humiliated, contributes to a loss of their autonomy, even their ability to make decisions for themselves. Many individuals recovering from sociopathic abuse adopt 'people pleasing' behaviour as a way of coping and dealing with others. The reason is that, as a defence mechanism, the targeted person has become conditioned to please the sociopath. Sadly, the only person the targeted individual does not set out to please is themselves until they wake to the abuse and take steps to remove the influence of the sociopath in their life.

The behavioural and emotional difficulties that follow gaslighting and abuse mean that, for the unfortunate few who have endured years of such abuse, life can seem rather hopeless. There can be a mix of emotional and physical responses brought on by high levels of stress hormones. Human beings aren't meant to endure high stress for prolonged periods. In a study on psychological abuse conducted in 2016 by the Society for Research into Empathy, Cruelty and Sociopathy (SoRECS), participants reported a myriad of stress-related symptoms after being gaslighted including hyper-vigilance (a state of increased alertness), general anxiety, social anxiety, physical conditions such as irritable bowel syndrome, skin complaints, respiratory conditions, poor sleep (sleeping for prolonged periods or the reverse, difficulty getting to sleep or experiencing disrupted sleep and nightmares) and changes to their weight (loss or gain). The long term effects reported included a lack of trust in other people with impacts on inter-personal relations, depression and PTSD. Fortunately most of us have the capacity to recover from psychological abuse, even if it takes some time. To that end, I discuss strategies for coping and turning things around in subsequent chapters. As emphasized in this chapter, apaths who aid the sociopath perpetuate sociopathic abuse. How and why otherwise ordinary and usually decent-minded people do this is important to understand if we are to change things for the better. In the next chapter, I take a look at the dangers of blind obedience and other influences on human behaviour.

5

Just doing my job! The perils of blind obedience

The sociopathic transaction introduced in the last chapter, which involves the Sociopath–Empath–Apath Triad (SEAT), occurs from the micro level of individuals and the family to the macro level of international politics. The reason why sociopaths, who constitute only a relatively small proportion of the human population, attain power and wreak havoc is the rest of us allow them immense influence. Most people are blind to the tactics and processes at play that see them fall under the sociopath's spell. We imagine that we can detect bad people and know how to avoid getting caught up in their games. It is other people who fall foul of sociopaths' deceptions is the line of thinking. Whether they are our political leaders, head up our institutions, lead our industries, are our parents or teachers, individuals in positions of power strongly influence our thinking and behaviour. A follow-my-leader mentality, and other psychological and social influences, can see us follow dangerous personalities and connive in cruelty, as discussed next.

Sociopaths at the top of the hierarchy

Historically, society has been based on hierarchy. Whole communities and nations form under leadership. This serves as a useful system of organization. It enables tasks to be delegated, individuals each play their part in their assigned roles and serve the needs of the whole.

A hierarchy is an arrangement in which the individuals are represented as being 'above', 'below' or 'at the same level' as one another. Every nation has a government, and every government is hierarchical. Socioeconomic systems are stratified into a social hierarchy. Most organized religions operate as a hierarchy with God at the top. Families are viewed as a hierarchical structure, as is ancestry, which is depicted in a family tree. Likewise, inheritance is traditionally based upon hierarchy, i.e. position within the family. In fact, all the fundamentals of a well-balanced life can be organized under a hierarchy of human needs.

Individuals make up the social body. If we do not take care of the social body's component parts (individuals), the whole structure can become overwhelmed and dysfunctional. To function effectively, a hierarchy must maintain the healthy functioning of its component parts. Contemporary culture is built on a model of society where fear and force maintain rigid understandings of power and superiority. The social structure can be described as a **dominance hierarchy** in which certain individuals are dominant over others. In such hierarchy, there is a single person or group with the most power and authority, and each subsequent level represents a lesser authority. Most nations, their institutions and public services are structured in this manner. When dominant individuals exhibit sociopathic tendencies like ruthless competition and grasping behaviour, it can influence the behaviour of the whole group. A dominator hierarchy influenced by sociopathic leaders, if left unchecked, can become an authoritarian structure with a high level of violence and abuse and a system of beliefs that normalizes such a society.

In a dominator hierarchy conditions are ripe for sociopaths to reach pole position. In their book *Snakes in Suits* (2006), Paul Babiak and Robert Hare identify several abilities that help sociopaths get the top jobs. They are motivated to, and have a talent for, 'reading people' and for sizing them up quickly. In other words, they have social intelligence. They identify a person's likes and dislikes, motives, needs, weak spots and vulnerabilities. Many sociopaths come across as having excellent oral communication skills. In many cases, these skills are more apparent than real because of their readiness to jump right into a conversation without the social inhibitions that hamper most people, and they are masters of perception management (strategies to alter another party's perception of past events and projections of future events); their insight into the minds of others combined with a superficial, but convincing, verbal fluency allows them to change their situation skilfully as it suits the situation and their ploy.

Humans seemingly have an inability to learn from past mistakes and experience some sort of amnesia when it comes to politics. Other countries, not our own, have corrupt government, despots and dictators, is the sort of complacent view. Hence, we take no active steps to prevent sociopaths from taking the helm. In fact, they are often heralded as saviours. There are no checks or screening processes in place with which to weed them out. Consequently, they flourish at the top of governments and in politics the world over and have done so since time immemorial.

Social and economic conditions can influence the type of leader we seek. In 2019, at a time when Britain was dealing with frustrating and protracted Brexit negotiations and a general election, a survey was conducted that showed that more than half of British people wanted political leaders who would 'break the rules'. The survey by Hansard Society, a research body on parliamentary affairs, revealed a growing clamour across the world for 'strong leaders', as seen in the rise of populist leaders elsewhere. 'People are pessimistic about the country's problems and their possible solution, with sizeable numbers willing to entertain radical political changes,' the report said. Indeed, Ruth Fox, the director of Hansard Society which produced the report warned that, 'Preferring a strong leader who is willing to break the rules ... would challenge core tenets of our democracy,' adding that the results of the survey were 'a potentially toxic recipe for the future of British politics'.[1]

Fundamentally, politics is about rulership and governance of people. Democracies entrust decision-making to people who are acceptable to the majority, whose power is defined and limited, and whose mandate is revocable. But according to Jonathan Sumption, a former Justice of the Supreme Court, who in 2021 wrote an article titled 'When fear leads to tyranny', the institutional framework of a democracy is not enough, because democracy can only work in a legal and social culture where there is freedom of thought, speech and association, uncontrolled access to reliable information, and a large tolerance of political dissent.[2] Hence, democracies and the cultures in which they are embedded are more fragile than might be supposed. In his article, Lord Sumption referred to the work of John Adams, one of the Founding Fathers of American democracy, who in 1814 observed that 'democracy never lasts long. It soon wastes, exhausts and murders itself. There never was a democracy yet that did not commit suicide.' Sumption argues that democracies fail from within. They are not usually overwhelmed by external forces, such as invasion or insurrection, or overthrown by internal coups. They fail because people spontaneously turn to more authoritarian forms of government.

Many argue that in Britain and elsewhere we are facing a crisis of political mistrust. If we permit political leaders to break the very rules they make for everyone else, if we don't hold these individuals to account or if we turn a blind eye to their poor treatment of other people, then we permit abuse of power. It is often said that how politicians behave in private is their own affair, but the way politicians conduct their private lives and treat other people provides important clues as to their true personality. If a sociopathic leader pursues self-interest above all else and lies to and manipulates their own family, colleagues and friends, they are just as likely to lie to and manipulate the public that pays their salary. Empathy corrosion in politics and government doesn't happen all at once, it is insidious. Sociopathic individuals in politics can be difficult to spot. Some display a grandiose air, are rumbunctious and have great charisma, thus they are easily identified, whilst others stay unseen, hiding convincingly behind a mask of civility. Consequently, those with a sincere persona often are the most dangerous, for their pernicious actions go unnoticed.

Democratic rule involves sharing power with those affected by its exercise and who have to live with its effects. People have a right to be consulted on how they are to be governed. A legitimate government is one where citizens, through participation, acquire a stake in the system. A government that only feigns to share power and consult its citizens is a government of trickery – an administration comprised of gaslighters. Psychologist Andrew Lobaczewski (1921–2007), author of *Political Ponerology: A Science on the Nature of Evil Adjusted for Political Purposes*, devoted his career to studying the relationship between psychological disorders and politics after spending his early life suffering under the Nazis and later living in Communist Poland.[3] He came up with the term 'pathocracy' to describe governments made up of people with personality disorders. He argued that pathocrats hate democracy. Once they attain power, they poke fun at democracy and do their best to dismantle and discredit democratic institutions, including the freedom and legitimacy of the press. They build bureaucracies that are destined to fail, establish institutions of scale that are so complex that their function cannot be understood. Their bureaucracies don't deliver what public services they are meant to. The intention is to deprive public access and to lower confidence in public institutions.

Governments that trample on freedoms and restrict public access to information head towards authoritarianism and tyranny. Sociopathically minded governments hijack democracy by appointing self-serving individuals (accomplices) to head up public institutions; those with little integrity who can be easily bought with honours and financial reward. In turn, public bodies become corrupted, a top-down spread of sociopathic behaviour in the organizations' culture. Over time, empathic failures in policymaking become apparent. Gaslighting operations are put into effect to cover up for failings and abuses. To distract the public, they put on a show by instructing public bodies to carry out internal reviews, thus avoiding accountability and close inspection. If a problem won't go away and the public demands justice, they engage in protracted independent public inquiries where the findings seldom see the light of day and after which no one in high office is ever held to account. They make it difficult to take to task public institutions by creating impregnable forms of redress such as complex complaints procedures. They obscure the view and befuddle the public by any means possible: new task forces, new public bodies and new appointees; high-level officials such as czars, brought in for public show to address a particular issue, and by false promises and downright lies. They conceal information through intricacies and misuse of privacy and secrecy laws. They privatize public services, transferring assets from the public sector to the private sector, sometimes through dubious practices and contracts. They ignore breaches to ministerial and civil code and when ministers do resign, they take up ministerial posts again after reshuffles or when new government is formed. They politicize the police, and other public services such as healthcare, and through them enforce harsh social control measures. In the process they give police draconian powers, whilst not holding them to account so risking the rise of a police state. They strip away the rights of citizens and curb dissent. They don't adequately fund or organize the judicial system, and as a result slow and dysfunctional legal processes become the norm. As they gain greater control and power, corrupted governments sense they are invincible. They distract, discredit, blame, barter (often with people's lives), catastrophize, create phoney hostilities and wars. They engage in all manner of diversionary activity that provides cover, leaving them untroubled to enjoy their ill-gotten gains. As Lord Sumption forewarned, the institutional framework of a democracy is not enough. The spirit of democracy is polluted and, in the end, is lost.

Sociopaths in pole positions do not need to satisfy the drive to bond with other people and can focus entirely on the drive to acquire. Whilst they may acquire power through a charm offensive, they rely on dominance tactics such as threats, coercion, intimidation, manipulation and violence to control others to get what they want. At best people only comply with them out of fear, whereas numerous studies point to their opposites – empathetic leaders – as personalities who increase cooperation, increase innovation, improve retention and help increase well-being. In light of what we know of the reality of sociopathic leadership then, it seems entirely absurd not to take the issue very seriously and make attempt to mitigate the risks. Yet typically, sociopathic leaders are churned out in substantial numbers, schooled in ideas which originate and feature in traditional schooling styled in ideas of punitive parenting. They tell others what to do and expect them to do it, often using external rewards and threats of punishment to motivate. Sociopath leaders may be stimulated by and driven on to behave badly toward subordinates owing to an over-reliance on base emotions such as envy, resentment, self-pity and anger, particularly when denied their perceived right to pursue self-interest. Yielding immense power such leaders often aren't brought to book for their mistreatment of others.

Without a strong sense of guilt or shame, they are immune to punishment and resistant to effort to bring about behaviour change. Why change when you always get what you want? They don't think twice about bringing down those who stand in their way or about putting other people in danger. The problem for all of us, individually and as a society, is that when we follow sociopathic leaders, tolerate them, collude with them or carry out their orders, our actions can have impact on others in harmful ways. A hierarchy dominated by sociopaths all too often has a crushing effect on everyone else and impacts upon us individually – our freedoms, rights, whether our most basic of needs are met.

Sociopaths at the top of the hierarchy have a knack of knowing who they can exploit to do their dirty work. They rely on apathetic individuals (apaths) low down the empathy spectrum to do their bidding, particularly egotistical sorts, and everyday sadists (those who engage in pleasure-driven aggression and enjoyment of cruelty in everyday situations) who carry out delegated cruelties such as defaming, defrauding, bullying or physical harm for some personal gain. While most people try to avoid hurting others, and will feel guilty, remorseful and distressed if they do hurt someone intentionally or unintentionally, an everyday sadist enjoys being cruel and may even find it exciting. All forms of cruel behaviour have the potential to be motivated by sadistic pleasure, including bullying and abuse of others. According to Erin Buckels from the University of British Columbia, who conducted research on everyday sadism, everyday sadists lack empathy and possess an internal motivation to hurt others.[4] Everyday sadists are not considered as dangerous to society as sociopaths except under certain conditions where cruelty is encouraged or is socially acceptable, because situational pressures are necessary for sadism to manifest with everyday people. War is an example of this convergence.

A recent example of sadism and cruelty emerging in an otherwise ordinary, if not a compassionate, group of people is the scandal that surfaced in 2018 surrounding serious sexual misconduct by staff of the charitable organization Oxfam in Haiti. Claims emerged that Oxfam employees, including a country director, used young prostitutes while based in Haiti after the earthquake of 2010. An internal Oxfam investigation led to several people being sacked and a few others resigning, but the internal report failed to mention sexual exploitation. The charity was severely criticized by the Charity Commission for the way it dealt with the misconduct of its staff. It said there was a 'culture of poor behaviour' at the charity; the incidents in Haiti were not 'one-offs', it said, and there were also issues at some of the charity's UK shops – the report highlighted incidences involving volunteers under the age of 18.[5]

Another example of abuse enabled by those working within a benign organization is the sexual abuse of children by priests of the Catholic Church, which has received significant media and public attention in recent years. Just how and why did the Church ignore, or worse aid, perpetrators of abuse in their midst? Church officials say that sexual abuse by clergy is generally not discussed and difficult to measure. This may be due in part to the hierarchical structure of the Church and stability privilege, as discussed in Chapter 2, where members of the group can't see harmful people within the group owing to a complacent attitude that 'there exists no danger amongst people like us', and also because of the public culture, which is still not open to discussing sexual abuse.

One more example of a group behaving outside the expected norms involved the ill-treatment of an academic by the Metropolitan police.[6] Dr Konstancja Duff was arrested on suspicion of obstructing and assaulting police after she tried to hand a legal advice card to a teenager in Hackney, London, who had been stopped under stop-and-search powers. She was later cleared of the charges in court. In 2022, the Metropolitan police were forced to apologize and pay compensation to her for 'sexist, derogatory and unacceptable language' used by officers about her when she was roughly strip-searched, held down on the floor and had her clothes cut off. The police apologized only after CCTV video capturing the officers' conversations was disclosed as part of a civil action against the force. In the subsequent reporting of the abuse, Dr Duff said: 'There was such a barrage of misinformation that they put out that I actually, even though I was there, and I knew that it was false, had almost started to doubt myself.' In other words, she was gaslighted. The CCTV footage of the police station custody area on the day she was searched showed one of the officers telling other officers to show her 'resistance is futile' and to search her 'by any means necessary'. 'Treat her like a terrorist,' he said. 'I don't care.' In a cell, three female officers bound her by her hands and feet, pinned her to the floor and cut her clothes off with scissors. Police officers are heard saying of Dr Duff, 'Was she rank?' and 'Her clothes stink'. Dr Duff described the ordeal, which left her with a number of visible injuries, as like a sexual assault. The case reveals how individual officers succumbed to dehumanizing and sadistic treatment of an individual held in custody and highlights the perils of blind obedience to authority, as officers acted on the orders of a senior officer.

Just doing my job!

We each make up the social body and our actions contribute to the whole. We therefore put in danger not only ourselves, but also everyone else if we aid a leader intent upon pursuit of self-interest whatever the cost to other people. Our unwillingness or inability to disobey a malign leader sees us wittingly or unwittingly contribute to abuse and injustice. As previously emphasized, empathic ability exists along a spectrum. People have different levels of empathy. Some have no ability to empathize and at the other extreme, some individuals have an almost unstoppable drive to empathize. As a reminder, Simon Baron-Cohen, who authored the book *Zero Degrees of Empathy* (2012), identifies seven default positions along the empathy spectrum:[7]

- **Position 0** No empathy and hurting others means nothing to them.
- **Position 1** Capable of hurting other people but have some regret if they do.
- **Position 2** Has enough empathy to inhibit acts of aggression.
- **Position 3** Compensates for a lack of empathy by covering it up.
- **Position 4** Low to average empathy.
- **Position 5** Slightly higher than average empathy.
- **Position 6** An almost unstoppable drive to empathize. Very focused on the feelings of others.

The distribution of empathy in the general population shapes up as a bell-shaped curve. Most people lie somewhere towards the middle of the curve with markedly fewer at each end. Sociopaths make use of those with low to middling default empathy to aid their abuses; the very selfish who seek to personally gain from the evolving situation, the everyday sadists among us who seek pleasure from inflicting pain, the fearful and the plain indifferent. These are all examples of apaths who involve themselves in sociopathic abuse.

Earlier I highlighted the psychological experiments of the 1960s by Stanley Milgram, a professor at Yale University, who set out to test the human propensity to obey orders. As a reminder, in the experiment, a participant in the role of 'teacher' was asked to administer an electric shock to the 'learner' whenever they answered a question incorrectly. The results demonstrated that a person of authority can strongly influence other people's behaviour with appalling consequences. In 2017, social psychologists reported on an experiment based on the original Milgram's obedience study. The newer study was conducted by researchers from the University of Social Sciences and Humanities, Wroclaw in Poland. It showed that people still blindly obey without resisting malign orders. Worryingly, this replica study found that 90 per cent of the people were willing to go to the highest level in the experiment; a level the participant's believed was fatal.[8] This suggests that the vast majority of people – nine out of ten – will follow orders even when their actions inflict extreme pain, suffering and even death on others. This may indicate that the level of societal compliance has increased over recent decades. The findings are truly disturbing.

In 1971, Stanford University psychology professor Philip Zimbardo led a research team who ran a study designed to examine the effects of situational influences on participants' reactions and behaviours in a two-week simulation of a prison environment. Twenty-four male students were selected to take on randomly assigned roles of prisoners and guards in a mock prison situated in the basement of the Stanford psychology building. The Stanford prison experiment was ostensibly a psychological study of human responses to captivity and its behavioural effects on both authorities and inmates in prison. Within one day things got out of hand in the mock prison, and the 'guards' used unmonitored brute force on many of the inmates. The experiment was cancelled after six days instead of the planned fourteen days.[9]

Like the Milgram experiment, the Stanford Prison experiment has been critiqued by other academics as one of the most unethical psychological experiments carried out. The experiment affected the way many universities approved research on ethical grounds. Nonetheless, the experiment raised uncomfortable questions about human behaviour and the conditions in which it can be manipulated.

In 2002, psychologists Alex Haslam and Steve Reicher conducted what became known as the *BBC Prison Study* to examine Zimbardo's themes of tyranny and resistance.[10] It was only a partial replication of the Stanford Prison experiment. The BBC supported the research and broadcast it as a documentary series called *The Experiment*. The results and conclusions led to a number of publications on tyranny, stress and leadership and saw mainstream psychologists distance themselves from the findings of Zimbardo's original prison experiment. Nevertheless, although Haslam and Reicher's study questions the notion that people slip mindlessly into role, their research, like Zimbardo's, points to the importance of leadership in the emergence of tyranny. In 2018, the authors of both experiments – Zimbardo, Reicher and Haslam – issued a joint statement asserting that both experiments were valid.[11] They also agreed that behaviours observed in all participants could have been caused by more than the situation. In their joint statement they concluded that 'the behaviours observed in the *Stanford Prison Experiment* and *BBC Prison Study* were a function of many factors, including roles, norms, leadership, social identification, group pressure, and individual differences, not all of which are necessarily mutually exclusive'. They urged people to continue research into toxic behaviours, arguing that their studies needed replications to demonstrate reliability and significance.

Clearly, setting up experiments to reflect real life is not without difficulty, as these studies show. The experimenters of the two prison experiments urged in their joint statement for the public release of information that aids in the interpretation of these and other studies. It is important to open our eyes and be alert to possible influences on social behaviour, which naturally will be complex and multifactorial. Cruelty in action does not make for easy viewing, and it is easy to understand why studies of these kinds create all sorts of defensive reaction and subconscious bias in a bid to protect ourselves from uncomfortable truths.

Let's explore the issue further by taking a look at an example drawn from real life that shows how abuse and violence is enabled in the workplace. In this example the organization is the police, which is based on 'command and control' principles (has authority to direct the actions of its personnel) and a strict hierarchical structure. It is a place where misogynistic and bullying attitudes have been highlighted recently by the police watchdog, the Independent Office for Police Conduct (IOPC), and where, as mentioned in Chapter 2, a 'blue line of secrecy' is known to exist:

Simone was a detective constable in a new role, working on rape and serious sexual offences. Little did she expect, when she embarked on the new role, to be sexually assaulted on the job by her boss!

Leading the team was Andy. He was popular amongst the officers. Charismatic though a little overconfident, even egotistical, he was known to demand a lot of those working on his team. At first, Simone found him a good source of support. He had made her feel special and capable. On the evening of the assault, he stayed behind and chatted about the case she was working on.

When the sexual attack took place, it came out of the blue. Unable to protect herself or to summon help in time, she succumbed to his abuses. Afterwards, still in shock and reeling she grabbed her things and stumbled out of the office to the car park. She drove home on automatic pilot. It wasn't until she got into the house with the door firmly shut behind her that she had any reaction to the earlier assault. She dropped her bag, leaned against the hallway wall with her coat still on. Hands covering her face she slid down the wall, ending up crouching and weeping. It was some time before she took herself off to have a shower and after to bed. She cried herself to sleep.

The next morning Simone went to work as usual. The ordeal of the night before had not yet sunk in. It was only at lunchtime when she was asked by a female colleague if she was OK that she sobbed and blurted it out. Another officer on their team named Pete was sitting nearby. Unbeknown to Simone, Andy had already attempted to cover up for the attack of the evening before. An arch manipulator, Andy knew just how to play it. He had already chatted to Pete over the coffee machine first thing that morning. He'd told Pete that he was concerned about Simone who, he alleged, had an obsession with him. 'You know, I wouldn't be surprised if she made up stories about me! She tried it on the other day. Flirted like mad when she thought no one was looking. Obviously, it is out of the question. She's a colleague and I am a happily married man! Female officers, eh? She's obsessed. Worries me, Pete. What should I do? How would you play it?' Pete took the opportunity to suck up to the boss, pacified him and agreed with everything he said.

Already groomed it was easy for Pete to accept Andy's lie rather than accept the truth that Simone had been sexually assaulted by his boss and colleague. So, when Pete noticed her crying and overheard some of the conversation between Simone and the other colleague, he stood up in disgust and rounded on Simone. 'Simone, if you have a problem with Andy, this is not the way to deal with it. You can't go around making up stories about him. Accept that the guy doesn't fancy you and get over it!' With that, he stormed off.

Poor Simone! Many colleagues in the canteen saw and overheard Pete's rebuke and now turned their backs on Simone. Over the next few months, Simone was sent to Coventry by her colleagues. She didn't report the attack out of fear of reprisal and worse, she feared she would not be believed. Work became a source of distress and seeing Andy at work every day filled her with fear and panic. Eventually after going off sick with low mood and stress, Simone applied for a new job and left the force for good.

In the context of the story Andy shows no concern for Simone or remorse for his abusive and anti-social actions. He takes on the **sociopath** role and involves others (the **sociopathic transaction** – often with the use of reward or punishment the sociopath persuades others to join in the abuse). Pete is the **apath** who unsympathetically sides with the perpetrator of abuse, Andy, and whose subsequent actions see other officers (also apaths) follow suit and snub Simone. She is labelled a troublemaker and avoided. These actions have a gaslighting effect on Simone and she is left feeling confused and humiliated. She is untrusting of her own perceptions after colleagues turn their backs on her and feels isolated and unsupported in dealing with the sexual abuse. In consequence, she takes time off work and later resigns from the job.

Apathy and the bystander effect

What prompts us to ignore the distress of other people? We have all found ourselves in situations – the times we have seen someone taunted and didn't intervene. We witness a problem a colleague is having, consider doing something, then respond by doing ... nothing. Something holds us back. So why don't we help in these situations? Influences on our behaviour are discussed next.

Apathy can immobilize us when we feel the impulse to flee and help at the same time. Researchers have studied the phenomenon and attribute the occurrence of the **bystander effect** (passive bystanding) to a **diffusion of responsibility**: when people believe there are other witnesses to an emergency, they feel less personal responsibility to intervene. They assume someone else will help. The end result is altruistic inertia. Researchers also suggest that we don't act on occasion due to the effects of **confusion of responsibility**, where bystanders fail to help someone in distress because they don't want to be mistaken for the cause of that distress. What is more, sometimes bystanders don't intervene in an emergency because they are misled by the reactions of the people around them. We succumb to what is known as **pluralistic ignorance**; the tendency to mistake one another's calm demeanour as a sign that no emergency is actually taking place. There are strong social norms that reinforce this; the

'Keep calm and carry on' mentality is one such. We adhere to these norms because it is embarrassing to get in a panic when no danger really exists!

What can further compound the issue of whether we will help another person out or not is how comfortable we are about feeling certain feelings in ourselves. Some people are fantastically empathetic and helpful when it comes to showing care and compassion for other people but have very little empathy when it comes to dealing with someone else's anger or outrage. Some close down in the face of violence and abuse, and some cut off completely from emotions they are frightened of in themselves.

Whilst passivity can be simply the first reaction to perceived danger and an avoidance strategy engaged in the hope that the problem will go away, it can also be something more sinister; say when someone passively or actively connives in hostilities they witness. The reasons people join forces with aggressors are manifold – they may fear punishment if they do not go along with the scheme, they themselves may bear a grudge towards the targeted person or persons, or just feel no real connection with them and shut off from feeling concern for them because of this. Or sadder still, they may go along with the situation on account of boredom or to revel in a sense of schadenfreude! In such cases apathy becomes not just a lack of empathy but a betrayal of it.

Clearly, apathy and collective follow-my-leader behaviour can be detrimental to ourselves and others. It is tempting to look at apathy as merely a problem of the individual, but it is not. It is a problem of global proportions and extremely hazardous. Turning a blind eye or joining in sadistic treatment of others can damage people and political systems. In her book *Cruelty: Human Evil and the Human Brain* (2009), Dr Kathleen Taylor recounts a harrowing example of cruelty: a German army photographer sent to the Lithuanian city of Kovno in 1941 witnessed a young man beat to death about 50 people with an iron crowbar; dragging them one at a time from the condemned group and killing them all. Onlookers, women and children included clapped. When he finished, they sang along as he stood on the mountain of corpses playing the Lithuanian national anthem on an accordion.

Taylor describes a continuum of cruelty from the mildest thoughts and behaviour to the most extreme. At one end lies the initial separation of 'them' (the 'other', the inferior outgroup) from 'us' (the superior ingroup). Its lesser implications include prejudices, poor taste jokes and mild verbal abuse directed at outgroup members. Moving along the continuum there are more vigorous verbal abuse, hostile and aggressive stereotyping and then increasing physical violence until the 'them' are destroyed. The term **otherization** is used to express the sense of creating a gulf between us and them and enables 'us' to treat 'them' as subhuman. Taylor argues that most people, in certain circumstances, would probably find themselves behaving cruelly, no matter how well-intentioned they were beforehand.

Arguably, apathy is worse than hate or anger. Not caring whatsoever, worse than having distaste for something. Many of us tend to see ourselves in a favourable light and don't believe that we are hateful, cruel or evil. So, can one do evil without being evil? This was the question that the political philosopher and Holocaust survivor Hannah Arendt grappled with when she reported on the war crimes trial of Adolph Eichmann, the Nazi operative responsible for organizing the transportation of millions of Jews and others to various concentration camps in support of the Nazi's Final Solution. Arendt found Eichmann ordinary and rather bland. He was, in her words, 'neither perverted nor sadistic', but 'terrifyingly normal'. He acted without any motive other than to advance his career in the Nazi administration. Eichmann was not an immoral monster, she concluded in her study of the case, *Eichmann in Jerusalem: A Report on the Banality of Evil* (1963). Instead, Eichmann 'never realized what he was doing' due to an 'inability ... to think from the standpoint of somebody else'. In other words, he lacked empathy. In the context of the theory of the socio-pathic transaction highlighted earlier in the book, he was an apath just doing his job and the leader's (sociopath's) bidding. Next, I identify some more influences that affect our behaviour towards others.

Blaming the victim mentality

Children and young adults brought up in a culture and in fam-ilies where punishment and control are the mainstay prop and tool of disciplinarian parents may accept and perpetuate a sim-ilar approach as they progress through their lives. Indeed, they may find it difficult to relate to other people in a more empa-thetic way. In fact, they may relate to other people in rather judgemental ways, especially if others do not appear to follow the expected norms and rules.

In 1966, Melvin J. Lerner, a professor of social psychol-ogy, conducted a series of experiments to investigate observer responses to victimization.[12] In his first experiment, 72 female participants watched what appeared to be an individual receiv-ing electrical shocks under a variety of conditions. Initially, these observing participants were upset by the victim's apparent suffering. But as the suffering continued and observers remained unable to intervene, the observers began to reject and devalue the victim. Rejection and devaluation of the victim was greater when the observed suffering was greater. Lerner theorized that there was a prevalent **belief in a just world**. He presents the belief as functional: the just world belief causes people to assume that people's actions always lead to fair consequences, meaning that those who do good are eventually rewarded, while those who do evil are eventually punished. Belief in a just world can lead to the tendency of observers to blame victims for their own suffering.

Research on belief in a just world indicates that it often correlates with religiousness, especially with faith in justice. Paradoxically, it is also associated with harsh social attitudes and anti-social tendencies, along with less social activism. Individuals with a strong belief in a just world may project a view of themselves as likable, competent and successful in a bid to maintain their position in the ingroup. One sign of effort to present oneself favourably in this way is by engaging in moral exhibitionism or virtue signalling, the practice of using moral talk or engaging in acts to enhance one's moral reputation. It can be observed to be engaged in on social media where disgust or favour for certain political standpoints or cultural happenings may be expressed in order to signal social competence and respectability. Individuals acting in this way are often quick to follow emerging cultural trends and are at greatest risk of behaving like the townsfolk in the tale of 'The Emperor's New Clothes' who, in order to be looked upon with favour, swore blind that the Emperor was wearing magnificent new clothes.

Those who most readily adopt a blame the victim mentality are the ones most concerned about other people's opinions. They are quick to adopt whatever stance helps maintain their position in the ingroup and readily fall for manipulation and propaganda. Sociopaths and malign actors influence public opinion by manipulating these super-compliant members of the ingroup. They know that these people can be depended upon to suck up their lies. They use manipulation, outright deception (disinformation) and diversion techniques. The tactics often involve the suppression of information or points of view by crowding them out, by inducing other people or groups of people to stop listening to certain arguments or by simply diverting attention elsewhere. They also encourage the spread of hate through the use of the **language of disgust.** Disgust, which is a survival mechanism, is exploited in such a way as to make us reject the abused. Calling people names, belittling them, ridiculing them has the effect of reducing them in our eyes. Reduced to 'less than us,' as unworthy objects and 'its' the otherwise decent-minded members of the ingroup permit themselves to hate and commit acts of cruelty.

People who hold a strong general belief that the world is just may have greater willingness not only to exploit and victimize others, but also to engage in dishonest behaviour. This can be best explained in terms of justification. Individuals confronted with a chance to cheat have to decide whether the potential gain outweighs the moral cost of cheating (and an impaired positive self-concept). Therefore, people justify cheating so that they can cheat (and gain) without having to suffer moral costs. In this way, justice in the world can be seen as independent of their own behaviour; their being dishonest does not affect what other people get, because others are believed to get what they deserve anyway. They may believe that even if their cheating harmed others, those others would be compensated elsewhere so that things would even out for those people in other ways. This reduces the moral costs of cheating in their own eyes because their own cheating is not believed to directly cause harm.[13]

There are many everyday examples of victim blaming: a woman might be judged harshly after being attacked if she walked home alone after dark, or people living in a flood prone area may attract little sympathy if flooded out on the basis that they should have known better than to live there. Comments made by the police following the murder of Sarah Everard by serving Metropolitan police officer Wayne Couzens in 2021 suggested victim blaming.[14] Sarah was kidnapped in South London, as she was walking home from a friend's house near

Clapham Common. Couzens claimed that he was arresting her for having breached COVID-19 regulations but drove her to near Dover where he raped and strangled her, before burning her body and disposing of her remains in a nearby pond. After the tragic event, a police commissioner spoke to the BBC where he discussed the murder. The commissioner said '[women] need to be streetwise about when they can be arrested and when they can't be arrested. She should never have been arrested and submitted to that'. His comment seemed to imply that Sarah was to blame for what happened to her because she submitted to arrest. In reality, she did what most people would have done and is socially expected, she followed the orders of a police officer.

Concerningly, people may go further than simply judging others; they may actively connive in abuse of the victim. A shocking real-life example was made into a docudrama, *Compliance* in 2012, based on true events that occurred in the US. It tells the true story of a strip search phone call scam that took place in Kentucky, in which the caller, posing as a police officer, convinced a manager restaurant to carry out unlawful and intrusive procedures on an employee. A young woman is detained over the course of an entire work day at a fast-food restaurant where she is subjected to horrific abuses by her co-workers. This abuse is prompted by nothing more than a man on the phone claiming to be a police officer who instructs the manager to detain the teenager. The man turns out to be a hoaxer.

Incredibly as the story unfolds, multiple individuals, including the manager of the fast-food restaurant, go along with various crimes against the young woman. It is shocking to think that otherwise ordinary people would go along with abuse just because someone ordered them to do so. It was reported that at the press screening of the docudrama, the audience broke into murmurs of disbelief, with someone calling out 'Oh, come on!' Much of the audience had become audibly uncomfortable with the representation of true events in which characters behaved in seemingly inexplicable ways. In a Q&A session after the screening, the renowned American psychologist Stanton Peele discussed cases of shocking compliance with authority, and Hara Estroff Marano, the editor-at-large of the US magazine *Psychology Today* pointed to the famous Milgram experiment highlighted in this book. People generally find it difficult to believe that they would behave in such a way, but sadly evidence points to such behaviour as commonplace. The story stimulates thought about political philosopher Hannah Arendt's theory of the 'banality of evil', which contends that the most heinous of crimes are frequently committed by everyday people who, in deference to an authority, view their wrongdoings as acceptable. The real-life events amplify the idea that even the least bad seeming of personalities can be swayed by the cruellest of commands.

A devastating real-life example of victim blaming that affected a whole group of people is the Post Office scandal that involved the wrongful prosecution of sub-postmasters for theft, false accounting and/or fraud. The problems began with the 1999 introduction of a new Post Office computer accounting system, called Horizon, which wrongly detected the existence of financial discrepancies at multiple post office branches. The prosecutions, civil actions and extortions resulted in criminal convictions, false confessions, imprisonments, defamation, loss of livelihood, bankruptcy, divorce and even suicide amongst the victims of this dreadful scandal. Melvin Lerner's research on a widely held belief in a just world is recognized as important for people to manage their fears about daily life.[15] Nevertheless, the world is not just, and people suffer without apparent cause. Victim blaming is a very real phenomenon as these examples highlight.

Conformity

Conformity is a type of social influence involving a change in belief or behaviour in order to fit in with a group. It is also known as group pressure and is used to signal an agreement with the majority position, brought about either by a desire to 'fit in' or be liked or because of a desire to be correct, or simply to conform to a social role. Once we are in a group it starts to shape us, pulling our attitudes and behaviour in line with others, threatening us with ostracism if we dare to rebel and, when facing rival groups, firing our competitive spirit.

Compliance occurs when an individual accepts influence because they hope to achieve a favourable reaction from another person or group. The individual adopts the induced behaviour because they expect to gain specific rewards or approval and avoid specific punishment or disapproval. Internalization occurs when an individual accepts influence because the ideas and actions are intrinsically rewarding. The individual adopts the induced behaviour because it is consistent with their value system. Internalization involves public and private conformity; a person publicly changes their behaviour to fit in with the group, while also agreeing with them privately. This is the deepest level of conformity where the beliefs of the group become part of the individual's own belief system.

Whether we conform and how we relate to other people is affected, among other things, by our beliefs. Beliefs are the things we hold true, regardless of whether we have any proof of their objective truth. Beliefs are inherited. As we grow up, we learn and take on the views of those around us, especially those whom we look up to. Parents, teachers, mentors, friends, they all pass their beliefs on to us, and we accept them or not. In time, we might turn them into our own beliefs or reject them. Beliefs about others and the world generate our stereotypes whilst beliefs about ourselves drive our self-image.

Together, they set the boundaries of what and with whom we feel comfortable.

The gap between our beliefs about others and ourselves creates our attitude and, eventually, shapes our belief about our world in general. Beliefs defend against disturbances or changes and create a common tie that binds us to other people. People use strategies to eliminate threats to their beliefs. These strategies may be rational or irrational. Rational strategies include trying to prevent injustice or obtain justice and accepting one's own limitations. But many of us, as we go about our daily lives, rely upon non-rational strategies including denial, withdrawal and re-interpretation of the event. Overlooking or denying the flaws in our beliefs can lead to the keeping of secrets. We do this to uphold a sense of dignity or to conceal a collective sense of shame. Whilst you might be willing to adhere and conform to most or some beliefs and rules set within the group, it is possible to feel resentful because of the undercurrents they set in motion. Unspoken rules are more powerful in affecting conformity and silence than written rules because they can always be denied. That is why, more often than not, sociopaths make unspoken deals with apaths during the sociopathic transaction, and why sociopath leaders tend to gain fearful compliance rather than wholehearted cooperation.

Groupthink is the practice of thinking as a group, which sees a loss of independent thinking. Combined with conformity it can play a significant role in the perpetuation of abuse. Typically, when groupthink forms, the 'ingroup' holds an inflated certainty about itself. It overrates its own abilities whilst underrating the abilities of its opponents (the 'outgroup'). Groupthink can be detrimental when different perspectives are not tolerated. It can produce dehumanizing actions against the 'outgroup'. Members of a group often feel under peer pressure to 'go along with the crowd' for fear of 'rocking the boat' or speaking out.

The socio-political thriller *The Wave* (1981) was intended as an after school educational TV drama. It illustrates the inherent dangers of groupthink and conformity. It is based on Ron Jones' real life social experiment *The Third Wave* (1967) and Todd Strasser's novel, *The Wave* (1981), and is the basis of later films, including the 2008 German film *Die Welle*. It fictionalizes the true story of an American high school history class's social experiment gone wrong. When a teacher struggles to explain to his students, perturbed by their studies of the Holocaust, how ordinary Germans could have allowed themselves to be swept up in the violence and hatred of the Nazi Party, he decides to show his students first-hand just how powerful groupthink can be. As the experiment gets out of hand it shows how groupthink and coercion can steer even the most well-intended individuals in the direction of cruelty and blind conformity.

The Wave experiment starts as a simple classroom exercise that demands discipline and conformity. The teacher urges his students to stand beside their desks. He begins by demanding that all students address him as 'Mr Ross', and practice drills. The students seem to appreciate the discipline, and work together even beyond the confines of the classroom. The teacher decides to expand The Wave by printing membership cards and implementing a Wave 'salute'. Before long, the groupthink and collective action that define The Wave begin to give way to mindless cruelty and blind pursuit of total conformity. When Wave members begin harassing non-Wave members into joining – and even don armbands bearing the Wave logo to more easily identify themselves to one another – it becomes clear that things have gone too far. Some students also notice that the experiment is out of control, and one writes an anti-Wave article for the school magazine. She begs her best friend to renounce her obsession with the Wave, pointing out that 'No one is thinking for themselves anymore,' and students have become 'a flock of sheep'. But the friend admits that she likes it.

The student with the anti-Wave stance is subjected to abuse. The teacher sees how his students have veered into coercion and violence. He tells the class that his experiment was really part of a wider plan to bring together a national youth movement. At The Wave's final rally, the teacher shows the class footage from a Nazi rally. As the rally draws to a close, he urges his students to take responsibility for their actions, to always question what they do rather than blindly follow a leader. The real social experiment and the subsequent film show that for some people, groupthink is more appealing than acting as an individual or doing what's right. Coercion and violence become a tool of the group as they pursue maintenance of the status quo. The above example demonstrates that in a crowd the moral principle can become displaced by the more powerful masses or an influential group leader.

Crowd psychology, also known as mob psychology, is a way of explaining the ways in which the psychology of a crowd differs from and interacts with that of the individuals within it. The seeds of the phenomenon were first planted in the book *The Crowd: A Study of the Popular Mind* by Gustav Le Bon as far back as the 1890s. Le Bon held that crowds existed in three stages: submergence, contagion and suggestion. During submergence, the individuals in the crowd lose their sense of individual self and personal responsibility. Contagion refers to the tendency for individuals in a crowd to unquestioningly follow the predominant ideas and emotions of the crowd. Suggestion refers to the period in which the ideas and emotions of the crowd are primarily drawn from a shared unconscious ideology. Crowd members become susceptible to any passing idea or emotion. Le Bon's work allegedly was avidly read by Lenin, Hitler and Mussolini, and became a huge influence on Edward Louis Bernays, Sigmund Freud's nephew and the inventor of modern public relations. The original hypothesis has been updated by Mattias Desmet, a professor of clinical psychology at Ghent

University in Belgium, whose ideas are detailed in the book *The Psychology of Totalitarianism* (2022). In the book Desmet demonstrates how governments, mass media and other large, 'mechanized' forces use fear, loneliness and isolation to demoralize populations to exert control, persuading large groups of people to act against their own interests, always with destructive results. He calls this **mass formation.**[16]

Mass formation is a technique used to influence large amounts of people at a time, persuading them to take action in some way. It is a very dangerous technique to employ because the 'mental intoxication' (a sort of hypnosis) that results makes people willing to do things that are clearly wrong and immoral. In short, masses of people become profoundly gullible and self-destructive. They become unable to recognize the lies and misrepresentations they are being bombarded with, and actively attack anyone who shares information with them that contradicts the ideas or propaganda that they have come to embrace. As mass formation progresses, the group becomes increasingly bonded and connected. Their field of attention is narrowed, and they become unable to consider alternative points of view. Leaders of the movement (politicians, cult leaders, etc.) are revered, unable to do wrong. Left unabated, a society under the spell of mass formation will commit unthinkable atrocities in order to maintain compliance. The most obvious example is how many Germans blindly followed Hitler's immoral and inhumane orders during the Holocaust, and actually believed it was for the 'greater good'.

Desmet identifies four psychological conditions that combine to create mass formation: a lack of social bond and isolation; experiencing life as meaningless or senseless (losing sight of human connection, family, etc.); focusing on everything material that is not fulfilling and losing the true meaning of life; and free-floating anxiety, frustration and aggression. Desmet states that mass formation follows a general distribution: 30 per cent are indoctrinated by the group narrative, 40 per cent in the middle are persuadable and may follow if no worthy alternative is perceived, and 30 per cent fight against the narrative. Those that rebel and fight against the narrative become the enemy of the brainwashed and a primary target of aggression.

Desmet made the observation during the COVID-19 pandemic that the lack of empathy and segregation during that time created conditions for mass formation. In these times of mass communication, fear and risk aversion we need to be on our guard for malign actors seeking to disrupt lives and create fear. In today's world, governments and other powers are capable of administering populations through a covert process aided by technology and mass communication. This process, called **governing from a distance**, is a way governments influence and shape the future of a nation, its citizens and their private lives without appearing to do so, by influencing everyday norms and behaviours. It can be done by the spreading and marketing of particular ideas and narratives through experts and institutions.

Nudge theory is a concept in political theory and behavioural sciences that proposes positive reinforcement and indirect suggestions are ways to influence the behaviour and decision-making of groups or individuals. Nudge units exist at the national level; the UK Nudge Unit was established in the Cabinet Office in 2010 by David Cameron's government to apply behavioural science to public policy, as well as at the international level (e.g. World Bank, UN and the European Commission). Nudging contrasts with other ways to achieve compliance, such as education, legislation or enforcement. Without the exercise of integrity by those employing such tactics these ploys can lead to social disaster. It is often argued that reliance on science and on experts is essential to the functioning of modern societies where knowledge is specialized and complexity is constantly growing, yet experts are not immune to the effects described in this chapter, nor are they excluded from the possibility of behaving improperly or misusing their influence. If psychological influences such as conformity, groupthink and mass formation can blind us to sociopaths and affect us in deleterious ways, should we really put blind faith in expert others to do our thinking or in them telling us what to do?

Wake up! Sound the alarm

Survival depends on us staying alert to the manoeuvrings of sociopaths. When we wake up to the sociopath's ruses, we can restore our ability to protect ourselves which means using our survival apparatus and conscience. Imagine operating as meerkats, those endearing creatures from the mongoose family. To look out for predators, one or more meerkats stand sentry to warn others of approaching dangers. When a predator is spotted, the meerkat performing as sentry gives a warning bark or whistle, and other members of the group run and hide. Meerkats also protect the young from threats, often endangering their own lives. On warning of danger, the young are taken underground to safety and the group is prepared to defend them if the danger follows. It is all our responsibility to defend individuals and the group from predatory behaviour of the worst kind.

Clearly, as highlighted, there are dangers to blindly following orders and following the crowd. It can mean you stop thinking for yourself and lose sight of your own conscience. So, just how do you enjoy a sense of belonging whilst not compromising your individuality or integrity?

- **Be yourself:** Everyone else is already taken (author unknown, but often misattributed to Oscar Wilde). Thinking for yourself is important in helping discover who you are and what you're about. As we mature it's only natural to want to reassess the beliefs you picked up along the way. It is up to us to decide what's best to hold onto or discard of the beliefs we grew up with.

- **Manage your emotional self**: Take responsibility for your actions. It's okay to permit feelings, which are neither good nor bad but indicators of your well-being. The resilient person is a problem-solver who doesn't paper over uncomfortable feelings and thoughts but acknowledges them.
- **Maintain good interpersonal boundaries**: Boundaries help us express our individuality. These are the limits we establish to prevent being encroached upon by other people. These can be material boundaries (money, clothes, food); physical boundaries (your personal space, privacy and body); mental boundaries (your thoughts, values and opinions). Whilst other people may try to over-step your boundaries, it's your job to uphold them.
- **Walk the walk, not just talk the talk**: There is a fable about a crab who admonishes her son, 'Why in the world do you walk sideways like that? You should always walk straight forward.' The little crab obediently replies, 'Show me how to walk, I want to learn.' The crab tries to walk straight forward but can only walk sideways like her son. The moral of the story – don't tell others how to act unless you can set a good example yourself.
- **Follow your conscience**: If we permit and conceal wrongdoing or maintain lies that may adversely affect other people, we become sharers in the guilt. Be prepared to speak your truth and follow your own conscience.
- **Take charge of you**: Don't think you or people around you can't alter entrenched positions. Studies on personality suggest changing patterns of thinking, feeling and behaving can eventually lead to permanent changes in a range of different personalities. One possible reason for this is that people change their very social identity, including how they see themselves. Exceptions include those with no conscience (sociopaths) because these individuals cannot empathize with, or accommodate, other people and are

highly resistant to change. Presented with other personalities like these, there's little one can do except protect yourself by upholding robust personal boundaries, especially if they pose a danger.

To take pro-social action against sociopaths requires courage and the ability to ethically reflect on the right course of action. To do this requires you to pause in daily life to ask yourself soul searching questions. What marks out those with high empathic ability from those with low empathy is the ready access to and processing of moral emotions such as guilt, shame and compassion. Empathetic personalities take heed of uncomfortable feelings inside themselves. They reflect on and make use of their feelings and experiences to arrive at ways of showing concern for other people and themselves; in other words, they think in a reflective way. Self-awareness comes about through a process of self-reflection. To self-reflect, a person accesses feelings inside themselves and has a language of emotions – a way of recognizing and labelling what they are feeling. Then they make use of their conscience and moral feelings to make decisions about the right course of action. Moral emotions such as guilt, shame, compassion, etc., help us determine how we can be reconciled with ourselves, and help us determine courses of action that are self-enhancing as well as enhancing of our relations with other people. This is emotional intelligence in action.

Those who have trouble self-reflecting can be compromised by lack of feeling within. This may derive from problems of emotion processing: some people find it hard to recognize what they feel inside (they may be traumatized, feel numb or depressed), or it may come from a problem of putting into words what they feel. There is a medical term for this – **alexithymia**, which is discussed further in Chapter 7. It is unclear what causes alexithymia although there is some evidence suggesting that environmental and neurological factors play a part in it.

Using emotions intelligently requires a highly developed sense of self-awareness, which comes with the ability to identify what you are feeling and experiencing inside yourself. Self-reflection helps you help yourself and other people in a number of ways:

- It leads to greater awareness of a problem, helps you recognize patterns in your own and others' behaviour, which in turn leads you to take affirmative, helping action, i.e. flex your empathy muscle.
- It helps you find 'frustration tolerance': 'I can remedy this situation if I am patient, and I have the facts. I know this is do-able, however difficult it seems right now' (positive self-talk).
- It helps you label feelings to help overcome unwelcome intense feelings and experiences.
- It helps you use this heightened self-awareness to process intense feelings like resentment and thoughts of revenge. Sometimes voicing notions of revenge can help if done with humour. It helps us see how daft our ideas of revenge are and diminishes this line of thought. Far better to shrug off all thought of revenge. Focus instead on improving your lot and seeking solutions, including justice.

It is often difficult to detect at first that abuses are taking place. This is why consulting your instincts and feelings is an important first step. This difficulty in detecting sociopathic ruses is because the nature of the abuse is almost always covert. Sociopaths use the tried-and-tested technique of perception management (sometimes called impression management); the process in which people attempt to influence others' perception about a person, group or event by regulating and controlling information in social interactions. Invariably, a sociopath intent on deceit attempts to alter the perception of a given situation to divert attention from what is really going on and to discredit the person or persons who calls out their abuses. They do so to present themselves in a way that satisfies their needs and goals. The end result is to psychologically abuse other people, to distort other people's reality – to gaslight them.

The techniques of psychological warfare have been used against peoples through history to justify wars and hostilities. Psychological warfare is used to denote any action which is practised by psychological methods with the aim of evoking a planned psychological reaction in other people. Modern tactics emerged in the twentieth century when there was much experimentation on humans, for instance, relating to stress and mind control especially during the Cold War era. Subsequently their use has become widespread in an era of mass communication. Various techniques are used and are aimed at influencing a target audience's value system, belief system, emotions, motives, reasoning or behaviour.[17]

The techniques are used by everyday sociopaths to reinforce attitudes and behaviours favourable to the originator's objectives, and are sometimes combined with **false flag tactics**, acts orchestrated in such a way to appear to have been carried out by a party that is not in fact responsible. The term 'false flag' originated in the sixteenth century as an expression to mean 'a deliberate misrepresentation of someone's affiliation or motives'. The tactic was originally used by pirates and privateers to deceive other ships into allowing them to move closer before attacking them. False flag operations are also known as a 'stitch-up' or 'set-up'.[18]

These days, operations of this kind are most often seen online. On the Internet, a **concern troll** is a false flag pseudonym created by a user whose actual point of view is opposed to the one that the troll claims to hold. Concern trolling is the action or practice of disingenuously expressing concern about an issue in order to undermine or derail genuine discussion.[19] The troll posts in forums devoted to a declared point of view and attempts to sway the group's actions or opinions while claiming to share their goals, but with professed 'concerns'. The goal is to sow fear, uncertainty and doubt within the group. Trolls hide behind anonymity. They are everyday sadists who aspire to violence and cause trouble in order to promote antagonistic emotions of disgust and outrage, which gives them a sense of pleasure. They often help out sociopaths who seek to bring a group or individual down.

Linguist Dr Claire Hardaker analysed the strategies of trolls. Their tactics include **digression**, which involves straying from the purpose of the discussion or forum, including malicious spamming or introducing entirely irrelevant topics; **(hypo) critizing**, which involves criticizing others for an offence to which the critic is also guilty (the word is derived from hypocrite, hypocritical, etc.); **antipathizing**, where the troller proactively and covertly exploits a sensitive discussion by being deliberately provocative or controversial; **endangering** where the troller masquerades as helper or advice giver whilst actually causing harm; **shocking** where the troller uses a classic strategy to be insensitive or explicit about a sensitive topic such as religion, death, politics, human rights, animal welfare and so forth, and lastly **aggressing**, where the troller openly and deliberately aggresses another person without any clear justification and with the aim of antagonizing them into retaliation.[20]

Sociopaths will persuade their hangers on (especially those who seek to gain from the evolving situation), to conduct Machiavellian **gaslighting operations** based on psychological warfare ideas. Most governments in history have employed a technique nowadays termed **controlled opposition** to trick and subdue their adversaries. Typically, governments have engaged with protest movements by covertly running them or infiltrating them. Nowadays it is not just governments who engage in such tactics. People are covertly surveyed and manipulated in everyday life by all sorts of malign actors, especially on the Internet. The controlled entity serves a role of surveillance and/ or social manipulation. Similar are undercover informants who nowadays are seen in a variety of other settings, for example, a business intent on surveillance and reputational damage of a rival. Another example is the police, who use undercover officers to engage in covert operations.

Ethical boundaries can be easily crossed when individuals are engaged in these covert practices, as an inquiry in England and Wales about undercover policing demonstrates. The inquiry, beset with problems and delays, was established in response to a string of allegations about the activities of undercover units, including the disclosure that police had spied on campaigners fighting for justice. During 2011, it was revealed by UK media that a number of undercover police officers had, as part of their 'false persona', entered into intimate relationships with members of targeted groups and in some cases proposed marriage or fathered children with protesters who were unaware their partner was a police officer in a role as part of their official duties. In late 2015, the Metropolitan Police force apologized to seven women 'tricked into relationships' over a period of 25 years by officers in the Special Demonstration Squad (SDS) and the National Public Order Intelligence Unit (NPOIU). The officers involved had eventually 'vanished', leaving questions and deceit behind, described by victims as 'psychological torture'. In 2016 further cases came to light.[21]

The aforementioned circumstances reveal a fundamental tension between two vital interests: preventing crime through covert operations and protection of members of the public (in this case from abusive police covertly operating!). The issues as they present themselves are also concerns that affect the UK national security service, MI5. Although MI5 has never openly admitted infiltrating extremist or political groups, a 2016 report by the Intelligence Services Commissioner suggested there may be occasions where agents engage in criminal activity in order to gather necessary intelligence.[22]

Since 2021, undercover informants working for the police and MI5 and other agencies including the National Crime Agency, Immigration and Border Officers, HM Revenue and Customs, Serious Fraud Office, UK military forces, Ministry of Justice (investigations in prisons), Competition and Markets Authority, Environment Agency, Financial Conduct Authority, Food Standards Agency, Gambling Commission and the Medicines and Healthcare Regulation Authority are explicitly permitted for the first time under British law to commit crimes. This is justified under the Covert Human Intelligence Sources (Criminal Conduct) Act 2021 (2021 c.4). The act makes provision for the use of undercover law enforcement agents and covert sources and the committing of crimes in the undertaking of their duty and in the 'greater good'. When the Bill reached the House of Lords in January 2021, peers defeated the government in passing two amendments to curtail use of children as informants, and to stop informants participating in the most serious crimes such as murder, torture and rape. The Act has far-reaching and concerning implications. Since the state would not be liable for the crime and officers are given immunity under the law, the rights of citizens who are victim of their crimes would be curtailed. Victims would be prevented from pursuing their attacker through the courts and receiving compensation through a civil claim.

Another common tactic employed by anti-social personalities who attempt to distort reality and harm their target is the use of **smear campaigns**. A smear campaign, also referred to as a smear tactic or simply a smear, is an effort to damage or call into question someone's reputation, by promoting negative propaganda. It can be a simple attempt to malign a group or an individual with the aim of undermining their credibility. It is not unusual for the individual or group orchestrating the smear campaign to be involved in the misbehaviour they accuse their target of. Common tactics involve spreading rumour that the targeted individual is a liar, a fraud or mentally unstable (i.e. otherizing). Smear campaigns are considered a low, disingenuous form of discourse. Smears often consist of attacks in the form of unverifiable rumours and distortions, half-truths or even outright lies. They can take place in the work environment, as the earlier case study of a smear campaign on the sexually abused police officer demonstrates, though often they take place online. In large-scale attacks of this kind, fake 'bot' accounts on social media spread misinformation and may hack into systems in order to leak sensitive information about the intended target of abuse. Unhampered by a conscience, sociopaths have no qualms in utilizing these harmful techniques for their own gain. They use them to control the group under their sphere of influence, most often enlisting indifferent individuals (apaths) to do their bidding (computer hacking, for instance), obtaining their compliance by overt pressure, some reward or subtler, unconscious influence.

How does one know if an individual one encounters in real life or online, is someone masquerading as benevolent who is really malevolent and intent on discrediting you? The truth is you may not know for certain, but you can trust your instincts about people, be mindful of what you disclose, uphold good boundaries of communication and if online, block accounts that have a pernicious effect on you. There is a language of hostility and a language of empathy if you tune into it. We transmit feelings when we express ourselves. Listen to your gut response to other's words in order to decipher the sender's real meaning. How does the communication make you feel? Hostile writers mostly aim for a fear or shock reaction and do not give much thought or weight to the subliminal messages their words convey. They sometimes give themselves away by inadvertently announcing their intention to offend ('No offence, but ...'). Their arguments may be impenetrable or authoritative, but on close inspection may prove to be nothing more than gibberish. They may make personal attacks. The type of humour used in communication is also telling; those who rely on affiliative (friendly) humour tend to have high empathy, whereas those who rely on sarcasm and put downs only to accuse others of having no sense of humour or being too sensitive tend to be lower in empathy.[23]

In many countries, the law recognizes the value of reputation and credibility. In the UK, defamation allows freedom of speech to prosper but keeps a check on telling lies that could damage someone's reputation or business. A defamation lawsuit in the UK is a civil action. The Defamation Act 2013 strengthened the criteria for a successful claim, mandating evidence of actual or probable harm, and enhancing the scope of existing defences for website operators, public interest and privileged publications. Nevertheless, a defamatory claim is open to anyone who suffers loss and damage as a result of it. An individual can pursue a claim in the civil courts though court cases can be sometimes expensive to pursue.

Another course of action is to report malicious communications to the police. The Malicious Communications Act 1988 (MCA) makes it illegal in England and Wales to 'send or deliver letters or other articles for the purpose of causing distress or anxiety'. It also applies to electronic communications. So, before you rid yourself of unwanted attention, it is important to gather evidence of the other person's wrongdoing so record all evidence before you block and delete. Take photographs or screenshots and keep audio messages, letters and text messages somewhere safe in case you decide to report to the authorities or take legal action at some later date.

Making overt the covert

Sociopaths are careful to keep their abuses hidden, often affecting an air of benevolence to mask their abuses; after all, they do not want anyone to know their real intentions. Often they are people that others least expect to behave badly. It can therefore take time to wake up to their abuses. If you are the targeted person, you may be feeling the effects of gaslighting, left bewildered, shocked and unsupported, especially if no one else seems to see what is going on. You may think twice before challenging the abuser. Nevertheless, once you are aware of abuse it is important to bring it to the open because to fail to do so puts other people at risk. But bringing the sociopath's behaviour into the open is in itself risky business, so you need to protect yourself. It is crucial to get right the timing of outing of abuse, just as it is crucial to look out for your own safety. This applies to situations of domestic abuse as well as work.

An important strategy is to gather documentary and other forms of evidence against covert abusers. Whilst it is important to abide by laws on privacy (data protection) and to conduct oneself in an ethical manner, a key strategy in defending oneself against distortion of the truth of a situation is by the acquisition of hard evidence. Emails, interviews, letters, video footage, social media messages, texts, photographs and other forms of documentary evidence will be very important, especially if the reporting of abuse leads to a disciplinary hearing or is reported as a crime. Maintaining contemporaneous notes is useful and can serve as an aid memoire. Keep evidence safely stored and consider keeping multiple copies in different locations.

There are practical approaches that one can employ to aid the outing of covert sociopathic abuse. These include:

Complying with a twist

It can be a frightening position to be in when an individual bears witness to abuse or wrongdoing. It may feel unsafe to openly challenge the sociopath especially if they are senior in position or if initially there is a lack of firm evidence to support any allegations. One approach at an early stage of bringing abuse out into the open is to **comply with a twist**. An individual taking on such a role does not actively collude in the abuse. Instead, they only *appear* to go along with the orders for as long as it takes to gather evidence of wrongdoing, i.e. they bide their time. The person who complies with a twist in this way is not a passive bystander. They take risks to actively help make overt the covert abuses going on inside the organization by gathering evidence. In time, they may find others who are alert to the abuses who are willing to lend support and join forces. Ultimately, the individual may become a whistle-blower or truthteller when they have enough evidence and have found a way to report their concerns safely. Ethically reflecting on one's conduct and relying on one's instincts in an emotionally intelligent way is important when trying to maintain this role in an effective way.

Truth telling/whistleblowing

Usually, the truthteller is a lone fighter who becomes the target of abuse (the empath in the Sociopath–Empath–Apath Triad – SEAT). They pose a threat to the sociopath and the status quo for speaking up about abuses or corruption. Their risk-taking often makes other people feel queasy. They may be willing to risk their job or put themselves in danger in speaking out, but one thing they refuse to do is go against their own conscience. They may be discredited or shamed by their detractors (the sociopath and their apath hangers on), made out to be bad, even criminal or deluded and mentally unstable. The sociopath may even accuse the truthteller of the very transgressions they themselves have engaged in. Though the truthtellers journey may be tortuous, and they may be judged harshly and in bad light by the rest for making a stand, they stay true to their original course and intentions. The sad paradox is, if more people were willing to make a stand in this way, abuses would be far easier to stop.

Society needs truthtellers: men and women who have courage to serve and protect the public, communities, families and one another. It takes courage to obey orders, but it also takes courage, perhaps greater courage, to disobey illegal or unethical commands. In fact, it is imperative that individuals do disobey if the command is illegal. The war criminal trials that followed the Second World War established the Nuremberg Principle IV that if a person acted in accordance with an order of their government or of a superior, it does not relieve them of responsibility under international law, provided a moral choice was in fact possible to them. Many Nazi defendants were executed or received life sentences despite their defence that they were 'following orders'.

Sometimes to act morally requires an individual to act in a disobedient way. The military have a term for this defiance based on morality. They call it **intelligent disobedience**.[24] It takes a certain level of intelligence and courage to know when and how to disobey. Disobedience can simply involve the professionalism to not execute an order that would clearly have negative operational consequences. It often involves moral courage. The individual in the follower role will need moral courage both to disobey unethical, illegal and immoral orders and to disobey orders that would inadvertently bring harm to the organization and its mission.

Edward Snowden, who escaped the US in 2013 before leaking shocking revelations of the US National Security Agency, is an example of a whistle-blower who some argue acted in an intelligently disobedient way. As an employee of the National Security Agency (NSA), he gained clearance to highly classified information relating to the agency's surveillance activities across the world. He leaked the information after becoming increasingly disillusioned by the legality and scope of the NSA's surveillance programme for its global surveillance was occurring on a far wider scale than most individuals had ever considered realistically possible. Snowden's case illustrates the tendency to define whistle-blowers as villains or heroes when in fact, there is a more nuanced way to look at what he did. He chose to act upon his conscience. To disobey in this way is a higher order skill than to obey. The intelligently disobedient address violations of values, ask tough and relevant questions to clarify orders, look beyond the rationale of those giving orders and show courage to resist the pressures to engage in wrongful and harmful acts.

Changing the culture

Our individual apathy, when added to the collective apathy, leads to a sociopathic culture where power, control and abuse predominate. Humans not only have a tendency to follow orders, but we also have a tendency to permit others to do our thinking. We function on automatic pilot surrounded by others doing the same. In short, we spend an inordinate amount of time in an inactive state, performing perfunctory tasks. This state leaves us oblivious to the world around us. Apathy then can leave us walking in and out of situations in a trance-like state, incapable of helping or supporting those around us when they are in need. We ignore humans who are suffering because we don't view them as our equals. We view them in a detached way as 'others' and 'its'.

Though callous and cruel behaviour spread out and diffuse within a community with relative ease, human behaviour can change and with the right influences around us, we can positively challenge the status quo and make shifts. As identified earlier, we are each lined up somewhere on the empathy spectrum and have a default position from where we may shift a little up or down. Only those at position zero, sociopaths with no empathy, are fixed at their default position and can't change at all. They lack the ability to experience guilt, remorse, compassion or other (moral) emotions that lead to self-awareness or the taking of personal responsibility. The rest of us, however, do have the ability to move up or down somewhat from our default positions, dependent upon external factors such as the circumstances we find ourselves in, and the influence of the leaders and peers in our daily lives.

Through human history we have not yet experienced a culture where punishment and control tactics are not applied by the governing bodies as a means of managing individuals and the masses. Coercive control generates fear, and it is fear of punishment, or social rejection that ensures individuals toe the line and do what they are told. But this approach is indicative of a society at odds with itself; it shows itself to be untrusting, one that fears people will not naturally cooperate and work towards common goals. Moral-emotional development occurs throughout infancy and adulthood. We have been schooled in punishment avoidance, but this does not encourage our morality to reach the heights of maturity; a place where we might operate according to our own conscience and in the knowledge that survival depends upon trusting relations and cooperation. As said repeatedly for emphasis, human behaviour is influenced by people around us. It is transmitted vertically by individuals at the top of the hierarchy downward and from one generation to the next, and it is also influenced by people around us (horizontal transmission) in our everyday lives. If more of us are exposed to, and adopt more emotionally intelligent ways of interacting, the general sway of behaviour could change for the better. All this, of course, takes effort – a shift of thinking and commitment to tip the balance. More empathetic cultures can be established. It doesn't take some massive overhaul or exploitative attempt at social engineering. Empathy, like its opposite number apathy, can be learned. Individuals can conscientiously opt in and practise being more empathetic. Over the course of the next few chapters I look at the importance of self-empathy and empathy for others in recovery from noxious relationships and discuss how to defend against further abuse.

6

Coping in the aftermath of a destructive relationship

> When the sociopath performs their cruel play, take your cue and exit the stage.
>
> *Fin McGregor*

That people can survive sociopathic abuse is testament to the fortitude of the human spirit. In this chapter I discuss what it takes to stop sociopathic abuse in its tracks and get your life back.

Witness or target of sociopathic abuse

So what should you do if you are aware that sociopathic abuse is taking place? If your brush with a sociopath is only fleeting, or you have witnessed someone else being abused, you will probably feel inclined to cease contact with the sociopath with immediate effect. But if you or someone else has been or remains in danger, you need to think about your obligation to report what you have experienced or witnessed to the police and other relevant agencies. In this way, you may prevent the same problem happening again. Evidence from victims and witnesses is important because it demonstrates the distress and damage that sociopathic behaviour can do in our communities. Apathy equates to collusion, so turning a blind eye is no option for a person of integrity.

Yet, in reality, many of us do find it hard to get involved. One of the barriers to speaking out is that sociopaths often work on evoking other people's pity. You should never agree to help a sociopath conceal their true identity, whether out of pity or for any other reason. If you find yourself pitying someone who consistently hurts you or other people, and who actively seeks your sympathy, the chances are you are dealing with someone with eroded or non-existent empathy. The best advice is not to listen. While there is still interaction between you and the sociopath, it is best to resist the temptation to join in their games. Trying to outsmart the sociopath or getting into arguments with them reduces you to their level – and distracts you from the task of protecting yourself. It is better to resist a showdown with a sociopath at all costs. In such situations their drive to win sets in. The best way to protect yourself is to avoid them, and refuse any kind of contact or communication. Sociopaths feel no obligation to you or anyone else. To keep a sociopath in your life is therefore to put yourself at risk of harm.

If you find it difficult to exclude the sociopath from your life, try to look at the situation dispassionately. Boundaries of communication are essential. If you find that your family, friends and acquaintances have difficulty understanding why you want to avoid a particular individual, and put unwanted pressure on you to continue the relationship, don't give in. Remain unmoved by those who don't comprehend the danger of the situation, and have the strength of your convictions.

If total avoidance is out of the question, for instance if the sociopath is someone you work with, limit contact as much as possible. As discussed in Chapter 5, it might be for a time that you decide to 'comply with a twist' until such time as you have mustered the courage and necessary evidence to make a bold stand and call the abuser out. Above all, make the rules of engagement ones that are right for you and then do your utmost to stick to them. View the boundaries on contact as non-negotiable and turn a deaf ear to those who ask for explanations. Conversely, don't be afraid to be unsmiling or serious when explaining your position.

It is important to keep at the forefront of your mind that the sociopath's behaviour is not your fault. It is far better to concentrate on your own behaviour and with sorting out your own life than to bother with things that you can't change.

Dealing with the draining effects of trauma

If you have been on the receiving end of direct and/or sustained sociopathic abuse, you may feel confused and bewildered in the aftermath. This section is intended to help you deal with the initial trauma and help you get back on your feet.

The very first steps towards recovery involve recognizing and accepting that abuses have occurred and taking steps to remove the sociopath from your life, or severely limit their influence. Recognizing and accepting the abuser and the abuse for what they are is a vital first step. Doing so helps draw the issue to the surface and lets you see and make sense of what has been happening to you.

If talking openly and directly to someone is too difficult at first, then 'talking to oneself' (self-reflection) is a pretty good start. Identify useful resources to aid your understanding, such as books, articles and online support. Online groups can provide instant support and advice, as well as the chance to practise a new and stronger voice to be incorporated with your real-life identity over time. Online groups also provide a level of anonymity, though it is important to protect your privacy, especially if you are feeling especially vulnerable and at a crisis point in your life. But a word or two of caution about use of the Internet: only discuss things you are willing to share and leave available in the public domain. Sociopaths and other anti-social types love to lurk online, as Claire from the earlier case study discovered (Chapter 2).

Identifying the problem can seem a mammoth task at first. In the aftermath of sociopathic abuse individuals can feel such an extreme sense of anxiety and confusion that they no longer trust their own judgement. Entering a sociopathic relationship is a one-sided and isolating experience. On exiting a socio-pathic relationship or group the isolation can be magnified as the abused person withdraws from social activities and becomes cut off from support. This is often the result of the immense shame abused people feel on account of their disempower-ment, and their maltreatment by the sociopath or sociopaths in their lives.

Shame

Shame is the greatest barrier for individuals trying to move on. Shame and a growing wariness of others can make it hard for such people to open up about the true extent of their unhappy situation. The situation becomes more desperate if earlier attempts to gain understanding have been met with incredulity. Wariness coupled with deep shame can render the abused person apathetic and inactive. Children, for instance, often learn from bitter experience that telling someone else about abuse at home can result in negative, even detrimental reactions. Most of the time shame is a normal and healthy human emotion. A healthy sense of shame keeps our feet on the ground, and reminds us of the boundaries. We are human and we make mistakes. Feeling shame is giving ourselves permission to be human. A healthy amount of shame can deepen our sense of personal power, helping us to recognize our limits and learn to redirect our energies to more fruitful pursuits. But too much shame and for too long can be harmful and demoralizing. Toxic shame can become internalized and a central part of oneself, leading to profound feelings of isolation. It can lead us to feel defective, beyond remedy.

It is not uncommon for people who experienced the shame and deprivation that goes with having a sociopath or sociopaths in the family to face difficulties in their adult relationships. Individuals who have experienced trauma at the hands of a sociopath in childhood may unwittingly seek out or attract similar domineering types of people in adulthood. Shame in the children of sociopaths can be intense and hard to shake off, for it originates from the trauma of abandonment as a child.[1]

In her powerful book, *The Drama of the Gifted Child* Alice Miller describes the notion of **abandonment trauma**.[2] This type of trauma occurs when damage is caused as a result of something not happening to an individual (for example not feeling loved, nurtured or protected). In essence, being abandoned by a sociopathic parent who is physically present but emotionally absent can leave a child bewildered to the point of despair. In order to develop as healthy human beings, children need to mirror the actions of an adult carer who is both physically and emotionally present. A baby is completely dependent on its parents and the parents' love and care is essential. Denied their basic needs, a child must find ways not to be abandoned. Many children in this situation try to reverse the natural order: they take care of their parents, as opposed to the other way round. But this often leads to a paradoxical situation where the child is nevertheless abandoned. Many children of sociopathic, neglectful parents try to make recompense by becoming caregivers. This can lead to excessive concern with pleasing and paying disproportionate attention to the care of others, at the expense of a proper concentration on oneself. Overwhelmingly, the children or partners of sociopaths tend to put others' needs first. They may feel they deserve the pain and trauma that goes with living with a sociopath; they usually rationalize that, after all, it was they and no one else that got them into this mess. This sort of thinking has a circularity about it, and if not interrupted and eventually terminated may drive a person near crazy.

Coping emotionally

The decision to change a situation of sociopathic abuse can be slow and laborious, or it may be experienced in a 'Eureka!' moment. One barrier to seeing the situation for what it is – abuse and trauma – is lack of self-confidence and self-belief, or fear of 'going it alone'; another might be that the relationship is a long-term one with children involved. In that case the timing and nature of the departure from the relationship can matter greatly. All the same, one day the abused person will find the courage to break free, or the sociopath in their life will walk out, probably without warning and leaving a whole lot of debris in their wake. Suddenly all alone, the abused person is left to contend with their grief and loss.

This phase can be bewildering and frightening. People react differently and take different lengths of time to come to terms with what has happened. Even so, you may be surprised by the strength of your feelings. It is normal to experience a mix of feelings. You may feel:

- **frightened** ... that the same thing will happen again, or that you might lose control of your feelings and break down
- **helpless** ... that something really bad happened and you could do nothing about it – you feel vulnerable and overwhelmed
- **angry** ... about what has happened and with whoever was responsible
- **guilty** ... you may feel that you could have done something to prevent it
- **sad** ... particularly if you or other people (your children perhaps) have been affected
- **ashamed or embarrassed** ... that you have these strong feelings you can't control, especially if you need others to support you

- **relieved** ... that the danger is over and that the cause of the danger has gone
- **hopeful** ... that your life will return to normal. People often start to feel more positive about things quite soon after a trauma.

The process is one of grieving. How we cope depends on our unique temperament and circumstances, but predictable stages of grief tend to follow.

Stages of grieving

Following a trauma of any magnitude many of us experience various stages of grief. We don't necessarily go through the stages one by one, in a neat linear way, and there is no typical response to loss. Grief is as individual as our lives. The most commonly recognized stages are denial, anger, bargaining, depression and acceptance.[3] Not everyone goes through all of them, or in that order, but knowing about the common experiences and stages of grief can equip us to cope better when we do experience them.

Denial

The first stage of grieving is concerned with surviving the loss. In this stage, the world becomes meaningless and overwhelming. Life makes no sense. We are in a state of shock and denial. We go numb. We wonder how we can go on. We find it difficult simply to get through each day. These are survival tactics that help to pace our feelings of grief. It is 'nature's way' of letting in only as much as we can handle. As we accept the reality of the loss, we start to ask questions and, unknowingly, begin the healing process. Without being aware of it we become a little stronger day by day, and the denial begins to fade. It is only as we proceed that all the feelings come to the surface, by which time we should be better equipped to handle them.

Anger

Anger is a necessary stage of the healing process. Be willing and unafraid to feel your anger, even though it may seem endless. The more you truly feel it, the more it will begin to dissipate and the more you will heal. There are many other emotions beneath the anger, and you will get to them in time, but anger is the emotion we are most used to managing. The truth is that anger has no bounds. It can extend not only to the sociopath who has left your life, but also to your people around you such as colleagues, friends and your family, and even to yourself.

Beneath anger is often pain. It is natural to feel pain at being deserted and abandoned, but we live in a society that fears anger. You may get angry at others now that you are no longer with the sociopath. Your anger is a driving force, something that has the propensity to propel you forward, and in that sense it is your ally, your friend. A connection made from the strength of anger feels better than nothing, so sometimes it is something we hold on to. We usually know more about suppressing anger than feeling it. The anger is just another indication of the intensity of your grief and sense of loss.

Bargaining

After a loss, bargaining may take the form of a temporary respite. Our conversations become full of 'If only ...' or 'What if ...' statements, such as 'What if I wake up and realize this has all been a bad dream?' We want life to be returned to what it was; we want it restored. The 'if onlys' cause us to find fault in ourselves and what we think we could have done differently. We are often willing to do anything not to feel the pain of a loss. In this state we may drink too much alcohol, take prescribed medication or illicit drugs to dampen or dull our senses, and we may eat too much or find whatever other means we can to block the pain. But doing so means we remain in the past, trying to circumvent the hurt.

Depression

After bargaining, our attention switches from the past to the here and now. Empty feelings may present themselves, and we may experience grief on a deeper level. This stage feels as though it will last forever. It is important to understand that this depression or period of low mood is not a sign of mental illness but an appropriate response to loss. We withdraw from life and feel intense sadness.

Depression after a loss is too often seen as unnatural: a state to be fixed, something to snap out of. The first question to ask yourself is whether or not the situation you are in is actually depressing and if so, whether depression is a normal and appropriate response. Not to experience some level of depression would be unusual after a marriage or family breakdown or an extreme emotional assault. Once you are fully able to take in the nature of the loss, the realization of what you have experienced is understandably depressing. Thus, we may need to accept that if grief is a process of healing, then depression is one of the many necessary steps along the way.

Acceptance

Acceptance is often confused with the notion of being 'all right' or 'OK' about a given situation, or of finding a place where one is able to forgive the other person (in our case the sociopath and/or their apath followers) for what has happened. This is not what I mean when I use the term acceptance here. Most people never reach a point of feeling all right about the losses and traumas they have experienced. What this stage is about is accepting the reality of the situation and recognizing that this new reality is permanent; in other words arriving at a point where we learn to live with it and where living with it becomes the new norm. In resisting the new norm, people cling to the hope of maintaining life as it was before. In time, however, we come to see that we can't maintain the past in the present. It has been changed and we must adjust. Hence, we learn to accept new roles for ourselves and others.

Finding acceptance may simply entail having more good days than bad ones. We can't replace our old lives and relationships, but we can make new connections and meaningful new relationships. Instead of denying our feelings, we must listen to our needs in order to move, change, grow and evolve. Once grief has been given its rightful stint, this is a time to live again.

Dealing with anxiety, stress and anger in the early days

Anxiety, stress and anger may result from continued association with a sociopath, or from the process of grieving for the relationship you thought you had with the sociopath before you discovered it was phoney. Left unchecked, anxiety and stress can build up and lead to anxiety disorders. When we become stressed or angry, our body's levels of fight-or-flight hormones such as cortisol and adrenalin increase. If we don't then either run or fight, the cortisol and adrenalin stay in the body, affecting the immune system, sleep and emotional well-being. These hormones have been linked with both heart disease and depression. It would not be surprising if a sizeable amount of referrals to psychiatric services for anxiety disorders, emotional distress and depression arise from circumstances involving sociopathic abuse. Psychological abuse is far more pervasive than is generally realized. To prevent this occurring to you, it is important to deal with anxiety and find ways to manage it.

If you find you have a particular problem with stress and anger, this section of the book may help you. Here some techniques are examined that may help you manage stress and anger in the early days after suffering a trauma.[4]

Pressing the pause button

The first step is to press the pause button and buy some time out from your anger and frustration. You might want to ask yourself the following questions:

What will I do to press the pause button?

You might try walking away, counting to ten, distracting yourself, keeping quiet or just biting your tongue.

What things might I try to stop me getting angry?

Possibilities include breathing, self-talk, exercise, talking to someone you trust, assertiveness.

One way to look at situations in which you easily get angry is by dividing up your thoughts into hot and cool ones. For example:

Hot thoughts	Cool thoughts
How dare he!	Don't let it wind you up
She's trying to humiliate me	I probably don't have all the facts
It's the same things over again	It might be different this time

It can be difficult to identify your thoughts, so another way of looking at the issue is to view thoughts as 'self-talk', or talking things over in your head. This is a normal thing to do and it can be really helpful. You can use self-talk to help when you are going into a difficult situation in which you may possibly get angry. You can also use it to get through a difficult situation, or to review what you did afterwards.

Tips for tackling stress

There are hundreds if not thousands of books on dealing with stress or anxiety, but to keep things simple here are my top ten tips for tackling stress, adapted from those of the UK mental health charity, MIND:[5]

- **Make the connection.** Could the fact that you're feeling 'not right' be a response to what the sociopath has put you through?
- **Take a regular break.** Give yourself a brief break whenever you feel things are getting on top of you.
- **Learn to relax.** Follow a simple routine to relax your muscles and slow your breathing.
- **Get better organized.** Make a list of the problems you need to tackle and deal with one task at a time.
- **Sort out your worries.** Divide them into those that you can do something about (either now or soon) and those that you can't. There's no point in worrying about things that you can't change.
- **Change what you can.** Look at the problems that can be resolved, and get whatever help is necessary to sort them out. Learn to say 'no'.
- **Look at your long-term priorities.** What can you off-load, or change? How can you get your life into better balance?
- **Improve your lifestyle.** Find time to eat properly, get plenty of exercise and enough sleep. Avoid drinking and smoking too much. However much you believe they can help you to relax, they tend to have the opposite effect.
- **Confide in someone.** Don't keep your emotions bottled up.
- **Focus on the positive aspects of your life.**

Relaxation exercise

Use the following simple exercise to help you learn to relax:

- Close your eyes and breathe slowly and deeply.
- Locate any areas of tension and try to relax the muscles involved; imagine the tension disappearing.
- Relax each part of your body, in turn, from your feet to the top of your head.

- As you focus on each part of your body, think of warmth, heaviness and relaxation.
- After 20 minutes, take some deep breaths and stretch your body.

Frustration

People with anger difficulties often talk about first becoming frustrated, and getting angry after the frustration sets in. Frustration is an emotion that we all experience from time to time. It develops when you are thwarted or hindered while trying to do something or reach a goal. It is the feeling you get when you expect a different outcome from what really happens. Although frustration can be helpful, as it leads to new ways of thinking about a problem, it is basically about not getting what we want, or getting what we don't want. Finding ways to manage frustration may improve our sense of well-being in everyday life.

There are a variety of factors that can trigger frustration. These include:

- **thoughts**: unrealistic expectations, plans, ideas for yourself or others (such thoughts may include the words *should, must, ought*: 'she *should* do what I told her')
- **situations**: particular places or tasks you would rather avoid;
- **relationships**: contact with people you would prefer not to see.

Frustration tolerance

Frustration often occurs when we have expectations for ourselves or others that are too high, or that are simply unattainable. In such cases we may have to alter our perspective or way of thinking. We may need to become what is called in the world of therapeutics **frustration tolerant**. To be frustration tolerant is to continue living a balanced, healthy life despite encountering repeated interferences and obstacles. How frustration tolerant we are refers to how robust we are in the face of life's stressors and challenges. If someone gets easily frustrated when they cannot get what they wants, they are said to have low frustration tolerance. Their frustration is intolerable and they can't cope. This way of thinking leads to the discomfort being increased. People with low frustration tolerance underestimate their ability to cope with discomfort (they might say 'I can't bear it!' or 'I can't stand it!'). Describing something as 'intolerable' frequently makes situations appear more daunting or off-putting than they actually are.

We can stand frustrating times if we choose to think about these situations in a different way. Therefore, the best approach might be to find ways of controlling the degree of frustration that we experience in daily life. This may be achieved by changing the things we do, or thoughts we have, when we feel frustrated. Alternatively, if there is nothing we can do, it may consume less energy if we are able to learn to accept and tolerate the uncomfortable experiences.

The most effective approach to overcoming low frustration is to develop an attitude of high frustration tolerance. This is the ability to tolerate discomfort while waiting to get what you want. Basically it is about toughing things out. Increasing tolerance for frustration helps us to experience normal levels of healthy annoyance in response to being blocked. High frustration tolerance enables people to be more effective at solving problems or accepting things that, at least at present, cannot be changed.

Examples of high frustration tolerance statements are:

'This is an uncomfortable situation but I can stand the discomfort.'

'This situation is hard to bear but I can bear it – some difficult things are worth tolerating.'

'Even if I feel like I can't take it any more, past experience has shown that I probably can.'

To increase your frustration tolerance, ask these types of questions:

> 'Can I remember being in this situation before and coping with it?'
>
> 'Is it true that I can't stand this situation or is it just that I don't like this situation?'
>
> 'Is this situation truly unbearable or is it really just very diffi-cult to bear?'

Being less extreme in our judgement of negative situations can help us have less extreme emotional responses, such as energy-depleting anger. Many situations are difficult to tolerate, but we need to remember at such times that we have tolerated similar situations in the past.

Venting

'Venting' means releasing pent-up feelings of anger or getting things off your chest. Venting is often explosive and can be an act of aggression. When people vent their anger, they often feel better immediately afterwards. However, not long after that, most people report feeling guilty, ashamed or sad for the hurt that they caused another person. Originally venting was thought to be helpful and healthy for reducing anger difficulties. However, recent evidence suggests that venting increases the chances of further anger in the future.

Reducing venting

The following steps may help you express your anger in a healthier way:

- Recognize and label your angry feelings: 'I am feeling angry because ...'
- Is the incident that has made you angry important or unimportant?
- If it is important, can you influence or control it?

- If it is important and you can control it, are there strategies you can use to implement the actions? If so, then list them. If it is not important, dismiss it and move on.

Rumination

Rumination involves dwelling on or thinking deeply about something. Everybody does it from time to time, but some forms of rumination can be unhealthy for us to indulge. People ruminate by bringing thoughts, memories and imagined events to mind and going over and over them. This can have a negative impact on our mental health. Ruminating about the darker side of life can lead to anxiety, depression and anger. Rumination can impair thinking, motivation, concentration, memory and problem-solving, and can drive away people who might be willing to support us. It can also increase stress. There are several types of rumination:

- **Anxious rumination.** When people worry, they go over thoughts about bad things that might happen to them or others. People with social anxiety go over what others might think of them, and over things they think they've done wrong in a certain situation. People with health anxiety think that they have serious illnesses.
- **Depressive rumination:** This involves dwelling on the causes and consequences of feeling depressed (lack of motivation or hopelessness). Depression can be related to a fear of anger, and ruminating can arise from fear of hurting others.
- **Anger rumination:** This may focus on injustice, angry memories, thoughts of revenge or angry afterthoughts. The way we think about things affects our emotions and our bodies. If, for example, you are hungry and see your favourite meal, your mouth will water. Nonetheless, just thinking or imagining your favourite meal will have a similar effect, because our thoughts stimulate areas of the brain responsible for

digestion. Likewise, ruminating about something will trigger the fight-or-flight response and get our bodies psyched up.

Know yourself

What happens when you ruminate or dwell on negative events? It helps to think about the physical, behavioural and emotional effects. What do you ruminate about? What are the usual triggers? What are the consequences? As with all aspects of anger, the first task is to recognize when you are doing it. So whenever you start to dwell on something that makes you feel angry, remind yourself that you are ruminating – 'WARNING! I'm ruminating' – and stop as quickly as possible. If ruminating has become a habit, however, this may be easier said than done. And as with all habits, patience and practice of new behaviours are essential.

When you find yourself dwelling on what has happened, say to yourself, 'Stop ruminating!' Calm yourself by breathing, relaxation, meditation or exercise.

Question the purpose and value of ruminating. Ask yourself:

- Would I advise a friend to think in this way?
- What would a friend say to me if she knew I was ruminating?
- Am I looking at the whole picture?
- Does it really matter that much?
- What would I say about this in five years' time? Will it be that important?
- Do I apply one set of rules or standards to myself and another to other people?
- Have I got the facts right?
- Am I just tired and irritable?

Challenge your own perspective on the situation:

- Maybe there's been a mistake or I've misunderstood?
- Have I checked that there's no other reason for this situation?

- Have I explained myself clearly?
- What's this doing to my health?
- Maybe I've jumped to conclusions too quickly?
- Ruminating like this may be harming me.
- I will act when I'm calm and have thought about it clearly.

Mindfulness

When people ruminate they tend to revisit past injustices or go into the future and fantasize about revenge. So bringing your mind into the present moment can be a powerful strategy. Say to yourself, 'Be here now!' Another mindfulness technique is to focus your mind on your senses and become aware of what is around you: the sights, sounds, smells and textures.

Rumination time

This is a useful technique to follow if you find you can't stop ruminating.

1 Set aside a regular time each day for ruminating – about 15 to 20 minutes once a day, and no more: set an alarm clock. Pick a time when you are free of interruptions.
2 Pick a place to ruminate, somewhere that you don't associate with relaxation (not your bed, or favourite chair). Some people sit at the foot of the stairs or at a table, on an upright chair. This will be the only place you should ruminate.
3 On a piece of paper write down the negative thoughts, all the things that you are dwelling on.
4 Stop when time's up – remember, set an alarm clock.
5 If any negative thoughts come up during the day, write them down on a piece of paper, and then tell yourself to stop thinking about them until your allotted time.

You will begin to understand your anger if you accept that your emotions and feelings are neither good nor bad, but that they are actually messengers. Then you can ask yourself what they are trying to tell you. When you feel angry or experience emotions related to anger (upset, annoyance, frustration, resentment, being judgemental), then ask yourself: Is my anger masking feelings of fear or loss? If so, then acknowledge those feelings. If not, ask yourself if it is your ideas and beliefs that are being violated. Try to revise these ideas by changing them to more flexible ones.

When the stress and anxiety aren't shifting

After exiting a traumatic relationship with a sociopath, and with sufficient support from friends and family, you might hope that it's possible to move straightforwardly through the stages of coming to terms with the situation, from initial trauma to acceptance. However, no one can predict the outcome of this recovery process. Even with the best intentions some people end up enduring persistent stress and anxiety – an experience similar to, if not the same as, PTSD. (Because it has primarily been identified by observing survivors of a specific range of traumatic events such as combat and disaster, the term PTSD fails to capture the consequences of prolonged, repeated trauma such as instances when a person is unable to flee and is under the control of an abuser, as may exist in families where abuse is taking place.)

PTSD is a severe anxiety disorder that can develop after exposure to any event that results in psychological trauma. According to one expert on surviving trauma, Judith Herman, captivity that brings the targeted person into prolonged contact with the perpetrator of the abuse creates a special type of relationship. She defines this as one of coercive control. This is equally true when the individual is rendered captive by physical, economic, social and psychological means, as in the case of battered partners or spouses and abused children.[6]

PTSD itself arises due to deregulation of the fear system. Fear is a necessary emotion at times of danger, and like anger is followed by a stress response – fighting, freezing or fleeing. This survival system depends on our ability to appraise threats in order to initiate survival behaviour. Once the threat or trauma is over, the fear system normally calms down after a few days or weeks. In PTSD this system fails to reset to normal, keeping the sufferer hyper-alert, on the lookout in case the event happens again.[7] The disorder is characterized by involuntary, persistent remembering or reliving of the traumatic event in flashbacks, vivid memories and recurrent dreams. Usually this is accompanied by problems such as depression, substance abuse and other anxiety disorders. The person may feel emotionally numb, for example feeling detached from others.

PTSD occurs when the trauma inflicted on an individual threatens their psychological integrity and overwhelms their ability to cope. As an effect of psychological trauma, PTSD is more enduring than the more commonly seen fight-or-flight response (also known as acute stress response), and is indicated by symptoms such as flashbacks, sleep problems, difficulty in concentrating and being emotionally labile (moods go up and down: the person is elated one moment, miserable the next). Chronically traumatized people are often hyper-vigilant, anxious and agitated. Over time they may complain not only of insomnia, startle reactions and agitation, but also of numerous other physical symptoms. Tension headaches, gastrointestinal disturbances and abdominal, back or pelvic pain are extremely common. Individuals also frequently complain of tremors, choking sensations or nausea. Repeated trauma appears to intensify the physiological symptoms.

For a formal diagnosis of PTSD to be made, the symptoms should have lasted more than one month and be causing significant impairment in the person's social, occupational, or other important areas of functioning. When the symptoms are mild

and have been present for less than four weeks after the traumatic events last occurred, the guidelines recommend keeping
a watchful eye and waiting. But managing the chaos, material
losses, grief and anger is down to the individual person, and
how and when they regain control.

The clinical literature points to an association between bodily
disorders and childhood trauma. Some survivors of prolonged
childhood abuse develop severe dissociation, cutting themselves off and becoming detached from their feelings and other
people. At the other extreme, one study conducted in 1989
described a process the researchers called 'mind-fragmenting
operations, where abused children were deluded into thinking
that their abusive parents were good parents'.[8]

Prolonged trauma at the hands of a sociopath may have emotional impacts, such as protracted depression. Here the chronic
symptoms of PTSD combine with the symptoms of depression,
producing what has been called the **survivor triad** of insomnia,
nightmares and psychosomatic complaints. The humiliated rage
of the traumatized person adds to the burden. They have been
unable to express anger at their perpetrator: to do so would
have jeopardized their survival. So even when released from
the perpetrator's grip, they continue to be afraid of expressing
their anger. Furthermore, the individual often carries a burden
of unexpressed anger against all those who remained indifferent and failed to help. Efforts to control this rage may further
exacerbate their social withdrawal and paralysis of initiative
while occasional outbursts of rage against others may further
alienate them and prevent the restoration of relationships.
Internalization of rage may result in self-hatred, even thoughts
of suicide. Even though major depression is frequently diagnosed in survivors of prolonged abuse, the connection with the
preceding trauma is frequently lost. Hence, patients are incom-
pletely treated because the traumatic origins of the intractable
depression have not been recognized.

Dealing with traumatic memories

Depression, severe anxiety and fear commonly stem from traumatic memories. People distressed by such memories may be constantly reliving them through nightmares or flashbacks, and may withdraw from their family or social circle in order to avoid exposing themselves to reminders of those memories. They may become physically aggressive, argumentative or moody, causing difficulties in relationships with their family, spouse or partner, and children. Sometimes they resort to substance abuse, drugs or alcohol in order to deal with the anxiety. If symptoms of apathy, impulsive behaviour, sleeplessness or irritability persist, the person may want to discuss this with their family doctor and to seek the help of a psychotherapist.

Most of us experience mild dissociation on occasion, such as bouts of daydreaming. Most individuals do not need help for mild dissociation unless it interferes with daily life. Dissociation is one way the mind copes with too much stress during a traumatic event like sociopathic abuse. Experiences of dissociation can last for a relatively short time (hours or days) or for much longer (weeks or months). If you dissociate, you may feel disconnected from yourself and the world around you. For example, you may feel detached from your body or feel as though the world around you is unreal. Dissociation can be a natural response to trauma that an individual can't control. An individual might have gaps where they can't remember anything that happened, or not be able to remember information about themselves or about things that happened in their life. These experiences are sometimes called **dissociative amnesia.**

You might feel like the world around you is unreal or see the world as 'foggy'. This is called **derealization.** You might also feel as though you are watching yourself in a film or looking at yourself from the outside, or as if you are just observing your emotions or feel disconnected from parts of your body or your emotions. This is sometimes called **depersonalization.** Another experience connected to dissociation is that you may feel your identity shift. For example, you may switch between different parts of your personality or feel as if you are losing control to 'someone else' or act like a different person, including a child. This is sometimes called **identity alteration.**

Dissociative symptoms arise as a way to cope with trauma and can be part of PTSD. The symptoms most often form in children or in individuals subjected to long-term physical, sexual or emotional abuse. When the symptoms interfere with a person's ability to care for themselves they may require treatment from a mental health professional. Individual therapy is the most common method of treatment for dissociative issues. People generally dissociate to cope with an experience that is too overwhelming for them to handle in an adaptive way. Therapy for dissociation generally focuses on acknowledging and processing the painful emotions that are being avoided. By changing how a person responds emotionally to a trauma, therapy can help reduce the frequency of dissociative episodes. A therapist may also teach coping skills for use during dissociation.

People may use their natural ability to dissociate to avoid conscious awareness of a traumatic experience while the trauma is occurring, and for an indefinite time following it. For some people, conscious thoughts and feelings, or 'memories' about the overwhelming traumatic circumstance may emerge at a later date. The management of traumatic memories is important when treating PTSD. Traumatic memories are stressful and can emotionally overwhelm a person's existing coping mechanisms. When simple objects such as a photograph, or events such as a birthday party, evoke traumatic memories, people often try to remove the unwanted memory from their minds in order to proceed with life, but this approach usually has only limited success. Over time the frequency of these triggers or memory joggers diminishes for most people, and for some the number of intrusive memories diminishes rapidly as the person adjusts to the situation. For others, however, they may continue for decades and interfere with the person's mental, physical and social well-being.

Several psychotherapies have been developed that weaken or prevent the formation of traumatic memories. Cognitive behavioural therapies have been found to be effective methods of reducing the emotional distress and negative thought patterns associated with traumatic memories in those with PTSD and depression. One such therapy is **trauma-focused therapy**. This involves bringing the traumatic memory or memories to mind and with the aid of a therapist restructuring the way the memories are thought about. Another effective treatment, which has gained favour in recent years is **eye movement desensitization and reprocessing** (EMDR). This involves elements of exposure therapy (where you systematically confront your fears) and cognitive behavioural therapy (which addresses unhelpful ways of thinking about your situation, and the things you do as a result). EMDR begins by identifying disturbing memories, cognitions and sensations. Then the negative thoughts are found that are associated with each memory. While both memory and thought are held in mind, the person follows a moving object with their eyes. Afterwards, a positive thought about the memory is discussed in an effort to replace the negative thought associated with the memory with a more positive thought.

Pharmacological methods for erasing traumatic memories are currently being researched, although this raises ethical concerns. The use of drugs to blunt the impact of traumatic memories treats human emotional reactions to life events as a medical issue, which may not necessarily be a good thing and may expose individuals to unnecessary risk. If drug treatments are administered unnecessarily – when for example a person could learn to cope without drugs – the person may needlessly be exposed to side effects. And the loss of painful memories may actually end up causing more harm than good. Painful, frightening or even traumatic memories can serve to teach us to avoid certain situations or experiences. By removing those memories their function in warning and protecting individuals may be lost.

Medication can sometimes be helpful following a trauma, but it is important for the person diagnosed with PTSD to see a medical doctor for regular check-ups.

Individuals with PTSD can also become ill with depression. Depression can be treated with talking treatments such as counselling or psychotherapy or with antidepressant medication. It is important in such cases, when the symptoms ascribed to PTSD persist, to speak about them openly with someone and get professional help. The important message to take from all this is that by reaching out for support, seeking medical advice and treatment, and developing new coping skills, individuals can at the very least learn to manage effectively the symptoms of PTSD and better still, overcome the problem in time.

7

Establishing boundaries and regaining control of your life

Once you have shaken off the sociopath, dusted yourself down and regained some control over your life, there are decisions to be made about the longer term. This chapter highlights the internal and external resources and know-how you will need to get back on track and guard yourself against further sociopathic abuse.

Coping in the aftermath of trauma

Re-establishing control after a one-off encounter

It is not sociopaths who change their behaviour; unfortunately they leave that responsibility to the rest of us. Sociopaths have no reason to modify their behaviour because the motivation and opportunities persist for them to carry on abusing other people.

In the case of a one-off brush with a sociopath, the chances are that all you need is to establish some boundaries to your relationship so you regain some control over the situation.

One of the first steps is stepping away from danger and considering what action can be taken to expose the abuse. It all depends upon your circumstances, and the circumstances within which the sociopath operates. Until recent years, UK law has offered little protection from psychological abuse and injury. However, in a number of jurisdictions, sanctions and remedies for psychological abuse are expressly and implicitly provided for within existing civil law. In England and Wales for example, these include non-molestation orders, occupation orders, restraining orders and the ground of unreasonable behaviour for divorce. In Scotland, non-harassment orders are covered by section 8 of the Protection from Harassment Act 1997. In Northern Ireland, the protection from harassment is covered by the Protection from Harassment (Northern Ireland) Order 1997.

Gaslighting has been a criminal offence since 2015 and is discussed in more detail in Chapter 8, where complex family situations are discussed. The coercive or controlling behaviour offence protects victims who 'experience the type of behaviour that stops short of serious physical violence, but amounts to extreme psychological and emotional abuse'. The offence carries a maximum five-year jail term, a fine or both. It is often difficult to address psychological abuse in the workplace. If this is the case in your situation, you made need first to consider making a formal complaint of harassment alongside report of any alleged criminality.

Bullying and harassment

Bullying and harassment in the workplace should not be tolerated. Sexual harassment is one of the most common forms of harassment and in the UK is specifically outlawed by the Equality Act 2010. The Advisory, Conciliation and Arbitration Service (ACAS), an organization devoted to preventing and resolving employment disputes, argues that it is in the interest of the company you work for to make clear what sort of behaviour would be considered harassment and what would constitute bullying. **Harassment** is unwanted conduct which has the purpose or effect of violating an individual's dignity or creating an intimidating, hostile, degrading, humiliating or offensive environment for that individual. **Bullying** is most often characterized as offensive, intimidating, malicious or insulting behaviour, an abuse or misuse of power through means that undermine, humiliate, denigrate or injure the recipient.

It is good practice for employers to give examples of what is unacceptable behaviour in their company. This may include the following:

- Spreading malicious rumours, or insulting someone
- Copying memos that are critical about someone to others who don't need to know
- Ridiculing or demeaning someone – picking on them or setting them up to fail
- Excluding someone from a team, colleagues or a task
- Victimization
- Unfair treatment, such as being asked to do unnecessary tasks, or penalized without cause
- Overbearing supervision, or other misuse of power or position
- Unwelcome sexual advances – touching, standing too close, display of offensive materials, asking for sexual favours, making decisions on the basis of sexual advances being accepted or rejected
- Making threats or comments about job security without foundation
- Deliberately undermining a competent worker by overloading and constant criticism
- Preventing an individual progressing by intentionally blocking promotion or training opportunities.

If the sociopathic bully is a friend or neighbour, be vigilant and record any unusual goings-on. If you are experiencing harassment or intimidating behaviour yourself, don't ignore it – most of the time it is unlikely to go away without some kind of action. Don't feel it is your fault, or fear being labelled as a 'troublemaker' for bringing it to the attention of other people and the relevant authorities. People who are involved in harassing behaviour often display it as a form of control and 'superiority' over your life; if you ignore it, this may be seen by the sociopath as a sign of success.

Even if you have only been harassed once, don't hesitate to contact someone for help. If the situation warrants it – if for instance your safety or someone else's is at risk, or property has been damaged – inform your local police and ask them for help. Ask them about the Protection from Harassment Act of 1997 (PFHA '97) and other legal avenues that might be open to you. The PFHA defines harassment as a 'course of conduct', meaning that for behaviour to amount to harassment it must occur on at least two occasions. Originally both occasions needed to involve the same person, but in 2005 the Act was amended by the Serious Organized Crime and Police Act so that 'pursuing a course of conduct' could mean approaching two people just once.

The Protection of Freedoms Act 2012 saw the inclusion of the offence of stalking in the PFHA '97. Its definition of stalking includes things like monitoring a person online, contacting a person, loitering in a public or private place, interfering with property or spying/watching a person. The offence of stalking involves fear of violence or serious alarm or distress. This requires there to be a person A whose 'course of conduct ... amounts to stalking' and a person B who is affected by the course of conduct. The course of conduct must either cause B 'to fear, on at least two occasions, that violence will be used against B' or causes B 'serious alarm or distress which has a substantial adverse effect on B's usual day-to-day activities'. Ask the police if they are able to take action on your behalf under the relevant legislation, and in particular the PFHA '97. Another option is to seek legal help from a solicitor.

You could also talk to a harassment adviser (you may have one in your workplace or company) or seek the help of a counsellor. Don't ever approach your neighbour or the person who is harassing you if you are in any way worried that there may be actual physical danger or that violence may be threatened. Call the police at once if this is the case. If you decide to approach the person responsible for harassing you, take due care over your safety. Do not go alone; take a friend or relative with you. Taking a witness will allow you to have a third-party account of what was said and done; the person harassing you cannot then claim that you didn't ask him to stop. Above all, your safety is paramount; do not place yourself in unnecessary danger.

Is it ever advisable to tell someone that they are sociopathic?

It is not advisable to confront someone with the notion that they are sociopathic, narcissistic or psychopathic, even if you are absolutely certain they exhibit the traits. Using terms like these might help us identify certain types of personality and see the behaviour for what it is, but name calling is not usually helpful. Even if the person concerned occasionally appears to be aware that they don't react like people around them sociopaths rarely think badly of themselves. They don't have the same emotional attachment to ideas and concepts that 'other' people do, and they may even get a sadistic thrill out of the idea that they are viewed as threatening to other people. This is why they often troll websites and social media sites that discuss the topic of sociopathy. They enjoy baiting other people. This all said, they may know they are different. Being relatively unemotional, they can be fearless. Often sociopaths use this to their advantage, staying calm when others are afraid. Trying to make them feel remorse, guilt or shame is useless and can encourage them to fake feelings, to go along with the game. Whether someone knows or is informed that they are sociopathic depends a lot upon their social and cultural background. But nowadays, with the terms in wide use it must be hard for sociopaths not to get wind of the concept of sociopathy or know something of the phenomenon. And their self-absorbed nature makes it highly likely that many of them have read widely on the issue and even diagnosed themselves.

Establishing control following prolonged contact with a sociopath

A full recovery from a traumatic encounter with a sociopath means recapturing your zeal for life. This requires a certain amount of self-growth. Getting over the experience is not always easy. It can be a battle, difficult and discouraging at times. The good news is that the vast majority of us get there in the end – but recovering from the experience often requires us to challenge the perspectives and rules that have sustained our belief systems and the belief systems of those around us.

This can cause conflict before it brings us release or resolution, because often the way we live our life is something handed down to us from our parents and shaped by the culture we're immersed in.

A growing body of literature suggests that recovery is characterized by predictable stages and milestones (see Figure 7.1). Within each stage there are developmental tasks and skills to master, perspectives to develop and issues to address before

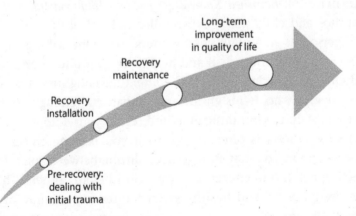

Figure 7.1 The recovery process

moving to the next stage. Change not only comes about in recognizable stages, but also is more likely to happen when changing is important to us, and we are confident in pulling it off. If this makes it sound easy, I acknowledge that it isn't. Most of us tend not to go through change in a neat and linear fashion; in fact the direction of travel can be a little bit messy, with movement back and forth. Things begin to steady as you gain confidence in the process and thankfully, most of us get there in the end.

Change requires us to actively engage in the process. We have assets, both internal and external, which support us in dealing with changing circumstances. Every one of us possesses internal reserves that initiate and sustain our own recovery, but sometimes we need a little help in identifying what we've got. Sometimes to aid the process we also need a change in self-perception, or somehow to 'repair' our identity.

It can help to seek out others who have a shared goal. People recovering from a traumatic relationship with a sociopath often find recovery-supportive friendships beneficial. Such friendships need to be natural (reciprocal), accessible to you at times of greatest need, and potentially enduring. It can also make a real difference if a positive person is around to witness your change. In her book *Banished Knowledge: Facing Childhood Injuries*, the author and child abuse expert Alice Miller identified this sort of person as an 'enlightened witness'; someone willing to support a harmed individual and help them gain understanding of their past experiences. In this context an enlightened witness is anyone who is insightful and empathetic enough to help you face up to your difficulties and regain your autonomy. The change process is often messy, so if you become engaged in peer support you may find yourself flitting between roles, from acting helpless to engaging in the act of helping others. This is entirely normal and healthy given the tentative nature of the recovery process.

Coping day to day

Establishing personal boundaries

It is important after you have experienced a trauma involving a sociopath to re-establish your personal boundaries. One of the best moves you can make is to introduce and reinforce new rules of engagement. This may or may not include a rule of 'no contact'. A rule of no contact is easier said than implemented, but can be very necessary in order to prevent further trauma. The move is a lot easier to carry off if at the final showdown the sociopath walks out of your life; nevertheless, *you* may have to initiate the rule and take affirmative action yourself. The right approach – whether merely to limit contact or to apply a no-contact rule – depends on your individual circumstances, but whatever route you take, stay alert to the sociopath's persistent games and stand firm; sociopaths have a tendency to draw you in again.

Limiting contact

Many people involved with a sociopath limit contact at the point when the drama reaches critical pitch. Each person's situation is unique, however, and it is best to determine for yourself what contact you are prepared to accept. For a parent whose partner is a sociopath, this is an especially difficult, stressful and confusing time. Not only are you dealing with the trauma of a destructive relationship, but you are working out how to handle future relations in order to protect your children.

It is not uncommon for a sociopath to behave badly and in an extreme fashion as soon as they realize you want to reduce or stop contact. They may become disruptive and manipulative in an attempt to regain control. On the plus side, most give up hassling and manipulating you eventually; usually when they set their sights on a new target. Nevertheless, limiting contact with a sociopath requires you to be firm. You have to learn to assert yourself and your needs, which will help you in your own recovery.

That said, if you think the sociopath is potentially dangerous, and you perceive that you, some other adult or any children are still at risk, you should seek help from the authorities: the police, social services and legal advisers. Another important piece of advice is to keep written records of all agreements and discussions involving adults at risk of harm, and agreements about the welfare of children. Keep all written statements in a safe place, as you will need ample evidence if you decide to take legal action at a later date.

No contact

In most other circumstances it is probably best to have no contact at all with a person you identify as a sociopath. While it can be quite straightforward to cut ties with someone who is relatively new in your life, if the sociopath is part of your social group or family, a friend or partner of long standing, it becomes more complicated. You should ensure that other friends and acquaintances know you are no longer in contact with the individual concerned, and ask them not to play 'go-between'. You will also need to make it clear that you don't want to discuss anything about the sociopathic person (or people). Refuse to accept information from a third party and if people try to involve you, tell them not to involve themselves in this way as it could damage relations between you.

The leaking of communication to and from third parties is the most common mistake people make following the establishment of a no-contact rule. Although it may be natural curiosity on your part to hear the third party out, it can reopen wounds to hear what the sociopath is saying about you or doing in their life, so stop people immediately if they begin telling you anything, and let them know you are not prepared to hear or say anything about the person who has abused you. If the third party refuses to respect your wishes, you should consider limiting contact with them as well.

For those whose lives have been heavily intermeshed with one or more sociopaths, in a family for instance, a no-contact rule can be extremely hard to apply. You will have to decide who to cut out completely, as well as what to do about communication with family members on the periphery of the situation. Again, you may have to spell out the boundaries to avoid further conflict.

Cutting ties is a painful and terminal step but typically a necessary one. On the upside, it is a significant step on the road to recovery. One way of doing it is to write a frank letter stating that the relationship is over and you don't wish to be contacted again. A phone call or email seems easy, but can lead to the mistake of getting into continued dialogue and bartering. Once a no-contact rule is set, there are things you need to iron out. Do you remove phone messages without listening to them? Block the person on social media? Do you accept apologies? Gifts?

If messages are left on voicemail, or you receive emails or calls from the person concerned, you must resist the temptation to respond. If the person catches you unaware and you pick up a call, hang up immediately. Call blocking is another option. Sociopaths like playing games with your emotions, and having access to you after a relationship is over is like letting the game continue. If your sociopath does harass you in this way, keep all their communications in case you decide to pursue a harassment charge at some later stage, as this is potential evidence. If you wish to save the evidence but think you would be too tempted to read it or to act on the contents, immediately give any communiqués to a trusted third party or to a solicitor, who can keep them stored away safely with your other important personal effects. It is probably advisable to block or change your email. If anything gets through, delete it as soon as you recognize the sender without opening or reading it (the exception to the rule being if you feel you need it as evidence). Do not get into games with the sociopath by entering into dialogue again.

Preventing lapses in judgement

Having an enlightened witness around will help to keep the person in recovery on the right path. It is not uncommon to feel isolated in the early days once you are removed from immediate danger, perhaps in completely new surroundings. After the initial relief has worn off, you may feel disorientated, ambivalent and lonely. Feeling alone is quite a normal response to change and unfamiliar circumstances, and it's one that the sociopath will play on, angered by your snub and the change you have made in the rules of engagement. Often at this point a sociopath will accelerate their games. They may make you question your sanity, your perception of what happened, everything and everyone you hold dear. They may even feign remorse to try to win you back, a response that is hard to ignore if you are feeling lonely and excluded.

Meanwhile others who don't know the full extent of your situation may make judgements and disparaging remarks, particularly if you have left a marriage, job or family. This sort of reaction sadly comes with the territory, as those who make a stand are often harshly judged by others who are uninformed and look on with untrained eyes. And let us not forget that most of those who criticize you are likely to belong to the apath majority, many of whom may fear or resent your newfound voice and strength. If this happens, just remember it is most likely your freedom of spirit and nonconformity that triggers social anxiety, rather than there being anything discernibly wrong with you. This is why it is important not to withdraw and become isolated at such a critical moment. Instead, the best route out of the situation is to keep good people about you and let them buoy you up until you are confident in your unconventionality and accept it as one of your strengths.

For all your good intentions about maintaining limited contact, or breaking it altogether, sometimes we trip up. There will be situations to look out for and set-ups to avoid until new behaviours and habits are bedded down and become the norm.

In the intervening period you need to learn how not to set yourself up and become entangled again in the sociopath's life. In some ways, weaning someone off a destructive relationship is like weaning them from an addictive substance or behaviour. In both situations the relationship and pattern of behaviour are often deeply entrenched and create an unhealthy dependence.

It takes time to gain confidence in our ability to make what are sometimes sweeping life changes, and time to adopt new sets of behaviour. It takes patience and a willingness to learn from trial and error to sustain changes and fully adapt. But one advantage the non-sociopathic in society have over the sociopathic is the ability to change. The sociopath is unable to do this; their persona is fixed. The sociopath lacks the insight and the ability to learn from their mistakes (they are unlikely to view their actions unfavourably). In addition the sociopath's behaviour is fairly predictable. In essence sociopaths behave the way they do because they are motivated by internal stimulus (stoked by feelings like self-pity, envy and anger or by boredom) and, unhampered by a conscience, seek out opportunities to take advantage of. Figure 7.2 sums this up diagrammatically.

Once you take this on board, it is up to you to identify ways to block opportunities for the sociopath to snare you again. Using the straightforward approach outlined overleaf, it is

Figure 7.2 Motivators for sociopathic behaviour

possible to identify cues and triggers to avoid relapsing into old ways and back into relations with the sociopath. Becoming more aware of our former ways and behaviours helps us gain insight, which helps prevent us inadvertently getting trapped in a cycle of sociopathic abuse.

Stop making seemingly irrelevant decisions (SIDs)

A seemingly irrelevant decision, or SID, is a decision or choice that may appear unimportant or insignificant on the surface but actually increases the likelihood that the person making it will be placed in a high-risk situation that can cause a relapse to their former behaviour. A person may ignore, deny or explain away the importance of these decisions and choices. The identification of SIDs is an important part of relapse prevention. Here I draw on the work of psychologists G. Alan Marlatt and J. R. Gordon.[1] It's a useful approach for weaning yourself off old behaviours that result in you succumbing to the sociopath's ploys. Examples of SIDs include:

- Driving past the sociopath's home on your way back from work
- Idly 'Googling' the sociopath or checking their social media accounts
- Asking after the sociopath to third parties who are still in contact with them
- Finding some reason to send the sociopath an email
- Texting the sociopath on their birthday or some other special occasion.

All these are seemingly innocuous, but can put you in the path of danger. Perhaps, as you drive past the sociopath's house, they see you drive by and wave. That one small act gives them licence to call you and you become hooked in again. Perhaps checking the sociopath's Facebook page makes you feel sad and you begin reminiscing – before you know it you have sent them a personal message. Curiosity is not a bad thing; it is natural in many circumstances. It is an emotion related to natural inquisitive behaviour and connected to learning. But in this situation we need to recognize its disastrous consequences and learn to control the impulse.

The rule violation effect

This effect is evident when we break our own rules and boundaries. It can apply to either a limited contact or no-contact rule that has been set in place. The rule violation effect (RVE) refers to the tendency of an individual, having made a personal commitment not to contact the sociopath, to revert to uncontrolled contact following a single lapse. The RVE comes into play when the person attributes the cause of the initial lapse to internal factors within themselves, such as a lack of willpower or believing themselves to be missing the sociopath (or rather, the person they *believed* the sociopath to be).

With these lapse and relapse prevention strategies the aim is to learn how to minimize the risk of relapse (i.e. prevent the RVE) by directing attention to the more controllable external or situational factors that triggered the lapse (e.g. high-risk situations, coping skills and anticipated outcomes), so that you can quickly return to the goal of no contact and not 'lose control' (i.e. get back in contact). Specific intervention strategies may help you identify and cope with high-risk situations and manage lapses. These are considered next.

High-risk situations
Moods
You may have low moods, bad moods, increased anxiety or irritability when you break off contact. These are temporary feelings and will get easier over time. You may over-react to things that normally wouldn't bother you. This is common. Try to find

new ways of coping with emotions like anger, upset, annoyance and stress. These tips may help you:

- Discover new ways of dealing with negative feelings rather than ruminating on the past.
- Remind yourself that the feeling is temporary; it will go away.
- Congratulate yourself for coping with life without the sociopath.
- Ask others to understand and be patient.
- Do things that make you feel good.
- Try to get a good night's sleep, and if having trouble sleeping, seek advice about improving your chances of sleeping well.

If you get good or bad news that affects your mood, dwelling on the past or seeking out the sociopath will not change the news, whether good or bad, or help the situation. It will only reduce your chances of changing your situation. Have a good cry; tell someone how you are feeling. Take slow deep breaths over a period of a few minutes to help you relax.

Habits and routines

You may have developed certain habits and routines in your life with the sociopath. It's therefore important to consider changing your routine so you don't experience cues and triggers about them; that's a situation that can lead you to take SIDs, to lapse or end up violating newly established rules.

Just as a reminder, here are the tips again for coping with stress:

- Work it off by taking a walk in the fresh air.
- Talk to someone you really trust.
- Learn to accept what you cannot change.
- Don't self-medicate with alcohol, too much coffee or tranquillizers.
- Get enough sleep and rest.

- Take time out for activities you really enjoy, or try out some fresh ones such as new forms of exercise, doing something creative or picking up a different hobby.
- Doing something for others can make you feel good too.
- Take one thing at a time.
- Prioritize your day ahead and only do the things you have to do.
- Don't be afraid to say 'no'.
- Eating good meals at regular times will help your mood.
- Know when you are tired and do something about it.
- Be realistic about what you can achieve. Forget perfection.

Triggers

A trigger is something that you associate with something or someone else, and to which you are likely to respond. Years of conditioning from a sociopath mean that a particular trigger will set off a reaction in you by a process of association, much as a dog can be conditioned to respond to a ringing bell in the same way as to food. Introduced here are some ideas of psychologist B. J. Fogg, who refers to triggers as phenomena that are either 'hot' or 'cold'. A **hot trigger** is something that affects you immediately: the sociopath suddenly in contact again and yelling at you or demanding something. A **cold trigger** is something that affects you indirectly: the sociopath's double or doppelganger passes you in the street. A hot trigger forces an immediate response, while the effects of a cold trigger build up over time. Triggers work as a call to action and can cause us to act on impulse. To avoid lapsing into previous behaviour it helps to find a way to disconnect our feelings from the object of association. The steps to breaking the connections involve:

- **Looking for patterns:** First we need to see clearly the things that make us think about the sociopath and other people we have removed from our lives or have lost as a result of changing our behaviour. Once we recognize the kind of things that work as hot or cold triggers – the sort that trigger an unhelpful reaction in us – it is useful to a make a mental note of them.

- **Becoming more 'trigger-savvy':** Give yourself a chance to analyse your own triggers and see if you can devise ways to break the associations. Maybe just being cognisant of the fact that a trigger can arouse unwanted feelings and memories is enough. Maybe you need to talk yourself out of reacting whenever a trigger arrives uninvited. Understanding how best to dampen the effects of emerging triggers is necessary in driving behaviour change forward. Here's an example.

Jill

Jill had not been in contact with her sociopathic father for several months when a message from him appeared in her email box. She immediately recognized this as a trigger, and knew that if she opened and responded to the email she would be in a high risk situation, in jeopardy of responding and thus lapsing. Because she was mindful of this situation arising, she recognized the position she was in and instead of responding on impulse, as she previously might have done, she calmly deleted the message and got back on with finishing her report, avoiding the high risk situation.

Managing your survival apparatus

Anger, sadness, fear, disgust. Why block emotions? Why be nice when you're angry? Why pretend that you aren't afraid? Why mute yourself when you want to talk? Why forgive someone when they have done something upsetting? We often block out uncomfortable thoughts and feelings, don't communicate how we really feel and end up frustrated or resentful. To improve our empathy and to avoid apathy, we need to decode feelings and use our emotions intelligently.

There are at least two systems for assessing the significance of events. One system leads to a conscious recall, through memory, of options for action. We use this system to reason with ourselves and decide what we will do. Another system, a more instinctive system and probably evolutionarily far older, acts before the first one. It activates feelings based on our previous emotional experience in comparable situations. These feelings affect the choices and reasoning strategies that we present to our conscious selves. We consequently do ourselves a disservice when we think of ourselves as solely rational or knowledge-driven and fail to pay attention to the role of our gut feelings and emotions in guiding our actions and behaviour.

Emotions are not consciously controlled, as we find out along the way. Emotion is expressed largely in the body, through posture and facial expression as well as through such internal processes as heart rate and blood pressure. When we experience any of the base emotions – sadness, happiness, anger, fear, surprise, disgust – our experiences express themselves physically, in ways that can be observed by another person. Emotional life is largely housed in the brain's limbic system, and it critically aids the formation of memories. It's thought that this part of the brain evolved early on in human history, making it quite primitive. Emotions, and where and how they originate, are not simply explained. There is debate about how many emotions people experience and if they are universally experienced. Nevertheless, base emotions like fear, apprehension (nervous excitement), disgust, sadness and anger can be employed as tools of survival. They serve to alert us to danger and help us protect ourselves. This explains why an emotional response is often quite straightforward, but very powerful: you want to cry, or run away, or shout to survive. These emotions are useful is that they get us to react quickly in response to danger.

Pain is both a physical and an emotional experience. If I fall and hurt myself, along with the physical pain, I am likely to feel embarrassed, humiliated or even angry with myself for being careless. When people feel emotional pain, the same areas of the brain get activated as when people feel physical pain: the anterior insula cortex (AIC) and the anterior cingulate cortex (ACC). The anterior insular cortex is thought to play a role in emotional awareness, defined as the conscious experience of emotions. Deficits in emotional awareness, discussed further in this chapter, are commonly seen in conditions associated with functional deficits of this area of the brain (e.g. some forms of dementia, depression and in some individuals who have experienced trauma).

The brain is interconnected with the rest of the body. It is thought that over the course of evolution, our bodies decided to take the economic route and use a single neural system to detect and feel pain, regardless of whether it is emotional or physical. There are direct neural connections via the brain stem and spinal cord. The circulatory and lymphatic systems also carry neurotransmitters (hormones and immune cells) that find receptor sites in the brain which feedback and regulate the links between brain and body.[2]

Recent research has identified that our gut acts as a second brain, controlling our enteric nervous system, which consists of a mesh-like system of neurons that governs the function of the gastrointestinal tract, whilst our 'upper' brain controls our central nervous system. In many ways the brain and gut are partners, they communicate with each other and have a strong, direct link between them. Sometimes the brain and gut miscommunicate. A common communication problem is irritable bowel syndrome, and this is due to neuronal hyperactivity. The gut and brain use the same 'language' or neurotransmitters. Serotonin is one of them. Intriguingly, serotonin once most extensively studied as a neurotransmitter of the central nervous system, is seen to be primarily secreted in the gut. About 95 per cent of serotonin is estimated to be found in the gut and dopamine is also found there. In the brain, dopamine is a signalling molecule associated with pleasure and the reward system.[3] It acts as a signalling molecule in the gut too, transmitting messages between neurons that coordinate the contraction of muscles in the colon. In the brain, the language of serotonin means a sense of well-being and happiness; in the gut it means a well-regulated immune system. Our gut therefore has the ability to affect our emotions just like our emotions influence our gut. It's a two-way process. Foods can help subdue stress and aid gut health in several ways. Some foods boost levels of serotonin (e.g. seeds and nuts). Other foods can cut levels of cortisol and adrenaline (e.g. dark chocolate, green tea, wholegrains), the stress hormones that take a toll on the body over time. A healthy diet can help counter the impact of stress by shoring up the immune system and lowering blood pressure.

When things go awry

When faced with a threat of aggression or violence, our instincts (survival apparatus) kick in. Those who are **instinct intact** prepare to fight or take flight, but some are **instinct injured** for various reasons and can't locate the feelings that ought to alert them to dangerous situations. If this early warning system is not in in good working order, we may find ourselves unable to determine a course of action to help ourselves get out of harm's way.

If your body can't distinguish between ordinary frustrations in daily life and truly life-threatening stress, it gears up to every challenge every single time. Our bodies get busy just in case we need to put up a fight or make a fast exit and release cortisol in readiness to do something physical. The formation of this body state is automatic, largely predetermined by our genes to respond not to a particular thing but to certain categories of things. Feelings, by contrast, are our conscious perception of all those changes happening in the body and to our thoughts. Rational thinking is too slow for handling a threat (e.g. the sound of a loud explosion) and we need to react more quickly. It is our base emotions, like fear and surprise, which help us do that. Most of what happens when an emotion is stimulated happens without us being conscious of it; for example, our body may already be in a state that represents anger (e.g. clenched fists, grimacing), before we know what is making us angry.

In some people, difficulty in locating and processing feelings is so marked that it affects their self-awareness, social attachment and interpersonal relating. They may have difficulty in distinguishing and appreciating the emotions of others, which is thought to lead to ineffective emotional responding, sometimes leading to inappropriate social behaviour. People who don't recognize many emotions in themselves or have difficulty identifying and describing their emotions may have what is known medically as **alexithymia.** Traumatization, both in childhood and in adulthood, has been identified as the most important known risk factor for developing alexithymia. Traumatic stress symptoms and PTSD are factors connecting traumatic experiences and alexithymia. Studies show that higher rates of alexithymia occur among individuals who have been repeatedly traumatized.

Research on alexithymia, traditionally defined in terms of difficulties identifying and describing one's own emotions, has focused relatively little on the ability to perceive non-emotional states from the body (termed 'interoception'). Interoception refers to the perception of a wide range of physical states beyond emotions, including heart rate, respiratory effort, temperature, fatigue, hunger, thirst, satiety, muscle ache, pain and itch. However, recent studies suggest that interoception may be a more significant feature of alexithymia than previously thought. The social consequences for individuals with alexithymia may also be more severe than originally supposed; it is possible that individuals with alexithymia struggle to identify not only emotion in others and themselves, but also signals of non-emotion interoceptive states, such as heat, nausea and hunger.[4]

Alexithymia can impair a person's ability not only to attend to their own needs, but also to respond to others' needs and successfully care for others. People who have alexithymia may find it hard to respond appropriately in social situations. For example, they may describe themselves as having difficulties expressing emotions that are deemed socially appropriate, such as happiness on a joyous occasion. Others may have trouble identifying their emotions. They may not have as strong emotions as their peers and may have difficulties feeling or expressing empathy. High levels of alexithymia occur in about 10 per cent of the population. Approaches to treating alexithymia are still in their infancy, with few proven treatment options available, although there are skills-based interventions for its treatment, often focused on addressing the following three areas: the relationship between alexithymia and early life experiences, identifying feelings and expressing feelings.

Some individuals working for organizations in which control of emotions is the norm (e.g. the police and military) might show alexithymic-like behaviour but not be alexithymic. Over time the lack of self-expression can become routine, and they may find it harder to identify with others. Difficulty with recognizing and talking about their emotions appears in men who conform to cultural notions of masculinity (for example, those who adhere to the 'men don't cry' sort of thinking). Reluctance to view some emotions as acceptable accounts for difficulties some individuals may have with 'describing feelings', but not by difficulties in 'identifying feelings'. Many people, more than is generally supposed, have a limited emotional range. Some severely restrict themselves; 'I'm happy', 'I'm sad' and 'I am p**d off' being their limit. Nevertheless, there is a wide range of emotions that go beyond these few and some emotions, interestingly enough, go in and out of fashion. Few talk of experiencing melancholia or feeling melancholic these days, for example. Sometimes what you feel is so much more than happiness or anger and hard to put into words because our emotional vocabulary is limited. Furthermore, what is considered a 'normal' range of emotion may differ from one era to another, one culture to another, from one household to another and from one situation to another.

Using emotions smartly

All emotions are impulses to act. The emotions of fear, anger, happiness, love, surprise, disgust and sadness send signals to the brain that release hormones to give strength to the necessary reactions. Emotional thought therefore can lead to action for coping and surviving. Being alert to our feelings is important to thought, and vice versa. Humans are of two minds: the 'emotional mind' and the 'rational mind'. One mind feels and the other thinks. Of course, these two minds interact. Emotion influences thought (reason) and vice versa. Emotions can inform the rational mind, which moderates the involvement and expression of our emotions. Feelings and emotions then are best viewed as indicators of our state of being, as opposed to 'good' and 'bad' experiences.

As already discussed, emotional empathy is when you feel along with the other person. Emotional empathy enables someone to tune into another person's inner emotional world. If one's range of feelings is limited; for example, a sociopath (restricted to base emotions such as anger, envy and self-pity), it may cause difficulty recognizing and empathizing with feelings in others that are not readily accessed or processed in themselves. For instance, a sociopath might not empathize with another person's fear or sense of shame. By contrast, an individual with an expansive emotional range can draw on this to aid them in empathizing with other people in many different situations, e.g. recognize fear in themselves but master it to find courage to help themselves or other people.

One downside of having a high level of emotional empathy is when people lack the ability to manage their own distressing emotions. I gave examples of this in Chapter 4 (in emotional instability disorder, for example). This can lead to emotional exhaustion and stress. In an attempt to manage personal distress, many people in their daily lives employ purposeful detachment from their feelings. Doctors and healthcare workers, for example, often employ purposeful detachment to protect themselves against stress and burnout. Of course, there is a danger that employing emotional detachment can lead to indifference, rather than well-regulated caring. Those who work with people in need – whose business it is to show care and concern for others – need to find ways to maintain a healthy balance if they are going to provide genuinely compassionate care.

Emotions help us aid one another and maintain relationships. They help us bond with one another and be sociable. However, being agreeable and sociable all the time has its drawbacks. Whilst being agreeable has been promoted as good for health and well-being, researchers have discovered something surprising: those who are described as 'agreeable, conscientious personalities' are more likely to follow orders (including delivering fatal electric shocks to innocent people when instructed!), than less agreeable personalities, who are more likely to refuse to hurt others. Anger and passion therefore can be beneficial. They are behind a lot of creative work: in a series of experiments, it was demonstrated that anger promoted unstructured or freer, more creative thinking.[5]

Pent-up and hidden emotions like anger often don't get you where you want, but keep you stuck where you don't want to be. That is because when anger is concealed, the other person in the relationship can't know about it, so has less chance of doing anything to remedy the situation. Anger can help us develop insight. If we can notice when we get angry and why, this can motivate self-change. Anger is a strong social indicator that things are not right and need to be addressed. Without the proper amount of anger, without moral indignation, we would lose the desire to protect our friends, communities, nation or the planet. So too, anger helps us negotiate a better deal for ourselves and other people, although negotiating while also staying in control of our anger can be a challenge, as the Greek philosopher Aristotle observed: 'Anyone can get angry – that is easy ... but to do this to the right person, to the right extent, at the right time, with the right motive, and in the right way, that is not for everyone, nor is it easy.'

It rarely pays to remain impassive to one's own or another's plight in the face of a threat. Playing dead, as some animals do ('tonic immobility', a state of paralysis or hypnosis), may be a way of avoiding or deterring predators to get out of a dangerous situation, but as a strategy of deterrence it cannot be maintained in the long term. So, what can we do to help ourselves? There are actions we can take that can influence our responses to other people. All of us use our emotion apparatus to influence and guide our actions. Some of us use this apparatus more often and to better effect than others. Nevertheless, most of us can learn to better exercise our emotion processing apparatus and put it to good use.

As we emotionally mature through childhood into adulthood, we learn and take on board ethical standards that we absorb from the individuals around us, from society at large and the people who make up the community we live in. All being well, the development of morality passes through several stages during childhood and adolescence, moving from avoidance of punishment to avoidance of disapproval and rejection, then finally avoidance of guilt and self-recrimination, i.e. acting on our own conscience. Unfortunately, some people dodge the last step in the process. Emotions such as guilt, shame, embarrassment and pride (the moral emotions), arise during the process of understanding how others see us. These are the emotions that the sociopath lacks.

Moral emotions influence future behaviour. It is thought that two requirements are needed for feeling a moral emotion. The first is the person needs to be capable of position-taking; in other words, knowing how your behaviours would affect or be perceived by others (self-perceptiveness). The second requirement is the individual needs the ability to imagine how the behaviour likely reflects upon their character (ethical self-reflection). For example, you are in a meeting with your line manager after your colleague complained about you. You are likely to feel some fear – your heart is beating fast, you feel nauseous and your palms are sweating. Fear is a base emotion. But the shame that might set in as you leave – 'I shouldn't have lied' – is a moral emotion. The moral emotions bind us to other people, to other people's or the group's expectations and ideas. These emotions require a heightened sense of self-awareness (self-perceptivity arrived at through self-reflection), which comes with the ability to identify what you are feeling and experiencing inside yourself. People with high **emotional intelligence** can recognize their own emotions and those of others, use emotional information to guide thinking and behaviour, discern between different feelings and label them appropriately, and adjust emotions to adapt to environments. Emotional intelligence is typically associated with empathic ability because it involves an individual connecting their personal experiences with those of others.

Harnessing instinct and intuition

As suggested, in terms of how we operate in daily life, humans have two very different systems at play. One system is our instinctual and often subconscious way of operating. The second is more analytical. Instinct is the innate inclination towards a particular behaviour in response to certain stimuli. It is instinctive, for example, to recognize when to run from a perceived danger. This is known as the 'fight or flight' response. Intuition is considered part of the fast system of thinking that draws from that collection in your brain to inform your decisions. This compares to the slow analytical style of thinking that follows rules to obtain your answer.

The word 'intuition' dates to late Middle English, when it denoted spiritual insight or immediate spiritual communication. It derives from the Latin *intueri*, meaning 'consider'. The intuitive system is more hardwired into humans than is commonly understood. Unfortunately, such gut feelings can also be silenced and suppressed. A childhood hijacked by abusive or neglectful people, for instance, can make it difficult to separate traumatic past experiences from gut intuition or instinct. And strong emotions, particularly negative ones, can cloud our intuition. A person's intuition may fail when they are alexithymic, depressed or angry, or in any heightened emotional state.

In recent times there has been a dismissive attitude towards intuition and its reliability in decision-making. However, intuition can be used in conjunction with evidence and can help us formulate questions in order to solve problems. For instance, if a scientist has a hunch or a gut feeling about something related to their field of study, they can use this intuitive thought to help formulate research questions and lines of inquiry. So too, doctors and nurses can use intuition in tandem with evidence-based practice to achieve good outcomes for their patients. It does not have to be one or the other. Humans can use their feelings wisely to aid rational thought.

It is interesting that we also call intuition, 'gut instinct' or 'gut feeling'. Researchers are only beginning to explore the mind-gut link. Is the mind-gut connection about our primal instincts? Or is it about instinct and this other phenomenon, intuition, working in unison? Much more research is needed to understand intuition. However, there's no denying intuition exists. Countless people acknowledge it and there are intuitive people who show signs and 'live' it. Intuition is defined from a psychology standpoint as the productive influence of non-conscious emotional information on an otherwise unrelated decision or judgement. It is a brain process that gives people the ability to make decisions without the use of analytical reasoning. Based on the 2018 research of psychologists from the University of Social Sciences and Humanities in Wroclaw, Poland, there are three types of intuitive abilities:[6]

1 **'I know something. However, I don't know the source of this knowledge'**: This is associated with an ability to subconsciously combine information stored in your long-term memory to make correct judgments based on fragmentary cues'.
2 **'I don't know that I know something'**: Implicit learning where someone can spontaneously learn and detect cognitive patterns (make connections, like doing a puzzle).
3 **'I think that I know something'**: This is subjective intuitive ability and relates to the people who like to daydream and have highly vivid and creative mental imagery, are open to new experiences, are intellectually curious and show a preference for intuition.

Today, as the aforementioned research work demonstrates, intuition is a legitimate subject of scientific inquiry. There is growing interest in how individuals can learn to use intuitive thinking. Soldiers, for example, often experience strong gut feelings or a sixth sense about situations and individuals. They utilize gut feelings to manoeuvre through potentially dangerous situations. In recognition of the significance attached to intuition, a number of years ago the US Navy began a programme to investigate how members of the military can be trained to improve their intuitive ability. The idea came from the testimony of troops in Iraq and Afghanistan who reported an unexplained feeling of danger just before they encountered an enemy attack or ran into an improvised explosive device. The researchers called this sense the 'Spidey sense' after the intuitive power of Spiderman.

Most of us, if not all, are connected to our intuition, but some people don't pay attention to it. Some people experience a visceral reaction when they are in the presence of a dangerous person or situation. Sometimes our bodies manifest such things as stomach ache or muscle tension; other times there is simply an unidentified feeling about what you should or shouldn't do. Neuroscientist and author of *The Feeling of What Happens*, Antonio Damasio theorized that we evolved to use bodily cues such as muscle tone, heart rate and endocrine activity (hormones travelling through your body to organs where they have an effect), in order to make rapid decisions about how to navigate the physical and social worlds. These 'somatic markers' translate unconscious emotions and sensations into felt instinct. This evolutionary strategy allows us to make quick decisions that require minimal thought to enhance survival.

Instincts and intuition can be interwoven with rational thought to improve decision-making and keep us safe. People are in a constant state of communication. We unconsciously 'leak' our moods, attitude and even intentions. Whether it be through a look, a posture of avoidance, tone of voice, gesture, movement, lack of speech or by talking too much, we are in constant communication with others. What we call a 'hunch' is often, in reality, an assessment of another and the immediate environment. That process evaluates the stimuli in relation to the immediate situation and the memory bank of past experiences. If something doesn't make sense to the unconscious, the alarms go off. We therefore can harness instincts and intuition in a helpful way. If you're considering forming a relationship with somebody but have a nebulous feeling of unease, let your mind start putting words to what it is about this person that is making you uncomfortable. It can start with something vague. 'I just have a feeling about him'. Then dig deeper and ask yourself, 'What about this individual is making me feel that way? Are they too charming? Too argumentative? Is it something in their body language? Something they said or the way they said it? It might be helpful to jot things down or enlist someone else as a sounding board to guide your reflection. Then test your feelings against available information. This way you use your survival apparatus in a balanced way, assessing emotional reaction alongside logical thought.

In this chapter I have discussed regaining control of your life by helping to repair your survival apparatus and then keeping it in good working order. If it all feels tough going at first, don't be disheartened. There is evidence that adversity can lead to post-traumatic growth, including increased compassion and pro-social behaviour. Researchers David Greenberg, Simon Baron-Cohen, and colleagues from the University of Cambridge, found that the experience of a childhood trauma increases a person's ability to take the perspective of another and to understand their mental and emotional states, and that this impact is long-standing. Trauma can therefore increase attention to emotion, environmental cues and increase emotional attentiveness in the post-trauma phase. This increase can improve the ability to recognize, understand and react appropriately to the states of others, i.e. improve empathy.[7]

8

Dealing with complex family situations

Coping with the fallout

After separating from or severing ties with a sociopath in the family you might think that things are finally sorted, but the sociopath is unlikely to cooperate as far as family responsibilities go. In fact, they are far more likely to try to turn things to their own advantage and lie about the situation.

Sadly, sociopaths' attentions often turn to their children, and not in a good way. They will frequently use their children as both shield and arsenal against you, the other parent. Co-parenting with a sociopath can be a daily challenge. In all parenting partnerships, there exists an ongoing need to negotiate and compromise; unfortunately, the sociopath neither negotiates nor compromises. Sociopaths are extremely good at manipulating others, including their own children, and will not hesitate to use them in a game of tug of war and attempt to harm their children's relationship with the non-sociopathic parent. Sociopathic parents have hallmark parenting traits that amount to psychological abuse, some of which can be seen in the case study presented earlier in the book of Rebecca's sociopathic mother. The hallmark parenting traits include:

- Lack of attachment, bonding, love
- Dismissiveness
- Disregard for the child's welfare
- Harsh expectations and demands

- Neglect, often extreme
- Purposeful attempts to corrupt a child (encouraging anti-social behaviour).

It is hard to accept this uncomfortable truth, but sociopaths don't love their children for themselves. Instead they view them as objects of manipulation. A non-sociopathic parent can thus be dealt a double blow at the hands of their former partner, and experience secondary trauma (a common term for the stress resulting from helping or wanting to help a traumatized or suffering person) whenever children or other loved ones are involved. To compound the situation further, children may be brainwashed by their sociopathic parent into believing that the non-sociopathic parent is the problem and the root cause of the family's difficulties. The child's mental health is often affected. Sociopathic parents instil fear, shame and a sense of worthlessness and self-blame in their children.

Being the partner of a sociopathic parent is like living on a minefield. On the whole sociopaths make poor parents. At best, they view their children as prized possessions. At worst, they actively try to corrupt them. Sociopaths see children as an inconvenience. This indifference to their welfare takes many forms. They may leave young children alone or in the care of unreliable babysitters, or fail to provide them with proper food and clothing. They may demand certain behaviour or accomplishments for their own benefit. They may inflict physical, sexual and emotional abuse, or deliberately try to corrupt a child through inappropriate or dangerous activities. So when a sociopath is involved with children, always be on guard.

Children can and do cope remarkably well if they sense they are loved and feel safe, but this is hard to achieve when a sociopathic parent is present and stirring up perpetual conflict. Many children eventually sense that there is no real bond between them and the sociopathic parent but it is, and will continue to be, a confusing and disturbing relationship for them. A good plan of action is to stay neutral whenever possible and say little about the sociopathic parent. Also, it is important to set boundaries in order to avoid children growing up thinking that sociopathic behaviour is acceptable. Over time you may learn to handle the new arrangement and situation effectively, like this father:

> 'My strategy now is not to give an inch on anything [with regard to the children], because she will take every possible opportunity to emotionally or otherwise manipulate every situation. You have to mean business and not get into a discussion or negotiation about anything. Zero tolerance is, unfortunately, the only approach that works for me.'

Do not accept into your life anything or anyone that you don't want your children exposed to. Sociopathic family members and their apath 'friends' will have an impact on your children whether you realize it or not. So take steps to become assertive and more self-reliant. Arrange things as far as possible so that you are financially as well as socially independent of the sociopath who was formerly part of your life, otherwise you are allowing them control over you.

If all this sounds depressing, remember that children usually work things out for themselves, so have faith. At some point they will realize that the sociopath cares only about themselves without you having to tell them and unintentionally pushing them away in the process. Nevertheless the systematic training and grooming of children in this way causes immense harm and damage to all sides. Many individuals who have gone through this experience say they didn't come to see what was going on until many years later, by which time a lot of damage had been caused to the individual and to family relations.

For children with one or more sociopathic parents it often takes years to come to terms with or understand their situation.

Some never come to terms with it, or 'see' the reality of their circumstances. Indeed, it is not uncommon for children of sociopaths to reach a certain level of maturity, perhaps middle age, before they gain any proper understanding of their experiences. This is possibly because childhood experiences of this kind are so overwhelming that there is a tendency to block the painful memories until we are more capable of facing up to the trauma of early life.

Child protection

Within the domestic sphere, a particular family member, often a child, is sometimes targeted by their sociopathic kin. This may not come to light until the child is grown up and ready to face their past, but it is conceivable that they might approach a family member whom they trust and try to unburden themselves about the abuse that is going on. In such situations it is immensely important that the child is properly listened to and commended for speaking out. The uncomfortable truth, however, is that adults don't always accept that abuse is going on, especially if the abuser is a close family member. Hence, children often learn to keep the abuse and their fears to themselves for fear of being rejected or told they are telling lies. In her powerful book *The Body Never Lies*, Alice Miller notes that the parent or primary carer is to blame for any damage they inflict upon their child, and must take full responsibility for participation in the abuse. Sociopaths don't own or take responsibility for the abuse they inflict upon others, but they must be held responsible all the same. And if other adults are involved in some way, albeit in not acting on an accusation of abuse or failing to 'see' the abuse, they must be held accountable for their inaction and negligence. Everyone who turns a blind eye to abuse of a child is, to some extent, blameworthy.

Let's recall the Sociopath–Empath–Apath Triad identified in Chapter 4. For sociopathic abuse to occur it usually requires the following threesome: the sociopath, the empath and the apath. As a reminder, the set-up goes like this:

- The empath is forced to make a stand on seeing the sociopath say or do something underhand.
- They challenge the sociopath, who throws others off the scent and blames the empath.
- The empath becomes an object of abuse when the apath corroborates the sociopath's side of the story.

If the empath is a child, and they come forward and tell another family member or friend, a neighbour, aunt or uncle, and that adult does nothing to help the child, then this behaviour is morally inept; the kind of behaviour that is usually the preserve of the apath. It means the sociopath is likely to get away with enduring mistreatment of the child, while the child is likely to be at even greater risk of abuse now the sociopath knows they are a threat and capable of making a stand. In such circumstances, it may not be in the best interests of the child to remain in the family environment. However, sociopathic abuse of this kind, especially emotional abuse, rarely comes to the attention of the authorities and remains hidden, leaving the child unprotected and unsafe.

Child welfare – what to do if you suspect problems

Different countries have different laws governing the protection and safeguarding of children, but in the UK there is a comprehensive child welfare system under which local authorities have duties and responsibilities towards children in need in their area. This covers the provision of advice and services, accommodation and care of children who become uncared for, and also the capacity to initiate proceedings for the removal of children from their parents' care. Risk of 'significant harm' to children covers physical, sexual and emotional abuse and neglect. The basic legal principle in the UK, under the Children Act 1989, is that the welfare of the child is paramount.

Emotional abuse can affect a child from infancy, through adolescence, and into adulthood. It sets back a child's physical as well as mental development (the child's intelligence and memory) and puts a child at greater risk of developing mental health problems such as eating disorders and self-harming. It can also hamper a child's emotional development, including the ability to feel and express a full range of emotions appropriately or control their emotions. It can put children at greater risk of developing behavioural problems such as learning difficulties, problems with relationships and socializing, rebellious behaviour, aggressive and violent behaviour, anti-social behaviour and criminality and negative impulsive behaviour (not caring what happens to them). In the UK, the National Society for the Prevention of Cruelty to Children (NSPCC) suggests emotionally abusive behaviour includes:[1]

- Not responding to a child's emotional needs by persistently ignoring the child or being absent
- Humiliating or criticizing a child
- Disciplining a child with degrading punishments
- Not recognizing a child's individuality and limitations, pushing the child too hard, or being too controlling
- Exposing a child to distressing events or interactions, like domestic abuse or substance misuse
- Failing to promote a child's social development, for instance by not allowing the child to have friends.

You may notice a child and its parent have a difficult relationship. If the relationship is nervous, fearful or distant, or if you think the child's emotions, mental capacities or behaviour seem very different from other children of the same age, this may indicate a problem. If as an adult you do have valid concerns about a child being emotionally or physically abused, you should take action by contacting your local social services or police. Emotional abuse especially is often overlooked, yet the scars take longer to heal than any physical ones. Sadly, emotional abuse is far too common and is experienced daily by many children throughout the world. It is important to stop abuse in its tracks or better still, prevent it entirely.

Children need to feel wanted, loved and safe; they also need consistency and boundaries. No parent or carer gets it right every time, and everyone has a bad day with their children, but emotional or physical abuse is different. Severe and persistent ill treatment undermines a child's confidence and self-worth. Trauma survival specialist Judith Herman argues that as long as the target (in this case the child) maintains strong relationships with others, the perpetrator's power is limited; therefore, the sociopath seeks to isolate the child. The sociopath will not only attempt to prohibit communication and material support, but will also try to destroy the child's emotional ties to others. When the child is isolated, they increasingly become dependent on the sociopath, not only for survival and basic needs, but also for emotional sustenance. Prolonged confinement in fear and isolation reliably produces a bond of identification between the sociopath and the victim. This is another form of traumatic bonding and may occur between a battered partner and their abuser or between an abused child and an abusive parent.[2]

Adult survivors of childhood abuse sometimes form intense, unstable relationships. Some find it very hard to tolerate being alone, but are also extremely wary of others. Terrified of being abandoned on the one hand, and of being dominated on the other, they may fluctuate between extremes of submissiveness and rebellion. This has been termed 'sitting duck syndrome'.[3] In the most extreme cases, survivors of childhood abuse may find themselves involved in abuse of others, either in the role of passive bystander or, more rarely, as a perpetrator. Nevertheless emerging evidence, referred to in the preceding chapter, offers hope that adversity in childhood in many cases can lead to post-traumatic growth, including increased compassion and pro-social behaviour. An example if ever there was one of triumph over adversity.

Assisting a child in overcoming abuse is a challenge, but children can and do overcome trauma. Helping children make sense of things by listening to them and acting on their behalf when necessary will make a lot of difference to their ability to recover from their childhood traumas.

Sociopathic relatives

It isn't just apathy but sociopathy itself that can be an entrenched problem within families. Siblings, grandparents, aunts and uncles may have some degree of sociopathy, or lack of empathy. Nor is it uncommon for the children of sociopaths, whether or not they are sociopathic themselves, to attract, and be attracted to, sociopathic partners in later life. In this way the cycle of abuse can often be transferred from one generation to the next. And sometimes sociopaths join forces, or pair up with others with conditions of zero or limited empathy such as narcissists or the almost sociopaths called everyday sadists. When these types combine they make for a potent and lethal mix. Such couplings can prove almost impossible to contend with in families.

Sociopaths rarely if ever improve significantly with age, though they may seemingly become more subdued owing to a reduction in the opportunities they have to inflict harm.

Family members often become the targets of manipulation, one against the other, with the consequence that the family is destroyed by the destructive elements within. More often than not other members of the family fall into line, taking on the role and function that suit the sociopath best once the sociopathic transaction has been conducted and the Sociopath–Empath–Apath Triad set-up is in place. All too often the empath, the family member who is more perceptive and sees the situation for what it is, becomes the target of family hostility, eventually ending up either walking away or being expelled from the family group.

In this chapter and the previous one, ways were proposed to help people in dramatic and painful circumstances deal with harassment, bullying and intimidation. Domestic abuse takes many forms and does not always involve the use of physical violence. As stated in the previous chapter, until recent years, UK law has offered little protection from psychological abuse and injury. To recap, there a number of jurisdictions, sanctions and remedies for psychological abuse expressly and implicitly provided for within existing civil law. In England and Wales for example, these include non-molestation orders, occupation orders, restraining orders and the ground of unreasonable behaviour for divorce. An occupation order, for example, allows the Court to decide who should live, or not live, in the home or any part of it. The Order can also exclude the other person from an area around the home.

England, Wales, Scotland and Ireland have adopted legal definitions and understandings of coercive control in recent years. In 2015, controlling or coercive behaviour became a crime in England and Wales for the first time. This made it a legally recognized form of domestic abuse. Gaslighting, a form of emotional abuse, is domestic abuse and is now recognized under coercive control legislation as a criminal offence in the UK. It became a crime in Scotland in 2019, and is recognized as criminal in Northern Ireland under the Domestic Abuse and Family Proceedings Act 2021.

Section 76 of the Serious Crime Act 2015 created a new offence of controlling or coercive behaviour in an intimate or family relationship. Prior to the introduction of this offence, case law indicated the difficulty in proving a pattern of behaviour amounting to harassment within an intimate relationship. The new offence, which does not have retrospective effect, defines an offence thus:

An offence is committed by A if:

A repeatedly or continuously engages in behaviour towards another person, B, that is controlling or coercive; and at time of the behaviour, A and B are personally connected; and the behaviour has a serious effect on B; and A knows or ought to know that the behaviour will have a serious effect on B.

A and B are 'personally connected' if: they are in an intimate personal relationship; or they live together and are either members of the same family; or they live together have previously been in an intimate personal relationship with each other.

There are two ways in which it can be proved that A's behaviour has a 'serious effect' on B: firstly if it causes B to fear, on at least two occasions, that violence will be used against them or secondly, if it causes B serious alarm or distress which has a substantial adverse effect on their day-to-day activities. For the purposes of this offence, behaviour must be engaged in 'repeatedly' or 'continuously'.

Another, separate, element of the offence is that it must have a 'serious effect' on someone and one way of proving this is that it causes someone to fear, on at least two occasions, that violence will be used against them. The phrase 'substantial adverse effect on B's usual day-to-day activities' may include, but is not limited to:

- Stopping or changing the way someone socializes
- Physical or mental health deterioration
- A change in routine at home including those associated with mealtimes or household chores
- Attendance record at school

- Putting in place measures at home to safeguard themselves or their children
- Changes to work patterns, employment status or routes to work.

It was reported in February 2022 in UK media that a high court judge gave credibility to the term 'gaslighting' in relation to coercive control legislation. This **landmark case** went to the Court of Appeal after a judge in an initial ruling warned the mother that if she continued with her claims of rape and abuse, her child would be taken into care and adopted. The judge also issued a consent order setting out times when the father could see his child. However, at the appeal, High Court Judge, Mr Justice Cobb, decreed that the mother was a vulnerable and naïve woman who had been subjected to emotional control/coercion. He also said there was no clear medical evidence that she suffered from bi-polar (the abuser's lies were given credibility because he was a mental health care worker). Agreeing that the use of the term gaslighting by the mother's representative, human rights lawyer was 'apposite,' Mr Justice Cobb said, 'the father's conduct represented a form of insidious abuse designed to cause the mother to question her own mental well-being, indeed her sanity.' The mother's case formed one of the four linked appeals in the Court of Appeal.[4]

Controlling or coercive behaviour towards another also can include or be committed in conjunction with a range of other offences including offences under: the Malicious Communications Act 1998; the Sexual Offences Act 2003; and the Offences Against the Person Act 1861. The consideration of the cumulative impact of controlling or coercive behaviour and the pattern of behaviour within the context of the relationship is crucial. Relevant behaviour of the perpetrator can include:

- Isolating a person from their friends and family
- Depriving them of their basic needs

- Monitoring their time
- Monitoring a person via online communication tools or using spyware
- Taking control over aspects of their everyday life, such as where they can go, who they can see, what to wear and when they can sleep
- Depriving them access to support services, such as specialist support or medical services
- Repeatedly putting them down such as telling them they are worthless
- Enforcing rules and activity which humiliate, degrade or dehumanize the victim
- Forcing the victim to take part in criminal activity such as shoplifting, neglect or abuse of children to encourage self-blame and prevent disclosure to authorities
- Financial abuse including control of finances, such as only allowing a person a punitive allowance
- Control ability to go to school or place of study
- Taking wages, benefits or allowances
- Threats to hurt or kill
- Threats to harm a child
- Threats to reveal or publish private information (e.g. threatening to 'out' someone)
- Threats to hurt or physically harming a family pet
- Assault
- Criminal damage (such as destruction of household goods)
- Preventing a person from having access to transport or from working
- Preventing a person from being able to attend school, college or university
- Family 'dishonour'
- Reputational damage
- Disclosure of sexual orientation

- Disclosure of HIV status or other medical condition without consent
- Limiting access to family, friends and finances.

This is not an exhaustive list and this conduct can vary to a high degree from one person to the next.

If a current or former partner has interfered with your money or economic resources to limit your choices – known as economic abuse – they can potentially be prosecuted for controlling or coercive behaviour. Previously, economic abuse could be prosecuted as controlling or coercive behaviour under the Serious Crime Act 2015 but now it is officially recognized in UK law, defined in the Domestic Abuse Act 2021.

Once you realize that you are being emotionally abused, keep a diary, record all events of lying or conversation during which abuse is trivialized or completely ignored. Seek comfort from friends and family, reconnect with those who you have been distanced from, and let them know what you are experiencing. If the behaviour becomes emotionally damaging and controlling or abusive, report it to the police. As a victim of emotional abuse, an individual has several options available to them – leave the family home temporarily or permanently or remaining in the home and forcing the person harming you to leave the property. Once you are safe, you need to consider your future options, which may include:

- Permanently splitting from your partner
- Taking action to keep your partner from harassing you
- Protecting your interests in the family home – whether this is if you decide to remain or leave the property
- Ensuring that child arrangements are taken care of.

Domestic abuse is not only an issue for adults, but also for children and teenagers. Young people's formative years are difficult at the best of times, but a lack of experience in relationships and issues with self-confidence can mean they feel they have nowhere to turn. As each person's circumstances differ some forms of support are more helpful than others. Family therapy, for example, is unlikely to prove helpful when there is a sociopath is in the family, because sociopaths do not respond constructively to therapy and may run rings around the therapist, however well qualified and experienced they may be. On the other hand, the non-sociopathic members of the family or household may well need this kind of psychological support; it may prove highly beneficial to have someone outside the experience who is able to listen to their concerns. But a word of caution: even trained and experienced counsellors and psychotherapists may not be *au fait* with the issue of sociopathic abuse. They may fail to appreciate the nuances of sociopathy and the abusive interactions that can occur in families where sociopaths lurk. My advice is to ask prospective therapists about their experience of working with families and sociopathic abuse, and only to engage in this kind of support if you feel confident in the therapist's ability to work effectively with this complex family dynamic and to handle the situation well.

Since those with first-hand experience of sociopathic abuse began to promote awareness about sociopathy and its harms, a significant amount of peer led help has become available and numerous support groups have been set up online to assist those overcoming sociopathic abuse. However, the issue of online support is fraught with difficulties, a situation that acts as a deterrent to would-be groups and campaigners, not least because it is vital to protect children and adults from the risk of further abuse.

Laying down the law with other family members

If the sociopathic family member happens to be someone other than a parent, for example a grandparent, aunt or uncle, then the situation can be equally murky. Adults with sociopathic parents or siblings are likely to feel torn between their parents' and society's expectation that grandparents, aunts and uncles should have access to their grandchildren, grand-nieces and grand-nephews, and their desire to properly protect their child from abuse. Such parents also have to contend with their own experiences of emotional, physical or sexual abuse at the hands of their own parents or siblings, and this prior experience can ring alarm bells about abuse occurring to their own children if contact is maintained. This situation may prove just too difficult for the parents to deal with and may deter them from allowing their children to have any kind of relationship with the sociopathic family member.

In the case of sociopathic grandparents it is fairly common for the parents to allow the grandparents to begin a relationship with their grandchildren, hoping that things will be different this time, but unfortunately this is rarely the case: sociopathy is a lifelong and untreatable condition. If contact is maintained, however, even in a limited way, the children involved may eventually be torn apart by the grief of having to sever a relationship with the unhealthy family member. And the parent is likely to experience secondary trauma if their children are abused by other members of the family. They may end up feeling mortified at having done more harm than good by allowing the sociopath access to their children.

It is important that parents consider the pros and cons of letting other family members have contact with, and access to, their children. The following questions can be used to provide help in the decision-making process. If the answer to the questions below is 'no', then a rule of no contact is probably safest and best:

- Is the previously abusive family member a very different person to you from the one you remember?
- Do you currently have a healthy, functional and stable relationship with the family member?

- Does the family member respect your choices and boundaries as a parent?
- Does the family member follow your requests about how you want your children to be treated and behave?
- Would you recommend your parent or other family member as babysitter to your best friend without any hesitation, and would you feel comfortable giving your word that the family member would never harm your friend's child?

If you find it very difficult to make a decision of this nature, seek professional help, as other family members will not be neutral or objective. Professionals may include an adviser from the local social services child protection department, a family therapist or a family lawyer.

In the UK family members like grandparents, uncles and aunts have no automatic rights in respect of their grandchildren, nephews or nieces. If family members wish to reinstate contact it may become necessary for them to obtain a court order. The implementation of the Children Act 1989 made it possible for the court to make a number of different orders in respect of children.

One of the most common types of court order is a **contact order**. This term has replaced the word 'access' but it is essentially the same thing. An applicant for an order of this type asks for the court to allow them to have either direct or indirect contact. **Direct contact** is where the person to whom the order is granted will be able to physically see the children and perhaps take part in activities with them. **Indirect contact** is where the person will talk to the child by letter, telephone, email and text messages. If one or both parents raise objections the family member will have to attend a full hearing in which both parties put forward their evidence. In light of this, the offending family member may occasionally continue to pursue this course of action for fear of their true nature being exposed. If an abusive family member does continue to pursue a contact order, make sure any letters, emails or other indicators of abuse are kept as evidence for use in court.

What if you suspect your child has sociopathic traits?

Although those who have children with a sociopath can have healthy, happy offspring, unfortunately some people experience years of problems with their children. There may be a number of reasons for this: the sociopath may have abandoned the children and left the other parent to raise them alone; the children may have been used as a pawn in the sociopathic parent's manipulation games; or – and this is the worst scenario of all – the children may turn out to be sociopathic themselves as highlighted in the case study of the child sociopath Thomas in Chapter 2.

Sociopathy in children is very much a hidden problem in society, but depictions in film allow us to glimpse the nature of the problem. The horror classic, *The Bad Seed* (1956) for example. The central character, Rhoda Penmark, was the first of her kind, a serial killer child, to be depicted on screen. Sickly sweet, she perfectly represented the wholesome, nuclear family of 1950s America. Rhoda is too perfect. Excessively polite, too unruffled, too calculating. She's effortlessly manipulative, knowing just how to sweeten her words and appear guileless before adults. And that's the unique danger she represents, how easily sociopath children are able to fool adults. All they see is the façade the child chooses to present – the perfect child who never misbehaves or disrupts anything.

The issue also is the focus of the contentious US thriller *The Good Son* (1993). The first thing to say is that the film was universally slated. Critics thought the sociopathic child, Henry, was too unrealistic, with one critic contending that 'This is a very evil little boy ... what rings false is that [the character] isn't really a little boy at all ... His speech is much too sophisticated and ironic for that, and so is his reasoning and his cleverness ...'[5] Nevertheless, for those who live in close proximity to a sociopathic child, the film, with the exception of its implausible ending, is not so far-fetched; in fact the main character's glibness, artificiality and indifference are an accurate depiction of real-life child sociopathy. For example, here's a passage of dialogue from the film. A grieving boy called Mark stays with his aunt and uncle and befriends his cousin Henry, who is the same age. But his cousin begins showing increasing signs of sociopathic behaviour. Henry, the cousin, has thrown a plastic doll over a highway overpass into oncoming traffic, causing a massive pile-up:

> Mark: Do you know what you did?
> Henry: Hey, come on. We did it together.
> Mark: You could've killed people ...
> Henry: ... with your help ...
> Mark: Hey, I didn't know you were gonna do that!
> Henry: I feel sorry for you, Mark. You just don't know how to have fun.
> Mark: What?
> Henry: It's because you're scared all the time.

The issue of child sociopathy is also the focus of Lionel Shriver's novel *We Need to Talk About Kevin* (2003), later a US/UK film (2011). In the film we see the problems through the eyes of the mother, Eva, who is the 'seeing' person in the family. Throughout her son Kevin's life (the sociopath) he has been detached and difficult. He does not bond with his mother and as a baby he cries incessantly, rebuffs her attempts at affection, and shows no interest in anything. While Kevin is still small, his mother Eva becomes frustrated with his intractability. Eva's husband (the apath) dismisses her concerns, makes excuses for his son, gives Kevin a bow and arrow set and teaches him archery. Kevin becomes an excellent marksman. There follows a series of disturbing accidents to the household. While the mother blames Kevin, the father insists that Kevin is blameless. Since her earlier concerns were dismissed, the mother keeps to herself her intensifying fear of her son. The story culminates with Kevin plotting and executing several multiple killings. The paradox is that no one other than his mother talks about Kevin or his disturbing behaviour. No one 'sees' the problem for what it is.

Callous unemotional traits

By the time a child with such tendencies (hopefully not as extreme) reaches school age, they are already on the way to developing into a sociopath. They may interact well with school friends but the signs of anti-social behaviour are already there. Some children exert control over others by bullying them in the school playground while showing a different personality at home (and even revealing different sides to their personality to different family members). They are therefore difficult to detect, a problem compounded by the fact that no psychiatrist or psychologist will label a child a sociopath because it is regarded only as a potential problem at that stage. Instead, if pushed, psychologists identify these children as having **conduct disorder** or **callous unemotional traits**. But more often than not, these children are not identified or brought to the attention of mental health professionals at all. Some may be passed off as anti-social and eventually get caught up within the criminal justice system, especially sociopathic boys.

All children make mistakes and have times when they are aggressive, lie and manipulate because these traits are on a scale and are part of human nature, but children with callous unemotional traits, conduct disorder or sociopathy display behaviour that is extreme because they are not reined in by the power of moral emotions (like their adult counterparts they don't feel compassion for others, guilt, remorse, etc.). Thus, these children are capable of acts of great harm carried out with intent. And, just like adult sociopaths, they seem to have no conscience about their actions or care about the consequences that befall others.

Identifying sociopathic children

In recent years doctors have performed fMRI scans of the brains of children with callous unemotional traits, focusing on an area of the brain called the amygdala, the part of the brain where fear and other emotions appear to be processed. In one study scientists showed children pictures of other people in emotionally distressing situations. Typically children have a strong amygdala response to other people's distress; however in this study it was found that children with callous unemotional traits showed no discernible amygdala response on fMRI scans when they observed other people in distressing situations. This was the first time such a study had been done involving children. It reflects what has been found in many other studies carried out on adult sociopaths, and the findings are changing researchers' perception of sociopathy. Some scientists now believe these traits result from an under-arousal of the amygdala in these children's brains.[6]

Most of us learn to care about how other people feel by seeing emotion and fear in them, which causes our own discomfort. If you don't feel discomfort or fear yourself, and you don't notice it in other people, you are highly unlikely to develop the higher-order human functions of empathy and moral conscience. As stated in Chapter 1, sociopaths recognize that other people have feelings and emotions and use them to their advantage, but they don't feel much themselves. Anti-social children with callous unemotional traits appear to be disconnected from other people's emotions just like adult sociopaths. Identifying children with these traits early and getting them into treatment is crucial. By the time these children reach puberty, it's often too late and they are untreatable.

So what are the warning signs? The **Macdonald triad**, proposed by J. M. Macdonald in 1963 and also known as the triad of sociopathy, is a set of three behavioural characteristics – animal cruelty, obsession with fire setting and persistent bedwetting (past the age of five) – originally thought to be associated with later violent tendencies.[7] However, this particular combination of behaviours has not been properly validated and the characterization has been more or less debunked. Today, younger children whose disruptive and aggressive behaviour takes place within the home but whose problem behaviours do not meet the criteria for conduct disorder may be diagnosed as having **oppositional defiant disorder**. Older children may be given a diagnosis of **conduct disorder**.

The key features present in older children with conduct disorder, sometimes referred to as high callous unemotional traits, vary in intensity and breadth, but hallmark tendencies include a lack of conscience, lack of empathy and lying and manipulative behaviour. According to the Royal College of Psychiatrists, there is no single cause of conduct disorder but many different possible reasons which lead to the condition. Children may be more likely to develop an oppositional defiant disorder or conduct disorder if they:

- have certain genes leading to anti-social behaviour – boys are also more likely to have these disorders than girls
- have difficulties learning good social and acceptable behaviour
- have a difficult temperament
- have learning or reading difficulties, making it difficult to understand and take part in lessons – it is then easy to get bored, feel stupid and misbehave
- are depressed
- have been bullied or abused

- are 'hyperactive' – this causes difficulties with self-control, paying attention and following rules
- are involved with other difficult young people and drug abuse.

In children with these traits, evidence suggests that there are genetic and physiological elements to the problem, although understanding of the condition is still in its infancy. The problem can also be exacerbated by the way the child interacts with their social environment, including what behaviours they learn at home, so in these ways the problem is perpetuated in families. It can be extremely tough on the parents of children with sociopathic traits: first, it is emotionally exhausting and shaming to deal with a child that doesn't care about others; on top of that the family are likely to have to cope with the resulting slurs and public humiliation.

What can be done?

So what if you are a parent with normal levels of empathy and your child is showing clear signs of callous unemotional behaviour? Of all the sociopathic relations to contend with, this must surely be the hardest, not least because options for both support and treatment are severely limited. As stated earlier, many boys with sociopathic tendencies end up within the criminal justice system, while girls with the condition often go undetected, their behaviour put down to all manner of things including puberty. The net result of failure to detect sociopathy in children and to have effective responses to the problem in place is that the situation perpetuates sociopathic parenting and the cycle of abuse.

What we do know is that there is no point in disciplining a child with sociopathic traits more severely. Children with these traits seem to be completely unmoved by punishment and will repeat the same sort of misbehaviour again. Therefore, it is important to appreciate that children with callous unemotional traits are **punishment insensitive**; they are very reward-driven but fearless, so they will not be prevented from doing harm or taking risks by being chastised. Parents need as much support as can be mustered, though sadly this is rarely available. A formal referral to a child psychologist or psychiatrist could be beneficial for diagnostic purposes and treatment, but this option is not readily available.

Is there anything you can do? At present a study is being conducted which suggests that increased physical contact and improved eye contact between parents or carers and the child may make some difference to the severity of these traits over time. Little is known of the parent–child emotional bond in such cases, but there is some evidence to suggest that these callous unemotional features in children are not immutable. Studies have found that children exposed to lower levels of physical punishment showed decreases in callous unemotional traits over time, while higher levels of parental warmth and involvement (as reported by the child) led to decreases in both callous unemotional traits and anti-social behaviour.

The researchers involved in the current study advise parents to look their child in the eyes to see if they can persuade them to look back. While to most of us this seems a natural response, young children with callous unemotional traits rarely look their parents in the eyes. Researchers are optimistic that this intervention can bring about a real difference; they consider that if they can train young children to look at their parents in this way, they can change the children's development. But only time will tell whether there is merit in this approach.

Increased physical contact and improved eye contact between parents or carers and the child may make some difference to the severity of these traits over time. At the time of writing, Parent–Child Interaction Therapy (PCIT) targeting callous-unemotional (CU) traits is thought to be effective at improving conduct problems among young children, according to results of a study published in *Behavior Therapy*.[8]

Before leaving this topic, I want to reaffirm a vital issue, and that is the importance of communication. Talking about the problem at home, at school, and among friends and relatives provides opportunities for early intervention. Not talking about it and ignoring it, hoping it will go away, may have disastrous consequences for all concerned. What we need to do is heed the message of the film *We Need to Talk about Kevin* and learn to talk about it.

9

Towards empathy

'Empathy is a skill like any other human skill – and if you get a chance to practice, you can get better at it.'

Simon Baron-Cohen, author of Zero Degrees of Empathy:
A New Theory of Human Cruelty, London:
Allen Lane/Penguin Books, 2012.

In previous chapters I discussed steps in the process of recovery from gaslighting and abuse. The initial step entails waking up from a comatose state. For some, there is a defining 'Eureka!' moment. For others, waking is a slow dawning where the fog of apathy gradually lifts. Living in apathy for a lengthy period often sees a person become engaged in self-defeating behaviours that become entrenched. It takes conscious effort to put such behaviours aside. We may find we have greater mistrust of others, and this leads us to retreat within, distancing ourselves from others as well as going inward. Over time as we waken, we take steps out of this entrenched position; most often not on the advice of other people but when we are ready: when it is important to us to make changes and we have confidence to pull those changes off. We don't yet know what aids this shift from this sleeping, hypnotized state to waking, though recently attempt has been made to understand it from a neurobiological basis.

For those who have been traumatized by a sociopath, some form of apology might be hoped for, but this is always denied them. An apology will never be forthcoming, not a genuine one at any rate. With a sociopath there is no satisfying end point or sense of closure to the situation and there is always chaos to clear up in their wake. Any change and improvement to your situation therefore has to come from you; driven by your own initiative. The process of recovery may involve making even more changes than you anticipated: a house move, a new job, seeking new horizons. On one hand this new state may lead to further alienation; a sense of having to 'go it alone'. Other people may not be going through a similar transformation process. They may struggle to come to terms with the changes in you, which can further add to the sense of alienation. On the other hand, the new situation feels good because it is indicative of your increased independence. Many people feel a newfound sense of freedom and confidence.

Empathy and its value in recovery

The next step is regaining meaningful connection with other people. Regaining empathy in the aftermath of abuse is about breaking out of isolation and reconnecting. To connect with others, we first have to revive our emotional apparatus; being able to empathize with ourselves as well as other people. So first, as discussed in Chapter 7, we need to recognize what we feel. It is quite normal to feel shame, guilt, sadness, relief – a whole gamut of emotions – after abuse. Allowing the full sweep of emotions is an important first step. Some people have difficulty accepting that they have been duped, especially if they are not the sociopath's primary target and along the way, inadvertently or otherwise, they helped the sociopath abuse other people. In such situations people make all sorts of irrational moves like denying it happened, blaming someone else or excusing the sociopath's behaviour. We see examples of this throughout history, when whole groups of people have been misguided in following a malign leader and where deniers attempt to rewrite history by minimizing, denying or simply ignoring essential facts. For those who have been in complete thrall of the sociopath coming to terms with our losses and trauma can take time. A period of reflection allows us to make sense of our experiences and see the bigger picture.

Reconnecting with other people is something else that takes time. After abuse, especially if we have lived in fear, we can find ourselves feeling pretty timid. Reconnecting with other people requires the acquisition of skills like paying attention to other people and listening to them. To empathize with someone else it is necessary to understand what it is they need. Actions that are critical to and aid recovery over the long term are often preceded by breakthroughs in one's capacity and willingness to listen. Such listening can come in many forms: listening to the stories of others, listening to what is not said, listening to the written word, listening to our own deepest aspirations or listening for the inner voice of wisdom (some may call this spiritual guidance). Listening is being receptive. It makes us more open-minded about life in general. This is vital if people wish to develop new friendships, repair old ones and build a prosperous life.

Regaining feeling means no longer being muted and anaesthetized. Instead, you may become more responsive to aesthetics and sensitive to sense-experience. You may find yourself greatly enjoying visual art, listening to music, reading poetry, experiencing a play or exploring nature. Interestingly, a research study using functional magnetic resonance imaging (fMRI) found that highly empathic people have significantly higher activation in their brains and, specifically, in the reward centres of the brain when listening to familiar music they like – meaning, they seem to find music listening more pleasurable than people low in empathy.[1] Being in a more receptive state enables you to get in touch with intense feelings such as anger, passion, joy. You can use these emotions intelligently towards taking appropriate action, such as seeking justice, helping others and pursuing passions. This in itself aids the recovery process as we shift identity from being helpless to becoming someone who can help themselves and other people.

Living in a culture of fear, risk and empathy erosion

It is morally inexcusable to look the other way when others are targeted and sitting on the fence is not an option for the empathetically minded. However, to take action against socio-paths is not for the faint-hearted and best not done alone or in an aggressive, confrontational way. Sociopaths are predatory and will fight hard and dirty, especially if backed into a corner. Bringing the sociopath's covert and harmful practices into full view requires us to smarten up and become socially savvy. This means understanding that as we re-enter the social sphere, we expose ourselves to the glut of malign actors in it. We there-fore need to be alert and stay alert to the manipulation games of sociopaths and the people they draw into their ruses – the apaths – and gain strength from empathetic people around us.

Whilst most people potentially can manipulate other peo-ple, how far and to what extent is influenced by our individual sense of right and wrong, and by how much empathy we have for others. Using our empathy and emotional intelligence we can act to control our worst impulses and behaviour. Empathy thus affords protection from engaging in cruelty. It gives oppor-tunity to step back, to put ourselves in others' shoes, reflect on past actions and gain insight. This ability to perspective-take is one of the reasons why empathetic people are both a threat and source of fascination to sociopaths who aim to dupe everyone with their ruses. They rely on the majority of people not having a clue what's going on or, worse, just not caring.

In Chapter 5, psycho-social influences that alter the way we behave and treat other people were identified. In most cases these influences have been known about for many years. They persist unconstrained because there has been no similar advance in effort to curb their influence through awareness programmes and education. Quite the contrary, experts in the mainstream have cast doubt on studies that shed light on the perils of conformity and blind obedience, whilst at the same time these influences are heavily exploited by governments seeking to influence social and health behaviours. Propaganda, which later evolved into public relations, was designed to rally domestic support and to demonize enemies, especially during the World Wars. This affected not only military, but whole populations. Contemporary approaches to behaviour manipulation of the masses are built on this and are explained by nudge theory, the concept of political theory and behavioural sciences that proposes positive reinforcement and indirect suggestions are ways to influence the behaviour and decision-making of groups or individuals. As discussed in Chapter 5, nudge units exist at national and international level. Nudging contrasts with other ways to achieve compliance, such as education, legislation or enforcement because it is done in a subliminal way. Heavy reliance on these concealed tactics suggests that governments fall on them because they fail to influence by more open means and by persuasion based on sound evidence. In the wrong hands nudging and nudge ploys, terms that sounds so innocuous, lead to deception and harm on enormous scale.

Humans abuse other humans by various tactics, brute force and by economic and psychological means. As revealed in Chapter 4 and subsequent chapters, abuse often comes in the form of gaslighting. Gaslighting is loosely defined as making someone question their own reality. It is used to describe a person or group who presents a false narrative to another group or person which leads them to doubt their perceptions and become misled, disoriented or distressed. It can take many forms and occur in different settings, including online. Gaslighting often occurs in domestic abuse, and as highlighted in Chapter 8 is now recognized as a serious criminal offence in the UK, although gaslighting also occurs on a much larger scale. Because of this, we need to extend our view of the concept to include distortions of reality and false narratives spread by malign actors in the corporate world and the arenas of national and international politics. As soon as governments or organizations start using subliminal methods of manipulation to influence people's behaviour that relationship changes. There is no consent and the situation, and form of government, becomes fundamentally unjust.

The era of propaganda, public relations and mass communication has impacted on people's fundamental freedoms and with this there have been impacts on mental health. Anxiety, depression and traumatic stress are examples. Often people cower in uncertainty, hesitant to voice their own minority views. They fear that their views and opinions will be chastised because their views violate the majority group's norms and understanding. This can lead to self-censorship and to pluralistic ignorance – people going along with a majority view because they dare not admit to holding an alternative view. Censorship in all its forms, and the deliberate silencing of people, is a tactic of those who seek to control and dominate.

To fight gaslighting and other forms of covert abuse requires people with high empathy for others and courage to expose the truth: to take on the role of the boy from the tale 'The Emperor's New Clothes', who refuses to go along with the lie and cries out that the Emperor is naked. We have a moral duty to call out covert abuse where and whenever we see it. More of us need to take an ethical stance, gather evidence, speak out, contest false narratives in order that sociopaths, wherever they do harm are brought to book. Gaslighting, when it is a part of a systematic campaign and on a large scale, causes immense human suffering and death. Trauma-induced apathy spreads down the generations. We have yet to properly grasp the lessons of past atrocities such as Nazism in Germany or fully appreciate the repercussions of the Second World War, a period heavily stained by gaslighting and from which many still have yet to waken. Gaslighting is a derivative of psychological torture used by the military and as political strategy to disarm and demoralize foe, but we, citizens of countries around the world, are not the foe of our own governments who use and abuse their peoples. Gaslighting undermines the very notion of democracy. It is targeted, sustained and deliberate psychological torment of peoples in order to acquire greater power and to oppress. It is a crime against humanity.

The inability of the many to see past the superficial charms of sociopaths has been an enduring pattern in history. It is one of the reasons they frequently rise to power. They stay in power even when they are exposed as fraudulent or morally defective. There they minimize, discount, project, deny and cover things up. No lessons are ever learned when mistakes or wrongs are exposed. They are promoted, re-designated or resign with substantial payoffs. They are seldom challenged because of their appeal to our worst impulses and for the reason that they are feared. Whole nations, institutions and organizations are sullied by their actions. As a result of their sustained influence, we see an ever-increasing environment of fear, mistrust and sociopathy.

We live in an age of fear and risk aversion where safety is regarded as a primary value. We identify the young as particularly vulnerable, viewing them as incapable of living with risk. We tolerate the intolerant for fear of raising our heads above the parapet or upsetting the status quo. Not only do we put up with anti-social behaviour from others, but we also fear holding separate views. Fearful thinking creates anxiety, affects our mental health, stops us from being courageous and creative. This is not a recipe for flourishing. If we fear to see things as they really are, if we don't allow dissent or the expression of ideas, we don't see change. We stagnate and lose freedoms.

Afraid of being bold, we become ever more dependent on experts to calculate and alleviate risks wherever possible. This leaves us almost entirely dependent on authoritative others to instruct us how to live our lives. Surrendering in this way leaves us vulnerable to abuse. Going back to the analogy of the tale of 'The Emperor's New Clothes' we become susceptible to fraudsters with false narratives when we cower in fear and submission. Fear creates fertile ground for authoritarian leaders and forms of government.

As emphasized throughout the book, sociopaths do not succeed unaided in their maltreatment of others. A great deal of the enacted cruelty is delegated cruelty. It is carried out on their orders by people who aren't necessarily sociopaths but have empathy deficits and something to gain. Empathy erosion gives rise to selfishism, which in turn gives rise to resentment, envy and sadism. Narcissism is increasing in modern Western societies and has been referred to as a 'narcissism epidemic'. The personal pronouns 'I' and 'me' are used more frequently than 'we' and 'us'. The scores of self-reported grandiose narcissism, as assessed using the Narcissistic Personality Inventory (NPI), have increased. This rise has occurred gradually in the aftermath of the Second World War, if media representations of real life tell us anything. In the 1960s TV dramas like *Cathy Come Home* and documentary *St. Ann's* (1969) about the slums of Nottingham put the realities of poverty and homelessness in Britain on the map. Both made for uncomfortable viewing. In 1974 the first reality show, *The Family*, appeared on British television screens. It was based on a 1973 programme, *An American Family*. Horrified viewers saw mum Margaret and dad Terry fighting over their children, cheating and money. The show was later parodied on Monty Python as 'The Most Awful Family in Britain 1974'. Several decades later, by the year 2000, reality TV programmes had transformed. Perhaps not wishing to see ourselves in an unfavourable light, these programmes were about tests of survival and cooperation, typified by a series titled *Castaway 2000*, where 36 men, women and children built a community on a remote Scottish island and lived there throughout the year. Another series, *Big Brother*, was also set up as a social experiment to see how 'housemates' would cope living together in an isolated house and avoid being evicted by the public. More recent formats are based on what's termed 'structured reality'; the *Real Housewives* series, *Keeping Up with the Kardashians* are examples. As a result, a new kind of celebrity culture was spawned. The culture is inherently tied to consumerism and narcissism where celebrities transform their fame to become product brands. A distraction from reality where most people's lives have become poorer.

Narcissism is a personality type belonging to the Dark Triad comprising narcissism, Machiavellianism and psychopathy (termed sociopathy in this book). Narcissism is characterized by selfishness, a sense of entitlement, a lack of empathy and a need for admiration; Machiavellianism is characterized as cunning, scheming and unscrupulous, especially in politics. In recent years, a fourth personality type has been added to the mix. Now known as the Dark Tetrad, the group comprises the same three personality types (narcissism, Machiavellianism, psychopathy) with the addition of everyday sadism. In everyday sadism, sadistic behaviour is unlikely to emerge unless the sadistic tendency is accompanied by some other personality deficit (e.g. anger prone, impulsivity, high envy) and a fertile social environment. In the main, the everyday sadist's behaviour remains within socially acceptable boundaries but when they get an opportunity, their sadistic side emerges (e.g. as seen in online trolling or bullying). Some possess a few moderating assets that make them appealing to society. For example, they may be wealthy, attractive, athletic or intelligent, which sees them gain attention and become influencers. This is how sadistic behaviour spreads and becomes an everyday experience.

This shift towards selfishism in an age of consumerism and commoditization has been moulded by corporations and governments seeking to maximize gain and profits. The monetization of just about everything, even blood and organ donation in some countries – in effect, the selling of our limp and near lifeless souls – exemplifies just how misled and misguided we've become. When you wake from this stupor and stop playing along, you might ask yourself, 'What on earth was I thinking?' In the thrall and under the spell of mesmeric leaders and mass media, chances are you weren't thinking much at all. To be fully awake in a sociopathic culture is a truly horrifying experience. Worse, when their frauds are exposed sociopaths leave destruction in their wake and leave it to others to clear up the mess.

Living in a sociopathic era profoundly damages relationships. As alluded to, the development of personality traits is closely related to the cultural environment. In a society characterized by marked empathy deficits, we no longer view others as similar or on a par with ourselves or our group. We emotionally disconnect from one another and reduce others to objects, to 'its'. On mass scale, empathic failure leads to human destruction, conflict and wars. In hostile environments we lose peripheral vision and a sense of perspective. Things become unsafe. We carve out enclaves and build high walls in order to protect ourselves. But from this restricted place we become disengaged from other people and polarized in our views.

Another indication that we are living in a culture of eroded empathy is that empathy is not given priority in politics. It is not often proposed as a way to find solutions and there is little importance given to diplomacy. Within the context of modern-day policymaking the emphasis on empathy is very small, if non-existent. Indifference to people's lives is shown in the way successive UK governments have dealt with tragedies that have befallen British citizens. The Hillsborough disaster, the contaminated blood scandal, historic child sex abuse, Manchester Arena Inquiry, the fire at Grenfell Tower, the scandal surrounding undercover policing, to name but a few, have led to protracted inquiries but no proper reparation or remedy. To pretend to do something to address concerns of the people and mechanistically say, 'We will learn lessons,' only not to, is a distraction technique of the unfeeling.

A recent example of non-empathetic policymaking was the government's response to the COVID-19 pandemic, which saw the government embroiled in scandal and wasting billions of pounds with regards to procurement of personal protective equipment (PPE). In foreign policy over the decades since the Second World War, successive governments have acted with superiority, foregone diplomacy and engaged in wars in many parts of the world. The results of such policies were seen recently in Afghanistan, where the rapid withdrawal of American and British troops left carnage and chaos in its wake. The positions and boundaries of the 'other' (e.g. other countries) are not respected and often crossed. Humanity in its many empathy failures teeters on the brink of a third world war.

Philosopher Henry David Thoreau (1817–1862) observed, 'Any fool can make a rule. And any fool will mind it.' In establishing a policy case questions should always be asked of governments as to whether an intervention or rule can stand on its moral base. Inevitably, we need to account for dominant socio-political realities, including the motivations and interests of political actors before arriving at decisions as to whether to adhere to new rules or not.

By contrast to the existing approach, empathic communication allows for different perspectives. We can each acquire the skills needed to critically analyse material we access in our daily lives. We can ask ourselves who has written the material and for what purpose. We can think about what their motivations might be and contemplate their intentions. It is potentially dangerous to rely on only one source of information and to disregard the rest. We can each learn to intelligently critique information for ourselves. Divergent thinking in children, according to educational expert Sir Kenneth Robinson, is an extraordinary gift. He argues that their open minds are full of possibilities and unusual, original and idiosyncratic reasoning. However, sometimes that creative potential disappears when children grow up in an educational system that standardizes the mindset of students, unifying their perspectives. Most of us know that having the courage to think differently is dangerous, but it should not stop us taking the risk. Robinson points to Galileo, the Italian astronomer, physicist and engineer who has been called the 'father' of observational astronomy, who discovered the hard way since he had to live out the final years of his life confined to a house in Florence due to his ideology. Open and questioning minds are those who defy the status quo, but they also help people move forward.

Coercion is not an effective tool for bringing about behaviour change with any permanence as anyone from the field of behaviour change knows. Instead at best coercion breeds fearful compliance and resentment and can undermine health and social programmes. In any case, with regard to the pandemic highlighted earlier, the rule-makers – the UK government – ignored the advice of their experts and became rule-breakers. When rule-makers break the rules they set, then one has rules that are really only made to keep the rule breakers in power. In such situations the rule-makers only make rules to restrain the rule followers. After the discovery that government officials had broken rules over social distancing and lockdowns by partying, no-one dared question *why* government failed to adhere to their own rules. Curiously, journalists from mainstream media did a poor job of asking the most obvious questions. Did top people have special protection from the virus? Or was the virus not as dangerous a public threat as the nation had been told? Ministers' authoritative pronouncements, denials, smirks, discounting, utter gobbledygook and innumerable distractions threw the public off the scent and infuriatingly, they got away with it. In the immediate aftermath the public was distracted by worrying events abroad.

UK government has granted immense powers to the police over recent years. Whilst the public was distracted first by Brexit and then the pandemic, consecutive governments introduced new laws giving police draconian powers. In 2016, then Prime Minister Theresa May introduced the Investigatory Powers Act (nicknamed The Snooper's Charter). The Act expanded the electronic surveillance powers of the British intelligence agencies and police. It gave police far-reaching powers to access the public's communications. The Act permitted the police and intelligence agencies to carry out targeted equipment interference, i.e. hacking into computers or devices to access their data for national security matters related to foreign investigations. It also gave police greater powers of surveillance of British citizens going about their daily lives. This means, for instance, that police can access individuals' communications and bank accounts, and through application of the banking compliance system close down accounts. Under the Proceeds of Crimes Act 2002, police can also confiscate money if they believe it has been fraudulently obtained. Police take this action behind closed doors and decisions are made in secrecy. Worryingly, despite these immense powers police seem unable to keep up with fraudsters. A recent Office for National Statistics (ONS) report shows that an estimated 5.1 million fraud offences were committed in England and Wales in the year to September 2021 – up 36 per cent in two years.[2] Fraud accounts for 40 per cent of all recorded crimes. Fraud, which is a common ruse of sociopaths and everyday sadists, seems to be almost impossible for the police to investigate, with only around 8 per cent of cases reported to Action Fraud. One explanation is that people don't trust the authorities will take meaningful action. This isn't unfounded scepticism for in 2018, the consumer watchdog *Which?* reported that 96 per cent of reported cases go unsolved and only around 1 per cent of police resources are spent on fighting fraud.[3]

There has been surprisingly little public concern about the increase in police powers over recent years. The body that oversees the police use of these powers is called the Investigatory Powers Commissioner's Office or IPCO. In 2019, the Home Office blocked the appointment of Eric King as head of investigations at IPCO, citing national security grounds. King had previously been director of the Don't Spy On Us coalition, and deputy director of Privacy International for five years. In an article of the newspaper, *The Guardian*, King commented, 'The problem, at its heart, is that there's a conflict as to whether my previous work and views are a positive or negative thing. They are both the reason I was hired and the reason my clearance was refused by the Home Office vetting team.'[4]

As stated in Chapter 5, since 2021 UK undercover informants working for the police and national security service, as well as other agencies, are explicitly permitted for the first time under British law to commit crimes. This is justified under the Covert Human Intelligence Sources (Criminal Conduct) Act 2021. The Act makes provision for the use of undercover law enforcement agents and covert sources and the committing of crimes in the undertaking of their duty and in the 'greater good'. The Act has far-reaching and concerning implications. Since the state would not be liable for the crime and officers are given immunity under the law, the rights of citizens who are victim of their crimes would be curtailed. Victims would be prevented from pursuing their attacker through the courts and receiving compensation through a civil claim.

The aforementioned circumstances reveal a fundamental tension between two vital interests: preventing crime through covert operations and protection of members of the public. Governments control the public by visible and less visible means. In the wrong hands, i.e. a corrupt government, these draconian powers, which are delegated to the police, could see government enact wrongs on the public and lawfully get away with it. Recently, the Commissioner of the Metropolitan Police, Cressida Dick, who resigned amid controversy about failings of the Metropolitan Police hit out at 'politicization of policing'. This should concern us all since this situation risks the rise of a police state.

Since politics is about people and issues that affect people's lives it demands more intelligent ways of working towards common goals. In the introduction of the book, I highlighted an operation of the British government of 1982, called 'Operation Regenerate' where, in the aftermath of a nuclear Armageddon, a future ruled by sociopaths was envisioned by a Home Office scientist. That the idea was rejected is surprising, for sociopaths in the corridors of power are nothing new; nor is associating sociopathy with 'survival of the fittest' or for that matter, human intelligence. Nevertheless, the understanding of what constitutes human intelligence is changing and where better to look at the changing nature of it than the bastion of the covert operation, the UK Secret Intelligence Service, which is tasked with gathering and analysing human intelligence in support of UK national security.

In 1948, in the immediate aftermath of the Second World War, the future of the intelligence service was set out in a defining document. Whilst the service apparently needed to take on recruits of 'character, integrity, and intellect' the document stipulated that it also required recruits who were 'more hard-boiled, in whom integrity and intellect ... are less essential' (i.e. those with sociopathic traits). More than 70 years on and the UK intelligence service has seen a major overhaul in the way it operates in the wake of the Iraq War and the

Chilcot Report – the report laying bare the appalling inadequacies and failures of the service in relation to the nation's role in the Iraq War. Consequently in 2016 the service, in an unusual step, publicly announced a campaign to recruit intelligence officers with *high* emotional intelligence. Speaking to the newspaper, *The Independent*, the head of recruitment at the service, explained that intelligence officers were required to have a blend of emotional intelligence and interpersonal skills. They were looking for people with a real passion for human interaction, understanding others and dealing with the sometimes complex nature of human relationships.

While emotional intelligence is gaining traction as a recognized skill set, this doesn't mean that our workplaces are awash with emotionally intelligent leaders. Far from it, recruitment of sociopaths to various top jobs, especially politics, is usually argued on the basis that only sociopaths know how to 'get the job done' or deal with arch manipulators. This isn't true, of course; the morally minded are far better equipped to deal with manipulators, for there is less risk of them becoming corrupted in the process. Already equipped with high emotional intelligence all the morally minded need acquire is the accompanying social intelligence, awareness about sociopaths and their abuse tactics.

Human intelligence is marked by complex cognitive feats and high levels of motivation and self-awareness. Through intelligence, humans possess the abilities to learn, form concepts, understand, apply logic and reason, including the capacities to recognize patterns, plan, innovate, solve problems, make decisions, retain information and use language to communicate. Several subcategories of intelligence are debated as to whether they are traditional forms of intelligence or distinct, although there is speculation that they tie into traditional intelligence more than previously suspected. These forms of intelligence, as highlighted in this book, are emotional and social intelligence. Emotional intelligence is important to our mental health and has ties into social intelligence. People with high emotional intelligence can recognize their own emotions and those of others, use emotional information to guide thinking and behaviour, discern between different feelings and label them appropriately, and adjust emotions to adapt to environments. Studies have shown that people with high emotional intelligence have greater mental health, job performance and leadership skills. Emotional intelligence is typically associated with empathy because it involves an individual connecting their personal experiences with those of others. Since its popularization in recent decades, methods of developing emotional intelligence have become widely sought by individuals seeking to become more effective leaders.

Social intelligence, on the other hand, is the ability to understand the social cues and motivations of others and oneself in social situations. It develops from experience with people and learning from success and failures in social settings. Most references to social intelligence relate to an individual's social skills. Not mentioned, and arguably more important, is how groups process information about the world and share it with participants in and outside of the group. This includes governments. The important issue of the influences on the behaviour of individuals and groups was raised in Chapter 5.

Building empathy in culture

Prosperous societies are most often orientated to taking risk although prosperity can negatively influence ethical behaviour as cheats will take advantage of the many opportunities, consequently societies must always be on their guard. But taking risks can also turn people into heroes and helpers of others. Risk-taking behaviour at high and frequent levels is seen in personalities at the opposing ends of the empathy spectrum –

sociopaths and the extremely empathetic/altruistic. This is likely why both sociopaths and empaths are considered effective leaders. Sociopaths have low fear arousal, so they aren't held back from acting on their impulses, whilst altruists are capable of mastering fear when courage is demanded. What distinguishes the two sorts of personality is what motivates them; the self-interest of the sociopath versus the drive to help others of the empath, and the resultant behaviour – anti-social versus pro-social.

If we take no risks, we live in evermore controlled environments and life becomes increasingly restricted. So just how do we become emboldened and take risk? It's all about managing our emotions and flexing our empathy muscle. Empathy isn't empathy if it isn't expressed as some form of action. Empathy isn't about being nice, placid or agreeable, or getting along for peace's sake. It can be an expression of any emotion; anger, outrage, sadness, joy, to identify a few. It can be a call to arms to fight injustice. As stated at the outset of this book, if more people, not just the extraordinary few, took risk and principled action and spoke up when a person or persons posed a threat, then the situation where the truthteller is left unaided would be avoided and dangers could be confronted. Standing up one by one rather than kowtowing to a malign force is how we bring about change.

Empathy, therefore, is about accepting risk as an unavoidable consequence of living. It is about being bold. It is about trusting one's survival apparatus and instincts. Moral courage and moral character are two elements of personality that work on two scales: fear and selfishness. Moral courage is defined as the courage to take action for ethical reasons despite the risk of adverse consequences. Finding ways to tell truths, to speak up or take action over dangers that one sees in everyday life, like the boy in the tale of 'The Emperor's New Clothes', is something more of us can do if we care to practise it. There is no point in waiting for others to give you permission to speak out or to take action for, as discussed in Chapter 4 and Chapter 5, the fog of apathy often obscures the vision of others and prevents them from seeing the true picture. Find courage, be prepared to stand out from the crowd. More of us doing this in daily life is the only way to prevent the empathy trap, where the individual who speaks out or stands up to an abuser becomes the lone fighter.

It is truly irrational when you think about it that humans in vast numbers don't challenge the few anti-social personalities (the estimated 1–4 per cent although actually we don't know the true number) who lead us to great harm. Using another folktale as an analogy, it is as if in a trance we allow ourselves to be led to obscurity like the children in the tale of 'The Pied Piper of Hamelin'. In the tale a piper is hired to rid the town of its plague of rats. Trailing after the hypnotic sound of the rat-catcher's magical flute, the rodents file through the city gates to their doom. But they aren't the only ones lured by his music. When the town refuses to pay the Piper for his service, the saviour turns into an evil seducer and comes for the town's children. Entranced by the notes of his flute, the mesmerized children follow the Piper out of town and simply vanish.

As mentioned, when we are introduced into a group, we respond to information about the world in ways that are subject to various effects. Amongst influences discussed in Chapter 5, I highlighted groupthink and the ingroup/outgroup effect. This effect refers to how we differentially treat those whom we see as 'in our group' versus those whom we see as some kind of 'other', or some group other than our own. I also highlighted how sociopaths and other anti-social personalities low down the empathy spectrum, like narcissists and everyday sadists, often use the technique of **otherization** and the language of disgust to single out individuals or other groups and class them as subhuman.

Here, I want to pause and reflect on the process of otherization. Otherization starts as a way of categorizing people. We organize and identify groups of people for all sorts of reasons. If I undertake research, I might organize people into different categories so that I can compare and contrast them. In this book I have grouped people into the categories of sociopath, apath and empath. I have done so to point out the dangers of a category of people who are harmful but aren't visible to the naked eye. Otherizing therefore can be used as a way to draw attention to the existence of 'others' who pose a threat to society. Pointing out, for instance, the existence and dangers of Nazis and terrorists' groups like ISIS has a pro-social purpose. The aim of otherizing in that context is to caution people from joining malign forces and to prevent people from getting harmed. Consequently, the exercise of grouping people is neither good nor bad; it is just a way of helping us identify different sorts of people. But otherizing can be used by dangerous people too; the process can be hijacked by those with motivations and intentions to harm, as the Nazis did when they otherized the Jews.

In present times, many look to experts (doctors, scientists) to do their thinking on a whole manner of issues to do with everyday life and eagerly await top experts' every pronouncement. But increasingly we see experts who refuse to engage in public debate. This is an indication of something amiss in culture.

Dominant hierarchies seek to subordinate those not in their group or league ('others') and tread on their human rights. By contrast, cooperative or empathic models of leadership don't oppress one group in order to satisfy the demands of another group. Whether in the arena of international politics, or at national or local level, empathic policies are not about taking over someone else's space, but about agreeing upon boundaries from where we can safely meet and interact. In an empathic space individuality is promoted and understood as important. Women, men and children are free to think, define and express their individuality. Nevertheless, there is a persistent danger of individuality being lost to the group if we don't observe personal boundaries. Conformity and other influences play a part in convincing us to blend in and do as everyone else does. But in the case of enacted wrongs and cruelty within the group it is never an acceptable excuse to say 'I was just doing the same as everybody else' or that 'I was just following orders' for we are responsible for our own conduct. Hence, in an empathic space, the right to freely express one's individuality comes with matching individual responsibility. We are individually responsible for our own actions including those actions that harm others. As author Booker T. Washington (1856–1915) said, 'A lie doesn't become truth, wrong doesn't become right and evil doesn't become good just because it's accepted by a majority.'

The idea of the existence of universal wrongs has been long contested, which is unsurprising since *wrong* is a concept only meaningfully understood by the morally minded, i.e. those with a functioning entity called a conscience, and as emphasized, not everyone has one. If we permit the amoral to set the rules, it becomes a mug's game. They restrict the lives of rule followers but don't follow the rules themselves. In an empathic society there is focus on liberty and on upholding the rights of citizens. Laws set the parameters and prohibit certain activities and behaviours that are deemed unjust. The law is intended to be applied equally and fairly, so that no one is above the law. Such law is meant to be understood by everyone, so that everyone can comply. Laws allow for the enforcing of restrictions on those who, in the exercise of their individual freedom, commit transgressions and violate social boundaries. Perceptions of wrongs change over time. Psychological abuse, which has been carried out for centuries but only criminalized recently, as we move out of an era of deference and strict adherence to the social hierarchy, is an example that demonstrates the changing nature of wrong over place and time.

Gaslighting may be pervasive in culture, but that doesn't make it any less harmful or any less wrong. Gaslighting has recently come under the gaze and scrutiny of lawmakers. It is now recognized as harmful behaviour and since 2015 it has been a criminal offence under 'Coercive control' legislation and recognized as a form of domestic abuse. As outlined in Chapter 8, in early 2022 the term gaslighting was used in a published High Court judgment in the family courts for the first time in a 'milestone' hearing. This involved a man who was found guilty of distorting his partner's reality, having said she was bipolar after he had raped, abused and controlled her. The abuser's lies were given credibility because he was a mental health care worker. The High Court judge was praised by the leading human rights barrister, who represented the woman who was gaslighted, for giving legitimacy and cred-ibility to the term. The barrister warned that abusers have long been warping victims' 'realities', yet until now there has been no legal term to shed light on the problem. This is empathic law-making in progress and challenges those who victim-blame. It is long overdue. Next it needs applying not just in domestic situations but broadly, wherever covert abus-ers conceal their ruses.[5]

There is a paradox in living in a tolerant society where members of the group live in the belief that they are of 'one mind' and in accord, because it can create complacency (stabil-ity privilege) and blind tolerance of intolerant persons. Going back to the analogy of 'The Emperor's New Clothes', most of us act like the townsfolk who pretend nothing is wrong when fraudsters emerge and play the crowd. And worse, some mem-bers of the group, in a bid to show their superiority, promote the scam of the swindlers and thereby spread the falsehood. In this book I have used fables to illustrate facets of human behaviour. Fables and fairy stories have at their base moral meaning and originally were intended for adults. However, from the late 1930s American animator and film producer, Walt Disney, began to transform many of these adult folktales into screen entertainment for children, after which many lost their earlier meaning. In creating these sentimental animations, Disney became a vastly powerful socialization agent influencing the way the West saw the world and made sense of their own relationship to it. The effects of Disneyfication are plain to see – infantilizing culture and downplaying morality. It is a shame that the often valuable lessons of the original tales, which were passed by oral tradition from one adult to another, one generation to the next, are now not readily understood, for in the past they served to alert generations of peoples to potential social dangers.

Not putting up with anti-social behaviour requires effective interpersonal boundaries. Empathy has to have an edge to it otherwise it isn't empathy, it's indifference. This means understanding that certain transgressions like deceiving, cheating, physically and psychologically hurting and maiming others are anti-social acts that people need protection from as far as possible. Boundaries are not about being cruel or about rudeness, but about creating personal space to think freely and be ourselves. It is up to each and every one of us to specify the boundaries that are most beneficial to us. The nineteenth-century philosopher, John Stuart Mill, in his essay, *On Liberty*, understood this and had this to say on individual rights and boundaries:

> 'We have a right ... in various ways, to act upon our unfavourable opinion of any one, not to the oppression of his individuality, but in the exercise of ours ...'

Mills also recognized the importance of alerting others to dangerous individuals:

> 'We have a right, and it may be our duty, to caution others against him, if we think his example or conversation likely to have a pernicious effect on those with whom he associates.'

Interpersonal boundaries allow for the separation between you and another person. As described in Chapter 5, they can be physical: to reach out and touch another person without asking or knowing they will be okay about it is a violation of a physical boundary. A boundary can be around space or around one's autonomy. A main purpose that boundaries serve is one of safety. The ultimate reason for, and function of personal boundaries, is to protect our hearts, our safety and our spirit from the harm of others. You need a sense of openness and personal responsibility in order to learn how to have good interpersonal boundaries. Good boundaries help other people to feel safe and respected in your company. Children can be shown how to set boundaries and put them to good use.

Although empathy is acknowledged as one of the defining characteristics of humanity, what has been discussed in the book suggests this trait is mutable. Just as high empathy is seen in every location around the world, so too empathy deficits can be seen in all cultures across the globe. These are not static traits; they shift back and forth over time. No one group has lasting protection from cruelty. Since we each make up the families, communities and societies we live in, if many lose empathy and display empathy deficits it affects the whole group. But this shift can work both ways. As highlighted in Chapter 5, we are heavily influenced by our leaders. If our leaders are emotionally intelligent, the majority of the group are likely to raise their game. This is top down, vertical transmission of empathy. Likewise, this route of transmission occurs if empathy is promoted by families through the generations. Furthermore, if more people act on their empathy, empathy becomes more noticeable in our daily lives and spreads throughout the group – this is horizontal transmission of empathy. Thus, we have the potential to correct the present imbalance – the lack of visible (acted out) empathy.

Our skill in empathizing can be impacted by difficult social and psychological conditions. Increased selfishism in culture, as now, can influence an individual's felt and expressed empathy. Other factors such as traumatic experiences and other impacts on mental health also can affect the ability to express it. Nevertheless, transformational experiences can occur after social and psychological turmoil. In 1955 a study surveyed for 32 years all the children born on the island of Kauai in Hawaii. Life there was beset with social problems – alcohol abuse, crime and poverty. Two thirds of children went on to develop problems such as violent behaviour and alcohol and drug problems. But every third child did not develop these problems, despite facing the same social conditions. The difference: each child who 'made it' had at least one person with whom they had an emotional connection – a sibling, aunt or uncle, a community leader, someone who helped them navigate through their difficulties. This strongly suggests that emotional connection with other people can help us thrive and overturn setbacks and difficulties. Emotional connection aids self-esteem and sense of worth.[6] There are many examples of people who have undergone a kind of awakening after difficult and traumatic experiences. Typically, they become more appreciative of life, more intensely aware of the world around them, less materialistic and more interested in improving their mind. They spend more time living in the present rather than being focused on the future and the past, enjoy solitude, and feel a powerful sense of contentment. This links with evidence reported in Chapter 7 that suggests adversity can over time lead to post-traumatic growth, including increased empathy and pro-social behaviour.

For the vast majority of people, empathy is a skill just like any other. It can be learned and when lost can be regained. A child as young as two to three months old realizes that they exist as a separate entity from others and that they continue to exist over time and space. Awareness of the self begins and arises in part due to the relation the child has with the world. For example, the child smiles and someone smiles back.

Empathy in children develops with a process that begins with an empathetic global feeling in which a child doesn't have a clear distinction between themselves and others. In the more advanced stages, an individual can empathize with others by knowing that there are physical entities other than themselves and that others have internal states independent from them. Interpersonal relations require recognition for the need of space between one person and another. Without boundaries we end up tolerating all sorts of undesirable behaviour that affects how we experience daily life.

There exists a continual struggle between the polar forces of empathy and apathy. Globalization has created a challenge, extending the reach of empathy far beyond its evolutionary origins – the family and the tribe. Opting for empathy in a situation of conflict is a risk, and the cost of the risk increases as we scale up from individuals to families, to communities, to nation states and the international stage. However, we can equip ourselves for the task. For the last 20 years or more an increasing body of research has shown that training the mind through various meditation techniques can enhance our capacity for altruism and compassion. Specific training in enhanced recognition of fear and suffering in others might also increase the propensity for altruistic behaviour. Altruism and showing empathic concern for others does not require that we suffer when helping others. It does not lose its authenticity if accompanied by feelings of profound satisfaction (sometimes called the Helper's High – based on the theory that helping produces endorphins in the brain that provide a mild version of a morphine high).[7] The very notion of sacrifice is relative: what seems like a sacrifice to some is experienced as profound fulfilment by others. This means that engaging in altruism reinforces itself – the gratification it incurs makes it more likely to be repeated. Parents who help their child understand the consequences of their actions produce children who have better moral development, compared to children whose parents use authoritarian methods and punishment.

What often stops people from speaking out about the problem of sociopathy in culture is the shame inflicted upon them by the rest of society. Jeremy Rifkin, author of *The Empathic Civilization*, describes a shaming culture as one that 'pretends to adhere to the highest possible standards of moral perfection'. We see this presently in the UK, where for example there are seven principles of public life, collectively known as the Nolan Principles. These principles apply to all postholders of public bodies including all those who are elected or appointed to public office, nationally and locally, and all people appointed to work in the Civil Service, local government, the police, courts and probation services, non-departmental public bodies and in the health, education, social and care services. The seven principles are selflessness, integrity, objectivity, accountability, openness, honesty and leadership where postholders of public office should exhibit these principles in their own behaviour and treat others with respect. Fine words and fine principles, but without accompanying integrity on the part of the individual the words mean next to nothing. Historically shaming cultures have been the most aggressive and violent because 'they lock up the empathic impulse'. We see this now in the way whistle-blowers are villainized, forced to suffer for speaking out and made outcast, often punished for embracing the very principles on which their positions are based. Such is social hypocrisy.

Breaking down the stigma of abuse requires individual and collective activity to expose the harms of anti-social behaviour. Thereafter each of us can contribute to a culture where empathy exists as a prized virtue with the potential to transform human beings into highly intelligent social beings. As emphasized throughout the book, empathic responses can be learned by means of cultural transmission. Parents, teachers, adults of all ages can be the next generation's enlightened witnesses, helping children make emotional connections and advance social behaviour in society. In his book, Rifkin highlights a study that is worth recounting here. Having observed the behaviour of adolescent elephants in an animal park in South Africa, zoologists noted that for unknown reasons the elephants had begun to taunt and kill other animals. It was only when the zoologists recollected that, years earlier, they had culled the adult male elephants in order to ease overcrowding and decided to bring back to the park two older male elephants that order was reintroduced. It transpired that the reintroduction of the older male elephants stopped the younger elephants from behaving in an anti-social manner. Rifkin suggests that we humans, like the elephants in the study, require adult role models to set the boundaries on social behaviour.

It is up to each and every one of us to set standards of social behaviour and maintain these by establishing clear boundaries. Getting a child to understand how their behaviour affects other children and how they would feel if the same misbehaviour was enacted on them requires a parent or adult with a well-developed conscience and empathy. The adult's role is to act as the child's guide, helping the child reflect on their own behaviour, feel remorse and prepare to make reparation for their misdemeanour. Through this process the positive human attributes of social behaviour and empathy are advanced. The benefits are likely to be substantial.

The post-truth era is a euphemism for a sociopathic age where truth is decoupled from reality. Sociopathy in culture will be reduced only when individuals stop colluding with abusers. Sociopathic abuse will be reduced only when individuals cease spreading untruths, and when less of us engage in selfish and sadistic behaviour. Change is brought about by conscientious people who are prepared to tell and defend the truth. It is brought about by spreading awareness of the destructive effects of psychological abuse and by outlawing it in all spheres of daily life.

Sociopathic abuse requires healing from so we don't pass on the trauma. Collectively, we need to recognize the importance of and need for high emotional intelligence in leaders and by making empathy an essential requirement for individuals seeking careers in public service. Change comes on a personal level by improving our individual empathy, modelling it to our children and by instigating interpersonal boundaries. We have the power to make it happen. There are more people with empathic ability than without. Whilst any of us can manipulate, it is good levels of empathy that keep our actions in check. Gaslighting in all its forms is a destructive force and a crime against humanity. We can be determined in our drive to stamp out gaslighting and all forms of sociopathic abuse by refusing to go along with cruelty. Collectively, we *can* learn lessons and change course.

Useful addresses

United Kingdom

British Association of Counselling and Psychotherapy: tel.: 01455 883300; website: www.bacp.co.uk

ChildLine: tel.: 0800 1111; website: www.childline.org.uk

If you think a child is in immediate danger and you live in the UK, contact the police on emergency number 999 or call the NSPCC on 0808 800 5000. If you suspect a child may be at risk but not in imminent danger, contact your local children's social services.

Family Law Society: helpline: 07747 540808 website: www.familylawsociety.org. An organization founded in 2004 to help families who are experiencing the pain of parental separation.

Mind infoline: tel.: 0300 123 3393; email: info@mind.org.uk; website: www.mind.org.uk

National Society for the Prevention of Cruelty to Children (NSPCC): tel.: 0808 800 5000; website: www.nspcc.org.uk

UK Council for Psychotherapy: tel.: 020 7014 9955; website: www.psychotherapy.org.uk

United Kingdom Psychological Trauma Society: tel.: 07979 994057; website: https://ukpts.org/

Women's Aid: website: www.womensaid.org.uk where there is an online chat service

EMDR Association UK: email: info@emdrassociation.org.uk; website: https://emdrassociation.org.uk/

Notes

Chapter 1

1 Barry, K. L., Fleming, M. F., Manwell, L. B. and Copeland, L. A. (1997) 'Conduct disorder and antisocial personality in adult primary care patients', *Journal of Family Practice* 45:2, 15–18. There is also an earlier study: Samuels, J. F., Nestadt, G., Romanoski, A. J., Folstein, M. F. and McHugh, P. R. (1994) 'DSM-III personality disorders in the community', *American Journal of Psychiatry* 151:7, 1055–62. This gave a prevalence estimate of 5.9 per cent of all types of personality disorders in adults in the community.

2 Babiak, P. and Hare, R. D. (2006) *Snakes in Suits*, New York: Collins.

3 Clarke, J. (2009) *Working with Monsters: How to Identify and Protect Yourself from the Workplace Psychopath*, Sydney, Australia: Random House.

4 Coid, J. W., Yang, M., Ullrich, S., Roberts, A. and Hare, R. D. (2009) 'Prevalence and correlates of psychopathic traits in the household population of Great Britain', *International Journal of Law and Psychiatry* 32, 265–73.

5 See BBC News (2014) 'The nuclear attack on the UK that never happened', 30 October, https://www.bbc.co.uk/news/magazine-29804446

6 Ibid.

7 Hare, R. D. (1993) *Without Conscience: The Disturbing World of the Psychopaths among Us*, New York: Guilford Press, 83–96.

8 Teicher, M. H. and Samson, J. A. (2016) 'Annual research review: Enduring neurobiological effects of childhood abuse and neglect', *Journal of Child Psychology and Psychiatry, and Allied Disciplines* 57:3, 241–66. doi.10.1111/jcpp.12507

9 The term derives from Narcissus, the figure from Greek mythology known for his beauty. Narcissus was exceptionally proud and vain. Nemesis (the goddess of divine retribution or revenge) saw this characteristic in him and lured Narcissus to a pool where he saw his own reflection in the water. Not realizing it was an image of himself he soon fell in love with it, but unable to leave the beauty of his own reflection, he died.

10 Pinel, P. (1801) *A Treatise on Insanity*, trans. Davies, D. D. (1806). Republished 1962, New York: Hafner, 150–56.

11 Pritchard, J. C. (1835) *A Treatise on Insanity*, London: Sherwood, Gilbert and Piper. He also published (1847) *On the Different Forms of Insanity in Relation to Jurisprudence*, London: Hippolyte Bailliere.

12 Hervey M. Cleckley's book *The Mask of Sanity* was first published
    in 1941 and described Cleckley's clinical interviews with patients
    in a locked institution. The text was the most influential clinical
    description of psychopathy in the twentieth century and the basic
    elements are still relevant today. See Cleckley, H. M. (2022) *The
    Mask of Sanity: An Attempt to Clarify Some Issues about the So-Called
    Psychopathic Personality*, Bristol: Mockingbird Press. (Original work
    published 1991)
13 Hare, R. D. (1993) *Without Conscience*, New York: Guilford Press, 23–24.
14 Baron-Cohen, S. (2012) *Zero Degrees of Empathy: A New Theory of
    Human Cruelty*, London: Allen Lane/Penguin Books. A full explanation
    of the empathy circuit can be found on pp. 19–28 of this book.
15 The emerging science on empathy is effectively conveyed in Keysers,
    C. (2011) *The Empathic Brain: How the Understanding of Mirror Neurons
    Changes Our Understanding of Human Nature*, Amsterdam: Social Brain
    Press.
16 Marsh, A. (2017) *The Fear Factor: How One Emotion Connects Altruists,
    Psychopaths, and Everyone In-Between*, New York: Basic Books.

Chapter 2

1 In June 2018, Netflix acquired the rights to the life story of Anna
   Sorokin and the *New York* article 'How Anna Delvey tricked New
   York's Party people' by Jessica Pressler, with plans to turn it into a
   television series. It premiered on Netflix on 11 February 2022.
2 Crawford, A. and Smith, P. (2022) 'Metaverse app allows kids into
   virtual strip clubs', BBC News, February, https://www.bbc.co.uk/news/
   technology-60415317?at_medium=RSS&at_campaign=KARANGA
3 See Elder, J. (2017) 'Are politicians natural-born psychopaths? Well
   you could say that', *The New Daily*, 17 June, https://thenewdaily.
   com.au/life/wellbeing/2017/06/17/are-politicians-psychopaths/;
   University of Oxford Research (2016) 'Presidential candidates may
   be psychopaths – but that could be good thing', https://www.
   research.ox.ac.uk/article/2016-08-23-presidential-candidates-may-be-
   psychopaths-but-that-could-be-a-good-thing. In the 2000s, a number
   of authors highlighted the dangers of sociopaths/psychopaths in
   everyday life. Over the next decade, peaking in 2016, the year of the
   US presidential election, the EU referendum on Brexit and release of
   the Chilcott report on the Iraq War, there was a shift to view their
   traits as desirable in leadership. Dr Kevin Dutton, a researcher at
   the Department of Experimental Psychology, University of Oxford,
   is among those who promoted this view and downplayed the
   psychopath's anti-social tendencies at this time. See also Dutton, K.
   (2012) *The Wisdom of Psychopaths: What Saints, Spies, and Serial Killers*

Can Teach Us about Success, Heinemann; Dutton, K. and McNab, A. (2014) *The Good Psychopath's Guide to Success*, Murray Bantam Press.

4 David Wilson is emeritus professor of criminology at Birmingham City University and a former prison governor. He is well known as a criminologist through his work with various British police forces, academic publications, books and media appearances. See Mail Online (2014) 'Tony on the couch: After Mail columnist Stephen Glover questioned the ex-PM's sanity, an academic who's studied the darker corners of the mind analyses the 'deluded, messianic, needy, narcissistic' Blair psyche', https://www.dailymail.co.uk/news/article-3680049/A-professor-criminology-analyses-deluded-messianic-Tony-Blair.html

5 See Elder, J. (2017) 'Are politicians natural-born psychopaths? Well you could say that', *The New Daily*, 17 June, https://thenewdaily.com.au/life/wellbeing/2017/06/17/are-politicians-psychopaths/

6 J. Maddison. Letter to W.T. Barry [4 August 1822] Writings 9:103–9

7 The Goldwater Rule is a statement of ethics first issued by the American Psychiatric Association in 1973 restraining psychiatrists from speculating about the mental state of public figures.

8 See https://www.nhs.uk/mental-health/conditions/personality-disorder/

9 The advertisement was on Twitter. The event was cancelled and the College issued an apology. See https://twitter.com/rcpsych/status/1508754068692520960

10 Güse, H. G. and Schmacke, N. (1980) 'Psychiatry and the origins of Nazism', *Int J Health Serv* 10:2, 177–96; Strous, R. D. (2007) 'Psychiatry during the Nazi era: Ethical lessons for the modern professional', *Ann Gen Psychiatry* 6, 8. doi.10.1186/1744-859X-6-8

11 The Jimmy Savile Investigation Report by Dame Janet Smith DBE, 25 February 2016. The full report is available for download at http://downloads.bbci.co.uk/bbctrust/assets/files/pdf/our_work/dame_janet_smith_review/savile/jimmy_savile_investigation.pdf

Chapter 3

1 Passive-aggressive behaviour takes many forms but can generally be described as a non-verbal aggression. It presents when one person is angry with another but does not or cannot tell them. Instead of communicating honestly when they feel upset, annoyed, irritated or disappointed such people shut off verbally, give angry looks, become obstructive or sulky. It can either be covert (concealed and hidden) or overt (blatant and obvious).

2 Harrn, A. (2011) 'What is passive aggressive behaviour?', *Counselling Directory*. Available at <www.counselling-directory.org.uk/counsellor-articles/what-is-passive-aggressive-behaviour>

3 Braiker, H. B. (2004) *Who's Pulling Your Strings? How to Break the Cycle of Manipulation*, New York: McGraw-Hill.

4 Babiak, P. and Hare, R. (2006) *Snakes in Suits: When Psychopaths Go to Work*, New York: HarperCollins.

5 For more about pathological lying see Dike, C. C. (2008), 'Pathological lying: Symptom or disease?' *Psychiatric Times*, 25, 7. Available at <www.psychiatrictimes.com/print/article/10168/1162950>

6 Carlisi, C. O., Moffitt, T. E., Knodt, A. R., Harrington, H., Ireland, D., Melzer, T. R., Poulton, R., Ramrakha, S., Caspi, A., Hariri, A. R. and Viding, E. (2020) 'Associations between life-course-persistent antisocial behaviour and brain structure in a population-representative', *Lancet Psychiatry* 7, 245–53. doi.10.1016/7.

7 Baron-Cohen, S. (2012) *Zero Degrees of Empathy: A New Theory of Human Cruelty*, London: Allen Lane/Penguin Books.

8 Marsh, A. A., Stoycos, S. A., Brethel-Haurwitz, K. M., Robinson, P., VanMeter, J. W. and Cardinale, E. M. (2014) *Neural and Cognitive Characteristics of Extraordinary Altruists*, Proceedings of the National Academy of Sciences of the United States of America 111:42, 15036–15041.

9 Gullapallia, A. R., Nathaniel, E., Anderson, N. E., Yerramsetty, R., Harenskia, C. L. and Kiehlab, K. A. (2021) 'Quantifying the psychopathic stare: Automated assessment of head motion is related to antisocial traits in forensic interviews', *Journal of Research in Personality* 92, 104093. doi.10.1016/j.jrp.2021.104093.

10 Wynn, R., Høiseth, M. H. and Pettersen, G. (2012) 'Psychopathy in women'; Nicholls, T. L., Ogloff, J. R., Brink, J. and Spidel, A. (2005) 'Psychopathy in women: A review of its clinical usefulness for assessing risk for aggression and criminality', *Behavioral Sciences and the Law* 23:6, 779–802. Also Kreis, M. K. F. and Cooke, D. H. (2011) 'Capturing the psychopathic female: A prototypicality analysis of the Comprehensive Assessment of Psychopathic Personality (CAPP) across gender', *Behavioral Sciences and the Law* 29, 634–48. Also Logan, C. (2011) 'La femme fatale: The female psychopath in fiction and clinical practice', *Mental Health Review Journal* 16:3, 118–278.

11 Wynn, R., Høiseth, M. H. and Pettersen, G. (2012) 'Psychopathy in women: Theoretical and clinical perspectives', *International Journal of Women's Health* 4, 257–63. doi.10.2147/IJWH.S25518

Chapter 4

1 'The perils of obedience' as it appeared in *Harper's Magazine* is available at www.age-of-the-sage.org/psychology/milgram_perils_authority_1974. The article was abridged and adapted from Stanley Milgram (1974) *Obedience to Authority*, Harper & Row.

2 Jean Decety is a French American neuroscientist specializing in developmental neuroscience, in particular affective and social neuroscience. He is the Irving B. Harris Distinguished Service Professor at the University of Chicago. His research focuses on the neurobiological mechanisms underpinning social cognition, particularly emotion, empathy, moral reasoning, altruism, pro-social behaviour, and more generally interpersonal processes. He is the co-editor of *The Social Neuroscience of Empathy* and *The Moral Brain* and the editor of *Empathy: From Bench to Bedside*, both published by MIT Press.

3 Salovey, P. and Mayer, J. D. (1990) 'Emotional intelligence', *Imagination, Cognition, and Personality* 9, 185–211.

4 Steiner, C. and Perry, P. (1997) *Achieving Emotional Literacy*, London: Bloomsbury.

5 Warneken, F. and Tomasello, M. (2006) 'Altruistic helping in human infants and young chimpanzees', *Science* 311:5765, 1301–03.

6 Bartal, I. B-A., Decety, J. and Mason, P. (2011) 'Empathy and pro-social behavior in rats', *Science* 334:6061, 1427–30. doi.10.1126/science.1210789

7 Louis de Canonville, C. (2011) *The Effects of Gaslighting in Narcissistic Victim Syndrome.* Available online at narcissisticbehavior.net/the-effects-of-gaslighting-in-narcissistic-victim-syndrome

8 Stern, R. (2007) *The Gaslight Effect: How to Spot and Survive the Hidden Manipulation Others Use to Control Your Life*, New York: Morgan Road Books.

Chapter 5

1 The Hansard Society's 2019 Audit of Political Engagement is a time series study. The annual audit commenced in 2004 and provides a benchmark to measure political engagement in Great Britain. The report was originally published on the Hansard Society's website but the links to the audit are now broken. However, there is a summary of the findings of the audit available at https://www.hansardsociety.org.uk/blog/finding-of-support-for-a-'strong-leader'-helps-provoke-responses-to-2019. Additionally the full 53-page report can be downloaded from The John Smith Centre: https://www.johnsmithcentre.com/research/audit-of-political-engagement-16-the-2019-report/

2 Essay by Jonathan Sumption, 'When fear leads to tyranny. Democracy is being quietly redefined', taken from the fourth and final lecture in the inaugural series of Sir Roger Scruton Memorial Lectures delivered at the Sheldonian Theatre on 27 October 2021. A copy of the essay is available to read online at https://unherd.com/2021/11/when-fear-leads-to-tyranny/

3 Lobaczewski, A. (2022) *Political Ponerology: A Science on the Nature of Evil Adjusted for Political Purposes*, 3rd ed., Grande Praire: Red Pill Press.

4 Buckels, E. E., Jones, N. J. and Paulhus, D. L. (2013) 'Behavioral confirmation of everyday sadism', *Psychological Science* 24:11, 2201–09.

5 Charity Commission Inquiry Report (2019) 'Summary findings and Conclusions', Oxfam, 11 June, Inquiry_Report_summary_findings_ and_conclusions_Oxfam.pdf (publishing.service.gov.uk)

6 This was widely reported in the media. For example, Simpson, J. (2022) 'Konstancja Duff: Video shows Metropolitan Police mistreating suspect in strip-search', *The Times*, January.

7 Simon Baron-Cohen, author of *Zero Degrees of Empathy: A New Theory of Human Cruelty*, London: Allen Lane/Penguin Books, 2012.

8 Doliński, D., Grzyb, T., Folwarczny, M., Grzybała, P., Krzyszycha, K., Martynowska, K. and Trojanowski, J. (2017) 'Would you deliver an electric shock in 2015? Obedience in the experimental paradigm developed by Stanley Milgram in the 50 years following the original studies', *Social Psychological and Personality Science*, online 194855061769306, doi:10.1177/1948550617693060

9 Haney, C., Banks, C. and Zimbardo, P. (1973) 'A study of prisoners and guards in a simulated prison', *Naval Research Reviews* September; Haney, C., Banks, C. and Zimbardo, P. (1973) 'Interpersonal dynamics in a simulated prison', *International Journal of Criminology and Penology* 1:1, 69–77.

10 *The Experiment* is a 2002 BBC documentary series in which 15 men are randomly selected to be either 'prisoner' or guard, contained in a simulated prison over an eight-day period. Produced by Steve Reicher and Alex Haslam, it presents the findings of what has subsequently become known as the 'BBC Prison Study'. Subsequently, Reicher and Haslam co-authored a number of publications including: Haslam, S. A. and Reicher, S. D. (2005) 'The psychology of tyranny', *Scientific American Mind* 16:3, 44–51.

11 After years of criticism of one another's work, in 2018, Haslam, Reicher and Zimbardo issued a joint statement in an effort to promote constructive scientific dialogue and in a bid to highlight where they were in agreement. The joint statement in two letters published by The British Psychology Society under a title 'Dealing with Toxic Behaviour'. The two letters on the Stanford Prison Experiment controversy, 10 September 2018, are available at https://www.bps. uk/psychologist/dealing-toxic-behaviour. See also Reicher, S. D. and Haslam, S. A. (2006) 'Rethinking the psychology of tyranny: The BBC Prison Study', *British Journal of Social Psychology* 45, 1–40.

12 Lerner, M. and Simmons, C. H. (1966) 'Observer's reaction to the "innocent victim": compassion or rejection?' *Journal of Personality and Social Psychology* 4:2, 203–10.

13 Wenzel, K., Schindler, S. and Reinhard, M-A. (2017) 'General belief in a just world is positively associated with dishonest behavior', *Front. Psychol.* doi.10.3389/fpsyg.2017.01770

14 BBC News (2021) 'Sarah Everard murder: Police box Philip Allott urged to quit over comments', 1 October, https://www.bbc.co.uk/news/uk-england-york-north-yorkshire-58762029

15 Lerner, M. (1980) *The Belief in a Just World: A Fundamental Delusion*, Plenum: New York.

16 There were many interviews with Desmet during the COVID-19 pandemic. He is a professor of clinical psychology in the Department of Psychology and Educational Sciences at Ghent University (Belgium) and a practising psychoanalytic psychotherapist.

17 Szunyogh, Béla (1955) *Psychological Warfare: An Introduction to Ideological Propaganda and the Techniques of Psychological Warfare*, United States: William-Frederick Press. Wall, Tyler (2010). U.S Psychological Warfare and Civilian Targeting. United States: Vanderbilt University. Taylor, Philip M. (1999) *British Propaganda in the Twentieth Century: Selling Democracy,* Edinburgh University Press. Kirdemir, Baris (2019) 'Hostile influence and emerging cognitive threats in cyberspace (report)', Centre for Economics and Foreign Policy Studies, JSTOR http://www.jstor.org/stable/resrep21052. Chung, Youngjune (2021) 'Allusion, reasoning and luring in Chinese psychological warfare', International Affairs. 97:4, 1007–23. https://doi.org/10.1093/ia/iiab070

18 Kert, Faye M. (2015) *Privateering: Patriots and Profits in the War of 1812,* Johns Hopkins University Press, p. 62. Politakis, George P. (2018) *Modern Aspects of the Laws of Naval Warfare and Maritime Neutrality,* Taylor & Francis, p. 281.

19 Buckels, E. E., Trapnell, P. D. and Paulhus, D. L. (2014) 'Trolls just want to have fun. Personality and individual differences', 67: 97–102. Andjelovic, Tamara, Buckels, E. E., Paulhus, D. L. and Trapnell, P. D. (2019) 'Internet trolling and everyday sadism: Parallel effects on pain perception and moral judgment', *Journal of Personality* 87:2, 328–40. doi:10.1111/jopy.12393

20 Hardaker, C. (2013) 'Uh ... not to be nitpicky ... but ... the past tense of drag is dragged, not drug: An overview of trolling strategies', *Journal of Language Aggression and Conflict* 1:1, 58–86. doi.10.1075/jlac.1.1.04har

21 BBC News (2015) 'Met Police apology for women tricked into relationships', 20 November, https://www.bbc.co.uk/news/uk-34875197

22 Report of the Intelligence Services Commissioner for 2016, The Rt Hon. Sir Mark Waller, Intelligence Services Commissioner – p. 34, para 2, of the report states: 'It is indeed in every individual's own interest to make sure that the guidance is complied with, because as the guidance itself says, compliance gives the best chance of an

individual not being complicit in what might otherwise be a criminal offence or an offence under International Humanitarian Law.'

23 Hampes, W. P. (2010) 'The relation between humor styles and empathy', *Europe's Journal of Psychology* 6:3, 34–45, www.ejop.org.

24 Thomas, T. and Chaleff, I. (2017) 'Moral courage and intelligent disobedience', *InterAgency Journal* 8:1, 58–66.

Chapter 6

1 Bradshaw, J. (1988) *Healing the Shame that Binds You*, Florida: Health Communications.

2 Miller, A. (2007) *The Drama of the Gifted Child: The Search for the True Self*, revised edition, New York: Basic Books.

3 Kübler-Ross, E. and Kessler, D. (2007) *On Grief and Grieving: Finding the Meaning of Grief through the Five Stages of Loss*, New York: Scribner.

4 The tips and strategies in this chapter are adapted from a guide on anger management by Garratt, L. and Blackburn, P. (2007) Newcastle Primary Care Trust, Newcastle, UK.

5 Available at www.mind.org.uk.

6 Lewis Herman, L. (1992) 'Complex PTSD: A syndrome in survivors of prolonged and repeated trauma', *Journal of Traumatic Stress* 5:3, 377–91.

7 Gersons, B. P. R. (2005) 'Coping with the aftermath of trauma', *British Medical Journal* 330, 1038.

8 Shengold, L. (1989) *Soul Murder: The Effects of Childhood Abuse and Deprivation*, New Haven: Yale University Press.

Chapter 7

1 Marlatt, G. A. and Gordon, J. R. (1985) *Relapse prevention*, New York: Guilford Press.

2 Eisenberger, N. I. (2012) 'The neural bases of social pain: Evidence for shared representations with physical pain', *Psychosomatic Medicine* 74:2, 126–35. doi.10.1097/PSY.0b013e3182464dd1

3 Banskota, S., Ghia, J. E. and Khan, W. I. (2019) 'Serotonin in the gut: Blessing or a curse', *Biochimie* Jun:161, 56–64. doi.10.1016/j.biochi.2018.06.008. PMID: 29909048

4 Brewer, R., Cook, R. and Bird, G. (2016) 'Alexithymia: A general deficit of interoception', *R Soc Open Sci* 3:10, 150664. doi.10.1098/rsos.150664.

5 Bass, M., Carsten, K. W., De Dreu, C. K. W. and Nijstad, B. A. (2011) 'Creative production by angry people peaks early on, decreases over time, and is relatively unstructured', *Journal of Experimental Social Psychology* 47, 1107–15. See also Van Kleef, G. A., Anastasopoulou, C. and Nijstad, B. A. (2010) 'Can expressions of anger enhance

creativity? A test of the emotions as social information (EASI) model', *Journal of Experimental Social Psychology* 46, 1042–48.

6 Sobkowa, A., Traczyk, J., Kaufman, S. B. and Nosala, C. (2018) 'The structure of intuitive abilities and their relationships with intelligence and openness to experience', *Intelligence* 67, 1–10.

7 Greenberg, D. M., Baron-Cohen, S., Rosenberg, N., Fonagy, P. and Rentfrow, P. J. (2018) 'Elevated empathy in adults following childhood trauma', *PLoS One* 13:10, e0203886.

Chapter 8

1 See https://www.nspcc.org.uk/what-is-child-abuse/types-of-abuse/emotional-abuse/

2 Lewis Herman, J. (1992) 'Complex PTSD: A syndrome in survivors of prolonged and repeated trauma', *Journal of Traumatic Stress* 5:3, 377–91.

3 Kluft, R. P. (1990) 'Incest and subsequent revictimization: The case of therapist–patient sexual exploitation, with a description of the sitting duck syndrome', *Incest-Related Syndromes of Adult Psychopathology*, Washington, DC: American Psychiatric Press, 263–89.

4 *Re H-N and Others (children) (domestic abuse: finding of fact hearings)* [2021] EWCA Civ 448.

5 Ebert, R. (1993) 'The Good Son', *Chicago Sun-Times*, 24 September.

6 Hawes, D. J., Price, M. J. and Dadds, M. (2014) 'Callous-unemotional traits and the treatment of conduct problems in childhood and adolescence: A comprehensive review', *Clinical Child and Family Psychology Review*. doi.10.1007/s10567-014-0167-1

7 Macdonald, J. M. (1963) 'The threat to kill', *Am J Psychiatry* 120:2, 125–30. doi.10.1176/ajp.120.2.125

8 Fleming, G. E., Neo, B., Briggs, N. E., Kaouar, S., Frick, P. J., Kimonis, E. R. (2022) 'Parent training adapted to the needs of children with callous-unemotional traits: A randomized controlled trial', *Behav Ther*, November 53:6, 1265–81. doi.10.1016/j.beth.2022.07.001

Chapter 9

1 Wallmark, Z., Deblieck, C. and Lacoboni, M. (2018) 'Neurophysiological effects of trait empathy in music listening', *Front. Behav. Neurosci.* doi.10.3389/fnbeh.2018.0006

2 Crime in England and Wales: year ending June 2022, Crime against households and adults using data from police recorded crime and the Crime Survey for England and Wales (CSEW). Office of National Statistics, https://www.ons.gov.uk/peoplepopulationandcommunity/crimeandjustice/bulletins/crimeinenglandandwales/latest

3   *Which?* (2018) 'Exclusive: More than 96% of reported fraud cases go unsolved', 24 September, https://www.which.co.uk/news/article/exclusive-more-than-96-of-reported-fraud-cases-go-unsolved-apfql3E0JxDz

4   Townsend, M. (2019) 'Home Office under fire for blocking new spy watchdog', *The Guardian*, 19 January, https://www.theguardian.com/world/2019/jan/19/edward-snowden-defender-eric-king-vetoed-top-surveillance-watchdog-job

5   The case formed one of the four linked appeals in the Court of Appeal, *Re H-N and Others (children) (domestic abuse: finding of fact hearings)* (2021) EWCA Civ 448.

6   Werner, E. E. (1989) 'High-risk children in young adulthood: A longitudinal study from birth to 32 years', *Am J Orthopsychiatry* 59:1, 72–81.

7   Dossey, L. (2018) 'The Helper's High', *Elsevier* 14:6, 393–99. doi.10.1016/j.explore.2018.10.003

Further reading

Books

Arendt, H. *Eichmann in Jerusalem: A Report on the Banality of Evil*. Penguin Classics; 1st edition, 2006.

Babiak, P. and Hare, R. D. *Snakes in Suits: When Psychopaths Go to Work*. New York: Collins, 2006.

Baron-Cohen, S. *Zero Degrees of Empathy: A New Theory of Human Cruelty*. London: Allen Lane/Penguin Books, 2012.

Behary, W. T. *Disarming the Narcissist: Surviving and Thriving with the Self-Absorbed*. New Harbinger, Oakland CA; 3rd edition, 2021.

Bradshaw, J. *Healing the Shame That Binds You*. Florida: Health Communications, 1988.

Bradshaw, J. *The Family: A New Way of Creating Solid Self-Esteem*. Florida: Health Communications, 1996.

Clarke, J. *Working with Monsters: How to Identify and Protect Yourself from the Workplace Psychopath*. Sydney, Australia: Random House, 2009.

Damasio, A. *The Feeling of What Happens*. London: Vintage, 1999.

de Becker, G. *The Gift of Fear: Survival Signals That Protect Us from Violence*. Canada: Little, Brown, 1997.

Desmet, M. *The Psychology of Totalitarianism*. United States: Chelsea Green Publishing Co., 2022.

Greenspan, S. L., with Benderly, B. L. *The Growth of the Mind and the Endangered Origins of Intelligence*. Reading, MA: Addison-Wesley, 1997.

Hare, R. D. *Without Conscience: The Disturbing World of the Psychopaths Among Us*. New York: Guilford Press, 1993.

Herbert, C. and Westmore, A. *Overcoming Traumatic Stress: A Self-help Guide Using Cognitive Behavioural Techniques*. London: Constable & Robinson, 2008.

Keysers, C. *The Empathic Brain: How the Understanding of Mirror Neurons Changes our Understanding of Human Nature*. Amsterdam: Social Brain Press, 2011.

Le Bon, G. *The Crowd: Study of the Popular Mind*. London: Pretorian Books, 2019.

Lewis Herman, J. *Trauma and Recovery: The Aftermath of Violence – from Domestic Abuse to Political Terror*. New York: Basic Books, 1997.

Marsh, A. *The Fear Factor: How One Emotion Connects Altruists, Psychopaths, and Everyone In-Between*. New York: Basic Books, 2017.

Miller, A. *For Your Own Good: Hidden Cruelty in Childrearing and the Roots of Violence*. New York: Farrar, Straus & Giroux, 1990.

Miller, A. *Banished Knowledge: Facing Childhood Injuries*. New York: Anchor Press; new edition, 1997.

Miller, A. *Thou Shalt Not Be Aware: Society's Betrayal of the Child*. New York: Farrar, Straus and Giroux, 1998.

Miller, A. *The Drama of the Gifted Child: The Search for the True Self*. New York: Basic Books; revised edition, 2007.

Miller, A. *The Body Never Lies: The Lingering Effects of Cruel Parenting*. New York: W. W. Norton & Co, 2006.

Rifkin, J. *The Empathic Civilization: The Race to Global Consciousness in a World in Crisis*. Cambridge: Polity Press, 2009.

Schiraldi, G. *The Post-Traumatic Stress Disorder Sourcebook: A Guide to Healing, Recovery and Growth*. New York: McGraw-Hill, 2009.

Simon, G. *In Sheep's Clothing*. Little Rock: Parkhurst Brothers, 1996.

Stern, R. *The Gaslight Effect: How to Spot and Survive the Hidden Manipulation Others Use to Control Your Life*. New York: Morgan Road Books, 2007.

Stout, M. *The Sociopath Next Door*. New York: Broadway Books, 2005.

Stout, M. *Outsmarting the Sociopath Next Door: How to Protect Yourself Against a Ruthless Manipulator*. London: John Murray 2020.

Taylor, K. *Cruelty: Human Evil and the Human Brain*. Oxford: OUP, 2009.

Taylor, K. *Brainwashing: The Science of Thought Control* (Oxford Landmark Science). Oxford: OUP, 2016.

van der Kolk, B. *The Body Keeps the Score: Mind, Brain and Body in the Transformation of Trauma*. London: Penguin Books, 2015.

Index

abandonment phase of
   manipulative behaviour 42–3
abandonment trauma 125
Action Fraud 212
Adams, John 79
aftermath of sociopathic behaviours
   see also regaining control
   anger in 130–1
   emotions in 126–7
   frustration in 133–5
   grief stages in 127–30
   limiting contact with sociopaths
      121–3
   outing sociopathic behaviour
      115–20
   and PTSD 139–40, 143–5
   rumination in 136–9
   shame in 124–5
   stress in 131–3
   trauma acceptance 123–4
   traumatic memories 142–5
   venting in 135–6
aggression 45–8
alexithymia 107, 165–8
Allitt, Beverley 30, 46
altruism 60
American Psychiatric Association
   (APA) 8, 9, 25
Amin, Idi 23
anger in aftermath of sociopathic
   behaviours 130–1
animal cruelty 47
anti-social behaviour 45–8
anti-social personality disorder
   (AsPD) 2, 9
apaths/apathy 52–8, 64–6, 83,
   91–4
Arendt, Hannah 93–4, 98
assessment phase of manipulative
   behaviour 41–2
authority figures 3–4

Babiak, Paul 2, 41, 77–8
Bad Seed, The 192
*Banished Knowledge: Facing
   Childhood Injuries* (Miller) 152
Baron-Cohen, Simon 10, 48, 86,
   175, 200
BBC Prison Study 88
Bejerot, Nils 71
belief in a just world 94–5
Bernays, Edward Louis 102
Big Brother 208
Blair, Tony 23
Body Never Lies, The (Miller) 179
boundary setting 153, 223
brain structure
   and aggression 47
   and empathy 11–12, 48–9, 58,
      60–1
brainwashing 33–4
*Brainwashing: The Science of Thought
   Control* (Taylor) 30, 34
Buckels, Erin 83
building empathy 216–28
bullying 46–7, 147–50
bystander effect 91–4

callous unemotional traits 194–5
Canonville, Christine Louis de 68
Castaway 2000 208
Cathy Come Home 207
Charity Commission 84
children
   building empathy in 224–7
   callous unemotional traits in
      194–5
   fallout from sociopathic parents
      176–9
   protection of 179–80
   sexual abuse of 37, 84
   sociopathic behaviours 20–1,
      192–9

welfare of 180–3
wider family contact with 190–2
Clarke, John 3
Cleckley, Hervey 8
Clinton, Hillary 23
Cobb, Mr Justice 186
collusion with sociopaths 52–8
Compliance (docudrama) 97–8
complying with a twist 116
conduct disorder 196–7
conformity 99–105
confronting sociopaths 150–1
controlled opposition 110–12
Couzens, Wayne 30, 96–7
Covert Human Intelligence Sources
    (Criminal Conduct) Act 2021
    213
criminal sociopaths 5–6
*Crowd, The: A Study of the Popular
    Mind* (Le Bon) 102
crowd psychology 102–3
*Cruelty: Human Evil and the Human
    Brain* (Taylor) 92–3
culture change 118–20

Damasio, Antonio 174
Davie, Tim 30
deception 45
Decety, Jean 58
defence stage of gaslighting targets
    71–2
depersonalization 143
depression stage of gaslighting
    targets 72–5
derealization 142–3
Desmet, Mattias 102–4
devaluation stage of gaslighting
    69–70
*Diagnostic and Statistical Manual of
    Mental Disorders (DSM-5)* 9
discarding stage of gaslighting 70
disbelief stage of gaslighting targets
    70–1
disgust, language of 96

dissociative amnesia 142–3
Domestic Abuse and Family
    Proceedings Act (2021) 184, 188
dominance hierarchy 76–85
Drama of the Gifted Child, The
    (Miller) 125
Duff, Konstancja 84
Dutton, Kevin 22

Eichmann, Adolf 93–4
*Eichmann in Jerusalem: A Report on
    the Banality of Evil* (Arendt) 93–4
emotional intelligence 24, 58–9,
    61, 107–8, 162–5, 168–71, 203,
    215–16, 228
emotional trauma 6
Empathic Civilization, The (Rifkin) 226
empathy
    and altruism 60
    and brain structure 11–12, 48–9,
        58, 60–1
    building 216–28
    as communication tool 59
    components of 12
    and emotional intelligence 58–9
    lack of as trait 48–50
    in leadership 24, 85–91
    in politics 209–10
    process of 59–60
    in recovery process 201–3
    as shared emotion 58
    and social intelligence 58–9
    societal erosion of 203–16
    and Sociopath–Empath–Apath
        Triad (SEAT) 64–6
    and sociopaths 12–13
    as spectrum 10–11
    those with targeted 5, 58, 63
    and well-being 62–3
empathy spectrum 10–11
Equality Act (2010) 147
Everard, Sarah 30, 96–7
eye movement desensitization and
    reprocessing (EMDR) 144

false flag tactics 109
Family, The (TV programme) 207
family situations
   child protection 179–80
   child welfare 180–3
   controlling behaviour in 186–8
   dealing with children with
     sociopathic behaviours 197–9
   fallout from 176–9
   wider family 183–92
Feeling of What Happens, The
   (Damasio) 174
fight or flight response 171–2
Fox, Ruth 78–9
fraud 212–13
frustration in aftermath of
   sociopathic behaviours 133–5

gaslighting
   as criminal offence 147, 184–6,
     221
   description of 66–8
   devaluation stage of 69–70
   discarding stage of 70
   effects on targeted person 70–5
   and erosion of empathy 205–6
   idealization stage of 68–9
   and leadership 81–2
gender of sociopaths 2, 3, 50–1
Goldwater, Barry 25–6
Good Son, The 192–3
governing from a distance 104
Greenberg, 175
grief 127–30
groupthink 100–2

Hansard Society 78
Hare, Robert 2, 5, 6, 8, 41, 77–8
harassment 147–50
Haslam, Alex 88
Haslam, Nick 24
Hayut, Shimon 17
Helper's High 225
Henry VIII 23

Herman, Judith 182
Hitler, Adolf 3, 23, 33
hunches 174–5
Hussein, Saddam 23

idealization stage of gaslighting
   68–9
identity alteration 143
Independent, The 215
instinct in regaining control
   171–5
intelligence 29, 117–18
intelligence services 214–15
intelligent disobedience 117–18
*International Classification of Disease
   (ICD-11)* 9
intuition in regaining control
   171–5
Investigatory Powers Act (2016)
   212
Iraq War 214–15

Jimmy Savile: A British Horror Story
   29–30

lapses in judgement 156–8
Le Bon, Gustav 102
leadership
   and apaths 83, 91–4
   and the bystander effect 91–4
   and conformity 99–105
   controlled opposition 110–12
   dominance hierarchy 76–85
   and empathy 24, 85–91
   false flag tactics 109
   and gaslighting 81–2
   impact of sociopaths 29–31
   and intelligence 29
   normalization of sociopathy in
     24–6
   outing sociopathic behaviour
     115–20
   perception management 108–9
   and politics 22–3, 25–6

protection tips 105–8
reluctance to label sociopathy in 26–8
and sexual abuse 84
smear campaigns 112–14
sociopathic figures of 3–4
and stability privilege 29–30
trolling 109–10
victim blaming 94–8
in the workplace 89–91
Lerner, Melvin J. 94–5
limiting contact 121–3, 153–6
Lobaczewski, Andrew 80
locating emotions 165–8
lying 43–5

Macdonald triad 196
Madison, James 25
manipulative behaviour 40–3
abandonment phase of 42–3
assessment phase of 41–2
Marano, Hara Estroff 98
Mask of Insanity, The (Cleckley) 8
mass formation 103–4
May, Theresa 212
McGregor, Fin 121
Messiah complex 38–9
Metropolitan Police 111
MI5 111–12
Milgram experiments 54–6, 86–7, 98
Mill, John Stuart 222
Miller, Alice 125, 152, 180
MIND 131
mind games 38
mood control 159–60

NSPCC 18
nudge theory 104–5

On Liberty (Mill) 222
online world
abuse on 17–18
trolling on 109–10

Operation Renegade 3–4, 214
oppositional defiant disorder 196
otherization 93, 218–19
outing sociopathic behaviour 115–20

paedophiles 37
parasitic lifestyle 39
Parent–Child Interaction Therapy (PCIT) 198–9
parents
child protection 179–80
child welfare 180–3
dealing with children with sociopathic behaviours 197–9
fallout from sociopathic behaviours 176–9
sociopathic behaviours 18–19
partners
manipulative behaviour 40
sociopathic behaviours 19–20
passive aggression 39
Peele, Stanton 98
perception management 108–9
physical trauma 5–6
Pinel, Philippe 7
pluralist ignorance 91–2
policing 212–14
political leaders 22–3, 25–6
Political Ponerology: A Science on the Nature of Evil Adjusted for Political Purposes (Lobaczewski) 80
Post Office computer system scandal 98
predatory behaviour 35–7
prevalence of sociopaths 2–3, 5
Pritchard, J. C. 7–8
Proceeds of Crime Act (2002) 212
Protection of Freedoms Act (2012) 149
Protection from Harassment Act (1997) 149
Psychopathic Personality Inventory-Revised' (PPI-Revised) 22–3

psychopathy 7
  diagnosis of 8–9
  and sociopaths 9–10
Psychopathy Checklist (PCL-R) 8–9
PTSD 139–40, 143–5
punishments 197–8

regaining control *see also* aftermath
  of sociopathic behaviours
  after prolonged contact 151–2
  boundary setting 153
  and bullying behaviour 147–50
  confronting sociopaths 150–1
  different circumstances for 146–7
  emotional intelligence 162–5,
    168–71
  and empathy 201–3
  and harassment 147–50
  instinct in 171–5
  intuition in 171–5
  lapses in judgement 156–8
  limiting contact 153–6
  locating emotions 165–8
  mood control 159–60
  routine changes 160–1
  rule violation effect 159
  seemingly irrelevant decisions
    (SIDs) 158–9
  triggers 161–2
Reicher, Steve 88
remorse 48–50
Rifkin, Jeremy 226
Robinson, Kenneth 211
romantic fraudster 16–17
routine changes 160–1
Royal College of Psychiatrists 196–7
rule violation effect 159
ruminating 136–9

St. Ann's (documentary) 207
Savile, Jimmy 29–30, 34, 39, 46, 58
seemingly irrelevant decisions
  (SIDs) 158–9
Serious Crime Act (2015) 184–6, 188

Serious Organized Crime and Police
  Act (2005) 149
sexual abuse 6, 37, 84
shame
  and aftermath of sociopathic
    behaviours 124–5
  and building empathy 226
  of victims 73–4
Shipman, Harold 30, 46
Shriver, Lionel 193–4
sitting duck syndrome 182–3
smear campaigns 112–14
Snakes in Suits (Babiak & Hare) 2,
  77–8
Snowden, Edward 117–18
social intelligence 12, 24, 36, 40,
  58–9, 78, 216
social interactions
  apaths 52–8
  collusion with sociopaths 52–8
  empathic people targeted 5, 58, 63
  gaslighting 66–75
  and Sociopath–Empath–Apath
    Triad (SEAT) 52, 64–6
  sociopathic transactions 63–6
Sociopath–Empath–Apath Triad
  (SEAT) 52, 64–6, 76, 116, 180
Sociopath Next Door, The (Stout) 2
sociopathic behaviours
  children 20–1, 192–9
  emotional trauma 6
  empathic people targeted 5
  online abuse 17–18
  of parents 18–19
  of partners 19–20
  physical trauma 5–6
  romantic fraudster 16–17
  sexual trauma 6
  at work 21–2
sociopathic transactions 63–6, 90
sociopaths
  as authority figures 3–4
  confronting 150–1
  description of 1

early studies of 7–8
and empathy 12–13
and gender 2, 3, 50–1
prevalence of 2–3, 5
and psychopathy 9–10
terminology for 7
threat from 2
Sorokin, Anna 17
stability privilege 29–30
stalking 149
Stanford prison experiment 87–8
Stern, Robin 70
stimulation, need for 37–9
Stockholm syndrome 71–2
Stout, Martha 2
stress in aftermath of sociopathic
behaviours 131–3
Sumption, Jonathan 79
superficial charm 33–5
survivor triad 141
Swindler, Tinder 17

Taylor, Kathleen 30, 34, 92–3
terminology for sociopaths 7
Thatcher, Margaret 30
Thoreau, Henry David 210
traits of sociopaths
aggression 45–8
anti-social behaviour 45–8
deception 45
empathy 48–50
and gender 50–1
lying 43–5
manipulative behaviour 40–3

need for stimulation 37–9
parasitic lifestyle 39
predatory behaviour 35–7
remorse 48–50
superficial charm 33–5
trauma acceptance 123–4
trauma-focused therapy 144
traumatic memories 142–5
Treatise on Insanity, A (Pinel) 7
triggers 161–2
trolling 109–10
Trump, Donald 23, 25
truth telling 116–18

venting in aftermath of sociopathic
behaviours 135–6
victim blaming 94–8

Washington, Booker T. 220
Wave, The 101–2
We Need to Talk About Kevin
(Shriver) 193–4
whistleblowing 116–18
Wilson, David 23
Without Conscience (Hare) 5, 6
Working with Monsters (Clarke) 3
workplace
bullying in 46–7, 147–8
leadership in 89–91
sociopathic behaviours in 21–2

Zero Degrees of Empathy (Baron-
Cohen) 10, 48, 86, 200
Zimbardo, Philip 87, 88

Acknowledgements

It is almost ten years since the original book was published. I thank Victoria Roddam, senior commissioning editor at John Murray, for encouraging me to update it and Purvi Gadia, senior desk editor, for her diligence when preparing the book for print.

Whilst sociopaths conduct their abuses in tried-and-tested ways, how they persuade otherwise decent-minded people to engage in their cruelties still needs demystifying. This updated version of the book attempts to explain the influences that see otherwise ordinary people become embroiled in abuse, drawing on research I conducted between 2016 and 2018 on behalf of the Society for Research into Empathy, Cruelty and Sociopathy. I am very grateful to the participants who shared their stories. I thank Dr Helen Oakley with whom I've had many thought-provoking discussions whilst on walks. Likewise, I am grateful to 'Mountain Man', whom I thank wholeheartedly for sharing his deep insights. Lastly, I thank Fin McGregor and Elena McGregor for their loving support and awe-inspiring bravery. Ordinary people may live life in submission, but the extraordinary refuse to and show us the way.